Major & Minor Adventures in Lah Lah Land

Martin Kiszko

First published in 2020 by Martin Kiszko.
Contact: contact@martinkiszko.com
www.martinkiszko.com
www.greenpoemsforablueplanet.com
ISBN 978-0-9568549-5-7

British Library Cataloguing-in-Publication Data:
A catalogue record for this book is available from The British Library.

Cover, book design and typesetting by Simon Bishop.
Printed in the Czech Republic via Akcent Media.

For

Serafina, Luka, Zita,

and my inner child.

Major & Minor Adventures in Lah Lah Land

Martin Kiszko

1

First Beat

The first beat of my heart to join the crazy symphony of heartbeats in the big wide world was in 1958. It was the year the singer Perry Como (1912–2001) released his hit single *Magic Moments*. My birth was not a magic moment for my mother. She decided there would be no other band members. If there was a music career ahead of me in Lah Lah Land, it was going to be a solo one. That was because of the two cries echoing around the delivery suite: me and mum. We were in a duet that would only reach the medical charts. After thirty-seven weeks, I'd decided to hold fast to my bum-first position and that's how I planned on coming out — end of story. It set the pattern for some, if not all, of my approach to life: doing things the way others wouldn't, taking the more challenging path, being unswervingly single-minded or ridiculously lateral! Unfortunately for mum, it was a painful breech delivery with forceps and an unwelcome episiotomy.

My mother, Edith, was the daughter of a miner and became a seamstress. For one of her first sewing projects she stole her father's gloves and refashioned them into a purse. She grew up in a house in Hunslet Lane, Leeds. Three rooms were lit by gaslight and the bedrooms by candlelight. She was convinced the house was haunted. Her sightings were a dog, an old man walking through a wall and a young woman who sat on the end of my grandparents' bed. Despite mum's admission of having a vivid imagination, the sightings were very real to her at the time. The family was very poor and due to a disability my grandmother was unable to work. My mum often scrubbed the doorsteps of house for a few pennies to buy a stale loaf for the family. Her playtime was spent with her brother Arthur on the 'hollow', an area of grassland near the house, where they had jam sandwich and lemonade picnics or waited for the 'Jack Lane boys' to come and have a punch-up with the Hunslet Lane gang. Apart from that entertainment, mum enjoyed chalking on the faces on advertising hoardings or sitting with a local nightwatchman who taught her how to make flowers with wire and strands of silk.

My father, Nikodem, was a Polish immigrant who escaped from incarceration in Germany, got to France, was assisted by the French resistance to get to Northern France and then by an American ship to Italy to rejoin the Polish and British armies. Given a choice to be demobbed to Canada or the UK, he chose the UK. He met my mother at Leeds Mecca dance hall and, fourteen years her senior, they married. He took the only jobs immigrants could get: in a textile mill, a warehouse and a tobacco factory. He played poker for a few ill-gotten gains, backed the horses and enjoyed vodka with friends. He was in love with music and played the guitar, mandolin and accordion. Music would also become a lifeline for me.

My very first word was 'bappit', my word for any branch or twig I picked up. I like the idea of this being my first word. The bappit is a symbol of my early connection to the environment and to creativity. I'm pleased I was fascinated with something that represented the invention of nature. Perhaps I saw opportunities to play with the bappit or create games using it. As for my natural habitat, we lived in a back-to-back in a vibrant immigrant community in Chapeltown, Leeds. The streets were full of life: kids playing games and kicking cans around, hand-pulled milk carts, the crashing and clashing of dustbin lids, the cry of the rag and bone man looking for 'any ol' iron', the lemonade delivery lorry, the coal men hauling sacks of coal into our coal-hole (I was convinced ours had a bogeyman and would never go in there) and the sound of our three-wheeled bubble car rattling over cobblestones. One of my first friends was a black boy, Bernard, who my mum occasionally minded. One of my best friends on the street was Muhammad. We played a submarine game under old beds stacked in his garden. It was based on the popular TV series *Voyage to the Bottom of the Sea*. My opposite neighbours were Pakistani. I was always in their garden waiting for chapati. One house down the street went up in flames. It wasn't me, though I did start a few fires at secondary school that were, at best, campfire size. My next door neighbour had a daughter who, along with another girl, once grabbed my hand and took me to her house where they promptly displayed their genitals. I liked what I saw but they then insisted on seeing mine. Twenty years later I would have given them the privilege but I was out of there in a flash! The next moment I'd be kicking a can around or playing the street games hopscotch and bulldogs.

One day I was once sent home from primary school for wearing a pair of green trousers my mum had made out of curtains. It wasn't a fashion statement. It was because we couldn't afford to buy any. Every Sunday night I bathed in a tin bath in front of the fire. Once I was dry and dressed, my grandma would often rock me in a rocking chair until the night she rocked so far back that I went over with her. I remember the old newspapers used as toilet paper in the outside loo. The loo was near steps leading down to the front door where rats rattled the milk-bottles and pierced their foil tops. I managed, as a toddler, to wheel myself in a pushchair along the path and down the steps. I still have the scar. But the point of this back-story is that if my mum had gone for another birth, I would probably never have had so many creative opportunities.

I was able to read before I started primary school especially the comics *The Dandy*, *The Beano*, *Topper* and *Beezer*. One of the first books I remember being given was totally unsuitable for a five-year-old and was responsible for promoting my hypochondriacal tendencies. It was a manual belonging to the St John Ambulance Brigade. It had illustrations of injuries and first aid and was given to me by my parents' friends Stan and Win who chain-smoked and kept two budgies. A few of my first books at school would be deemed politically incorrect by today's standards and have been struck off the list. I do remember moving at hyperspeed through the *Janet and John* reading series and enjoying the fluency of my reading and spelling. My father was keen for me to learn Polish in the home but my mother fought against it. Why would he need it? I regret my father never pushing for it or speaking Polish to me during those early years.

My first primary school introduced me to vernacular language. Once, in the playground, a boy in a tight fitting knee-length coat came up to me. His first words were, 'Your mum and dad shag don't they?'

Not only was it shocking, but the weird thing is that I understood what the word meant even at that age. How? I've no idea. It was my very first lesson in sex education. On another occasion I was sent on an errand by a teacher to give a message to another teacher. Arriving at the classroom, I knocked and went in to be confronted by the class watching their teacher hold a girl over her lap, pull her knickers back and spank her bum. Back then, that was as common as getting a detention is nowadays. Apart from rolling a car tyre through a classroom window, being sick in school dinners, painting my hands blue and meeting my first girlfriend Teresa, for whom I bought a packet of Parma Violet sweets most days, the first two years at primary school passed relatively uneventfully.

My first memories of music were twofold. First, it was watching dad play his guitar and accordion. He played folk melodies remembered from the days he and his three brothers, Victor, Fabijan and Edward, had a band that played for village weddings and rural events in my ancestral homeland — a part of Poland which is now Belarus. He also played songs from during and after the war, especially tangos. There were many happy times watching mum and dad dance but it was soon over in exchange for a lifetime of 'grin and bear it' for her. He showed her little respect and never complimented her. He ridiculed her love of reading, television, and second-hand shops. There were always arguments. In those days it was hard to walk away, especially with a child. My second music memory was of an old gramophone with a large horn, a felt turntable and a rickety handle. From the age of three I loved winding it up and playing through a large pile of old 78 rpm records. My favourite was the popular WWII song *Run Rabbit Run* sung by the comedy duo Flanagan and Allen. I wasn't interested in the classical music discs. Who would have thought that one day I'd end up composing classical music? Not me.

My escape from Chapeltown came as a result of the compulsory purchase and demolition of our house. The escape almost didn't come off. I was once nearly run down by a car — so close it touched my coat buttons. My dad blamed my mum for the incident — a precedent for the naming and blaming in their married life. Another time, when out on a walk to the shops to get my favourite bubble gum and cards — a wonderful pictorial set of aliens and monsters from the TV series *The Outer Limits* — I was stopped by a motorist who told me to hop in because he was a friend of my parents and could 'take me home'. I suppose if supernatural protection (or protection from aliens of *The Outer Limits*) was ever available, it might have been at that very moment as, at age five or six, I declined the offer and ran off for dear life.

I was a 'latch key child' from an early age. Dad did shift work on the buses and mum worked in a wholesale stationers. We didn't have a phone and I was on my own most of the time. It gave me the freedom to raid the biscuit tin or help myself to the gas meter money to spend on bubble gum. When my parents were home, I liked to wrestle with dad or sit with mum whilst she was knitting a jumper for me. We ended up on a council estate: Belle Isle in South Leeds. 'Beautiful Isle' it was not! Yet for a child, it was a place where imagination, adventure and naughtiness could flourish. The house was a three-bed semi with only a gas fire for heat. The kitchen had a combustion stove that had to be stoked up with wood and coal to heat the water. The kitchen had mould everywhere and the hot water was always brown from a rusty tank the council refused to change. My father's hobby was making guitars but he couldn't afford to buy the tools to construct them. Instead, he set about building many of the clamps and tools himself. He used the hot pipe of the combustion stove to bend wet wood to fit into a home-made mould that held the body of the guitar together. My children and I still have the four guitars he made.

The house's porch had a coal storeroom, toilet, and a tool room where my dad built a makeshift vodka distillery. One day a police officer arrived at the house to get information about an accident my father had witnessed. There were nail-biting moments as the officer walked past the secret distillery room on his way in and out. I often used the porch to create 'environments' such as Halloween ones with cobwebs, skeletons and ghouls. I also used the tool room to store fireworks for Bonfire Night. In those days boys kept them in their pockets too. I used to stuff my pockets full of Bangers, Jumping Jacks and the odd Roman Candle or Air Bomb. I was able to buy them straight over the counter, no questions asked. Me and my friends would throw the bangers and crackers at each other or split open the bangers, pour out the powder and then put a match to it. We called it the 'genie' effect – a big blue flash. We were blessed by luck or something else to still have our eyeballs today. We certainly didn't have the slightest bit of common sense and health and safety hadn't been invented. Although the council house was cold, damp, and featured a fireplace with hordes of creepy-crawly silverfish under the rug, the house was near the edge of the housing estate and bordered fields of crops and a long stretch of land we called the 'spare ground'. The spare ground had grass growing to waist height and it was where the local houses dumped everything they didn't want. I once found a brass plate embossed with the image of a group of revellers in a tavern. I thought I'd found treasure. The spare ground was great for war games, hide and seek, and chumping. 'Chumping' was the term used for the collection of wood and any old rubbish for November 5th bonfires. Old prams were also dumped there and we used the wheels and wooden planks or boxes to make a bogie. We'd nail on a short stick to act as a handbrake for one of the back wheels and tear down the street at breakneck speed hoping no cars were on the way up.

Cars were also an interest. Each week I'd save my pocket money and I managed to build a fine collection of twenty die-cast vintage cars. They were my pride and joy. One day, my father announced he had made friends with one of the passengers on his bus route. My father was originally a tramcar conductor and later became a bus conductor on Leeds City Transport for the rest of his life. When I was often interviewed during my composing career, I used to mention my dad was a famous conductor.

'Oh', the interviewer would say, 'which orchestras did he conduct?'

I would smile, 'the number 21 to Belle Isle and the number 19 to Middleton. He was a bus conductor!'

The man my father had made friends with on the bus got invited to tea. One Sunday the man turned up and my mum prepared a meal for him. The conversation was lively and the man was very friendly. He mentioned he worked for a children's charity and wondered whether I had any spare toys the children would like. I don't know what possessed me except a deep sadness for those children without toys. I went over to my vintage car collection and picked out not one or two, but I gave him the entire collection bar one. I insisted he should take them. My parents didn't say anything. A few weeks later my mother became suspicious about the man. We hadn't heard anything from him. My father wasn't bothered and said he'd bump into him again on the bus. My mum, however, wasn't going to leave it there. She had the man's address and one day, while my dad was at work, she decided we'd take the bus to Headingly and find the man's house. We walked the man's street a few times. There was no house with the number the man had given. We never saw him again. This was my first encounter with a confidence trickster who had taken all my toys. The incident set up what became a lifetime's distrust. Perhaps it was a good thing? I was always on my guard when asked for things and never believed anything on first hearing.

My other fascination with cars was an obsession with car mascots. These were the round decorated car manufacturer nameplates set in the middle of a car's steering wheel or sometimes on the bonnet. Along with my pals, I started a collection by going to car scrap yards. When the owners weren't around, we'd climb stacks of cars, scramble inside and prise out the mascots with a crowbar. I had a fine collection from cars such as the Anglia, Consul, Cortina, Zodiac and Zephyr as well as the Morris Oxford, Jaguar, MG, Hillman Minx, Triumph Herald and VW Beetle. I used the memory of mascot collecting as the basis for the opening scene of my second screenplay *Junkworld* in which four children on a council estate discover a world entirely made from the junk of humankind. As for my original collection of car mascots, I made a bad move in swapping it for a Subutteo football game which I then swapped for a collection of birds eggs. I know! Back in the sixties on a council estate, boys didn't know any better. There was no teaching at home or at school about how to protect wildlife and the environment. Along with a gang of boys, I added to my egg collection by climbing trees or stealing eggs from hedgerow nests. My knees were always bruised from climbing and my arms full of scratches and cuts from hedgerow thorns. We'd stick a pin through the top and bottom of the eggs and blow out the contents. It makes me feel sad and physically sick to think about it now. I'm glad I eventually mended my ways and ended up doing work connected to protecting wildlife and saving our planet such as my long connection with the BBC Natural History Unit as a composer and my work as the 'UK's green poet' with my environmental campaign *Green Poems for a Blue Planet*.

The woods, meadows, and fields were the places I collected caterpillars and caught butterflies. I was crazy about butterflies and chased them for ages. The large tortoiseshell was one of my favourites but to find a red admiral or a peacock was the best prize. My ambition was to see a swallowtail but most of the time I had to put up with the cabbage whites. I kept caterpillars in a large goldfish bowl and watched their metamorphosis from pupa to the glorious butterfly I'd let out into the big wide world. I also collected tadpoles and newts. I'd often run from my estate and cross the M1 Motorway being built nearby at the time. In those days boys ran everywhere, partly because it was the boy thing to do but the other reason was to escape the bullies on the estate. If you were moving, there was less chance of an ambush from their gate or from behind a hedge to give you a good thrashing. I collected newts from ponds in the woods at the other side of the motorway or sometimes when out on woodland trips with my father. Young people today cannot ever imagine those poor newts being whisked away from their habitat and stored in an old sink and buckets in my garden. I adored them.

I guess it was my father that set me up to be interested in animals and the environment. He grew up in a wilderness of marshes, icy lakes and rivers, silver birch and pine forests in what is now Belarus. He loved nothing more than sitting in a meadow, walking in the woods, stroking a bee in the palm of his hand or examining a plant. When out on our walks, he often carved a small flute for me out of a fallen branch. A few of my excursions in search of adventure were dangerous. The Middleton Broom Colliery was just up the road from my house. I'd go there to play with my mates Margie and Moira and we'd climb the massive slag heaps full of all the waste materials and by-products of coal mining. As I stood on one, the spoil beneath my feet ran away like shifting sand. The heap was often steaming hot and I had no idea it could swallow me up or create a black avalanche to engulf and suffocate. One day the heap was so hot it burnt holes in the soles of my sandals. On arriving home, my parents saw the shoes and wanted to know where I'd been. Needless to say, they were extremely angry and told me I was lucky to be alive. A group of boys from school kept insisting I visit the 'wanking plank' in the woods at Middleton. I wasn't even brave enough to venture and take a peek at what anyone might get up to on it.

The nearby farmland was also a place where adventures could be had when we weren't being chased by the farmer for stealing his peas and beans or for making dens in his fields. One evening a gang of us all probably no more than eleven years old was out exploring and chanced on a large cardboard box tied up with string. It was under a bush on the edge of the farmer's field. The excitement mounted as we untied the knots and opened the box. Everyone stared goggle-eyed. We looked at one another and smiled. Then the first hand went in and pulled out a *Playboy* magazine from a box of many. We flicked through the pages and couldn't believe our luck. But once we'd thumbed through all the pages of the bare-breasted beauties, we had to decide what we were going to do with the magazines. We each tore out a few pages to keep and decided to hide the rest under a hedge in the garden of the local church. A few days later, someone in the gang leaked information on the location of the magazines and another gang of kids turned up at the church garden to look for them. Our gang rolled up too and a mighty free for all tussle for that box of delights ensued. Where all the magazines ended up I can't remember but a few of us kept a few torn out pictures and articles. They greatly enhanced our knowledge of female anatomy.

The church was also the venue where the Cub Scouts ran their activities. I was a Cub Scout but only got a couple of badges. I was hopeless with knots, didn't fancy fishing and hated the idea of ropes and tents. In fact I was so bewildered by knots I was the last person in my school year able to tie their shoelaces. This was the beginning of what I later identified as a problem with spatial relations and the following of diagrammatic or verbally listed instructions. Good job I was never put on an assembly line. That aside, it was at Cub Scouts where I learned life lessons about lying. Akela, the leader, had set a task to design a flag and colour it in. The illustration was required at the next meeting and for some reason I never even started the task. I had no coloured in flag. The next meeting came around and everyone was asked to show their flag illustration. It got to my turn.

'Where's yours?' asked Akela.

I felt a stomach churn.

'I've left it at home.'

I was pretty sure I was out of the woods but then Akela took a step towards me.

'You live close by. Could you pop home and get it?'

That was very awkward. I couldn't say no and found myself forced into a yes. As I left the group and walked home, my mind kept turning over several strategies for saving my bacon. My mum was surprised to see me arrive home so early.

'Why are you back?'

I explained what happened and began to cry.

'Have you done your flag?'

I shook my head.

'I told Akela I'd done it but left it here and she sent me to get it.'

My mum asked me to get the piece of paper the flag was supposed to be drawn on. Once I'd found it, she put on her coat, grabbed my hand and marched me down to the meeting. She took me to Akela and made me explain what I'd done. I was gutted. After my mother left, Akela got me to colour in the flag. It was a hard lesson that taught me about the consequences of the lie. The toggle, cap and short trousers went soon after that.

Luckily, I enjoyed going to school. I enjoyed writing stories, watching black and white projected films about Scott of the Antarctic, learning Scottish dancing and entering the school 'hobbies competition', a competition in which everyone submitted a model based on one of their hobbies. I submitted a hover-car. The body was created from two cereal packets. The interior had fake fur seats and the dashboard had a colour television. I used the inner tube of a bicycle tyre wrapped around the boxes to create the hover element of the design. I painted the car peacock blue. It won the coveted special prize at the competition. I was also determined to win the weekly 'best polished shoes competition' which took place in the school assembly. I only achieved it by giving them a brilliant shine and walking to school with a plastic bag covering each shoe. Apart from that event, I found the school assemblies boring. I passed the time by reading the hymnbook upside down and developed a skill useful in later life — the ability to read documents from the other side of someone's desk. Useful if you wanted to become a spy! My major ambition at school, however, was Linda. Linda was in my class, my recorder group, my Bible club group, my school house group and was the girl of my dreams. She lived in the posh part of Middleton in her parents privately owned house. Some days I ventured up there to gaze at the house and once I was bold enough to knock on the door and ask her out to play, but her mum said no. I was in love with Linda all the way through primary school but she never reciprocated my love. I should have learned my lesson and forgot about her, but I didn't and made the same mistake in a long term relationship in my fifties with a woman to whom I gave everything but who couldn't love me back.

Some of the worst days I ever spent in my childhood were with the school dentist. I'm sure he gave me unnecessary fillings but I must admit to eating mountains of bubble gum, gobstoppers, sherbet lemons, liquorice sticks, and whatever chocolate I could get my hands on. My father's cousin who worked at Cadbury in Birmingham was also responsible. Whenever he visited, he would bring a pack of chocolate rejects. It was chocolate heaven before dental hell. The school dentist's surgery was in an old building. The waiting room was uninviting with drab painted walls. The dentist's chair looked like something out of the cockpit of a fighter bomber that had seen better days. I hated the feel of the mask that supplied the anaesthetising gas. It had the sickly smell of old rubber and I've never forgotten the odour. I also hated the feeling of coming round after the procedure to the taste of blood and the room swirling with fragments of the voices of the dentist and nurse. I always had the most awful nightmares under anaesthetic and it made me reluctant to go there again. But I did and had many extractions as my small jaw couldn't accommodate all my teeth. It all came to an end when an orthodontist removed a tooth growing out from behind my front teeth. Years after those early visits to the school dentist, I still find it difficult to fully relax in a dentist's chair without all the memories of the gas mask and nightmares flooding back. Yet thinking back on it, perhaps the removal of the tooth growing behind the front teeth actually improved my clarinet and saxophone embouchure.

Indeed it was music that became the common thread in my life's embroidery and the first stitch came in the form of Gertrude Paul (1934–1992) from the Caribbean island of St. Kitts. Gertrude was the first black teacher in Leeds and went on to become the first black headmistress. It was Gertrude who created an enthusiasm in me and my classmates for music at Belle Isle's Clapgate Primary School. She quickly got me started on descant recorder, then tenor, and with the passion but also hard line pressure of my music obsessed father, they both got me learning the clarinet at age nine. We couldn't afford clarinet lessons and I was too young for music college so my father taught me even though he knew nothing about the instrument. By age ten I was taking lessons at the Leeds City College of Music as well as basic music theory. For some reason I became fascinated with counting the beats of music and I liked the puzzles music theory presented: writing out intervals, harmonic, melodic and chromatic scales, and the later challenges of four part harmony, transposition and ornaments. By the age of twelve my clarinet teacher suggested I should take up the tenor saxophone. My parents could ill afford it but my father was always of the opinion that if we could afford something for me then it had to be a music or educational item. The saxophone — a *Keilworth New King* — cost £65. It was almost as big as I was and quite a weight to be slung from my neck. It came in a very heavy wooden case my mum had to carry to work twice a week. After work, she'd carry it across town whilst also doing the family food shopping. She was a strong and resilient lady and wanted to do the best for me. So, she'd meet me after school at the music college and hand over the instrument. She'd then walk back across town and get the bus home.

Meanwhile, my father repeated his mantra that I should practise as much as possible and his insistence led to me being sent to perform in a mass concert of school orchestras at Leeds Town Hall. Still somewhat feverish and delirious from a bout of rubella, I turned up at the venue with my clarinet. There were hundreds of young musicians on stage, and feeling unwell I lost my way. The concert was about to start and I couldn't find the orchestra in which I was meant to play the third clarinet part. I quickly selected a seat and found myself in a different orchestra to the one in which I'd rehearsed! When the orchestra began to play their piece, I realised the clarinet section was so massive I could easily hide behind the lines of players and unashamedly mime my way through the music. I felt really bad about it, but felt a whole lot better when I realised it was done all the time on BBC music charts programme *Top of the Pops*! I was annoyed, however, at the way I'd been pushed into participating in the concert and was resolute that if I was going to pursue music it would be at my own pace with my own approach.

To that end, every Saturday morning I took the bus into town. I'd go to the basement café of Lewis's department store and order a coca cola ice cream float. After that I'd browse the LPs (long-play) in Barkers' music shop. I'd usually buy a 45 rpm single and the first one I ever bought was *Fire Brigade* (1968) by The Move. The same year I bought and played over and over again the tracks, *Guitar Man* by Elvis Presley, *The Legend of Xanadu* by Dave Dee Dozy Beaky, Mick and Titch, *Kites* by Simon Dupree and the Big Sound, *The Bonnie and Clyde* by The New Vaudeville Band and Glen Campbell's *Wichita Linesman*. After buying a record, I'd move on to the Leeds City Music Library where I'd borrow LPs — usually of the classics along with their accompanying music scores. It was totally time consuming as I had to check all the discs for scratches and scrapes prior to borrowing. There was nothing worse than putting on an LP and finding the record player's needle got stuck on a scratch. I spent many hours in front of our radiogram. I particularly liked Ron Goodwin's score for the movie *633 Squadron*, Holst's *The Planets* suite, and Beethoven's fifth and sixth symphonies. I loved conducting the music and, if I had the score, I'd be able to bring in every instrument as it made its entry.

Performing in clarinet duos, trios, quartets, and playing the sax in the Leeds Schools Concert Band was a joy. The repertoire consisted of music I loved — mainly from the movies: *Sound of Music*, *South Pacific*, *Carousel*, as well as Sousa marches. I also formed a band, Rosanna and the Rascals, with my friend Eddie and his sisters. I began to arrange music for the line up: alto saxophone, tenor saxophone, piano and tambourine. We played the Polish club, a hospital gala and a talent contest at Leeds Town Hall. Sometimes on a Sunday, a friend would come to my house or I would go to his. He encouraged me to buy large format sheets of manuscript paper and start composing for orchestra. I had absolutely no idea how to compose for orchestra and not a clue about transposition or the different ranges of the instruments. I simply listed all the instruments at the side of the staves and wrote music notes along each stave. If it had been played it would have sounded diabolical! But what I loved was the aesthetic, the look of it. I was engrossed with the pattern of music notes on the page. This was the catalyst which spawned a hidden ability to orchestrate — a skill that blossomed at the start of my professional music career. I also started to buy sheet music of pop songs I liked. I knew the lyrics to all of the songs in the charts and memorised them from the magazine *Words* a weekly publication of song lyrics. The first two sheet music songs I bought were Jethro Tull's *The Witch's Promise* and The Carpenters *Close to You*. I attempted to arrange them both for orchestra.

There were other preoccupations too. I loved board games. This was as a result of being bought several games when I was around four or five: Snakes and Ladders, Ludo, and my favourite game Airport Flying Game. Some years later I saved and spent all my pocket money on games such as Monopoly, Buccaneer, Totopoly, Spy Ring, Cluedo, Careers, Risk and James Bond 007 Game. I always wanted a snooker table but we could never afford it (or my parents didn't want me to have one!) However, I spent many an hour with my friend Victor playing snooker on a table in his garden. One day he asked my friend John to smell a handful of iron filings. Did Victor raise his handful of filings a tad too close to John's nostrils or did John breathe in too deeply? The jury is still out on that one but it almost ended in a hospital visit. If I wasn't playing there I was with my friend Robert taking *Action Men* on another dangerous mission. Another pastime was making Airfix model aeroplanes. It was really finickity to get the pilot into the cockpit and I always ended up with him glued to my fingers. I also enjoyed ten pin bowling and played in a team most Saturdays. There is no way all this could have taken place without being an only child with a latch key and with few material luxuries in life. When you are an only child, your imagination is your best friend and the portal to a world where you have to work extra hard to entertain yourself. I had friends, of course, but we didn't have telephones. Instead, I'd run across the estate to a friend's house and knock on the door.

'Is your Paul coming out to play?'

His mum would say, 'Not today,' or 'He's still having his tea. Come back later.'

Sometimes I'd simply stand and shout outside a house.

'You coming out to play?'

Often no-one would be available and I'd be out on my own. I remember the rainy days – staring out of the window and feeling glum. It was at those times I'd ask my mum when she was going to have another baby. Her face and the shake of her head said it all.

On some rainy days I'd head for the deserted playground and climb the frames or watch oil create spectrums of swirling shapes in the puddles. One of my first childhood poems was about rain and those swirly coloured psychedelic patterns. Hmm, come to think of it, perhaps I'd eaten too many Midget Gems! One of my favourite indoor pursuits was creating radio plays with a miniature reel to reel tape recorder my parents bought me for my birthday. I'd write a script, perform the characters and create the sound effects: crumpling newspaper to create the effect of burning fire, shaking a box of drawing pins back and forth to create the sound of footsteps walking on gravel or I'd open a large dictionary and slam it shut to create the sound of thunder or an explosion.

This kind of creativity was essential for my well-being as an only child and it stood me in good stead for my professional creative journey as a composer, screenwriter and poet. As I journeyed through life and met many people, I discovered something about my 'onlyness'. I found that at parties or networking events I unknowingly started up conversations with other only children. This may have been simple coincidence but I often wonder whether there is a magnetic attraction between only children or even a neediness that draws only children together in search of a sibling. I once met a young actress at the Cannes Film Festival and we agreed to meet when she was next working in London. We met at the British Academy of Film and Television Arts (BAFTA) in the bar. We had the usual conversation about work and our projects but I detected something in her that was also in me. I identified a need for someone to be close to her. Her passion for her work was effusive and she spoke with great gusto and commitment as if her imagination and vision was a jack-in-the-box waiting to spring out. I stopped the conversation dead at that point.

'Can I just pause us there?'

She stopped talking and gave a quizzical look. I smiled.

'Can I tell you something about you?'

She looked even more perplexed.

'What about me?'

'You're an only child.'

She gasped in astonishment.

'How did you know that?'

She went on to tell me about how she had always longed for a sibling but family circumstances had made it impossible. That scenario of gravitating to only children has happened many times.

Although I had many friends at school, I always felt different. Perhaps it was because I was the son of an immigrant and had a strange surname no-one could spell. Indeed, I've spent the rest of my life with people spelling it incorrectly. I even have close friends who still misspell my name and I simply can't understand why people don't make the effort to check spelling if they are unsure. Having an odd sounding surname and being an immigrant's son also hit home the prejudice of people. My father never got naturalised and was always proud of his Polish nationality, but because his accent was so strong and his syntax all over the place, passengers made fun of him on the buses. It became especially obvious to me when our next door neighbour leaned over the fence and shouted, 'Hey you, Polish pig!'

I also felt different at my second primary school because I excelled at music rather than having a passion for rugby, football or cricket. One of my primary school class teachers, Harry Jepson OBE, was the secretary of the Hunslet Rugby League Football Club. He later became chairman and club president. As he was my class teacher, it was unavoidable that I'd be press-ganged into joining the school rugby team. I was right prop and hated every moment of it. If I got the ball I would get rid of it as quickly as possible. I did get a knee injury and persuaded them the game was not for me. Cricket was also not my sport. I lived in fear of the Corky ball. We had batting pads at that time but if you got hit on the hand or body it really hurt. One of the games I preferred was 'kiss and catch' in the playground. The games were so politically incorrect in those days and the catch part of the game often involved losing your pants or knickers.

What also made me so different was that I was the only boy to pass the eleven-plus examination. The pass was a guaranteed passage to grammar school. But there was a problem. For a lad who'd grown up on a rough council estate, attending a grammar school was like throwing yourself into the lions' den. One would have to put up with taunts and bullying on the estate day after day and most mornings you might never even make it to the school bus especially if you were wearing a uniform and more so if you were wearing the uniform's cap! All the other boys were going to a very rough secondary modern school. If I was going to avoid grammar school, my only other option was to go to a comprehensive. I persuaded my parents to go for Matthew Murray School in Holbeck. It was a streamed comprehensive. It still had a uniform and my father even made me wear the cap. Only one other kid at the school had one and it had been beaten into a rag! I had to watch my back on the school bus. It was a good job I had a team of security guards: an older girl, Susan, who sat next to me, and my friends Margie and Moira who lived opposite to where the school bus picked up. The three girls formed a force field to repel any bullies. In the case of Moira, she only did it because I used to help her with her maths homework — often scribbling it down on the bus ride to school. Moira went on to get a Certificate of Secondary Education in Mathematics. I failed the O level twice. It's extraordinary to think I got all my O levels, five A levels, a BA, a Post Graduate Certificate, a PhD and a DLitt honorary doctorate but still failed to acquire that elusive O level in Mathematics. In any case who cares? I'm a wizard at mental arithmetic and quick with numbers and that's all I need. Thus far, I haven't required geometry, quadratic equations, logarithms or algebra. People often equate musicians with being great mathematicians. I guess I had all the maths I needed for my music.

The transitional time between primary and secondary school was a challenging learning curve. At home my mum had started a job at a toy warehouse and often brought home toys or books that were thrown out as seconds. It was the books that became a mainstay of interest. Our house had very few books. There was one on gardening and one on winemaking as my parents liked to make wine from raspberries, rhubarb and marigolds – all of which we had in abundance as well as a very well stocked vegetable patch. Our living room book shelf had the Bible and a few supernatural novels since my mum was an avid reader of ghost and horror stories. My dad called them rubbish. When my mum came home with some of the abridged classics and Enid Blyton, I voraciously read one book after the other: Anna Sewell's *Black Beauty*, Robert Lewis Stephenson's *Treasure Island,* Herman Melville's *Moby Dick,* Jules Verne's *Twenty Thousand Leagues Under the Sea,* Daniel Defoe's *Robinson Crusoe* and my favourite *Brer Rabbit's a Rascal* by Enid Blyton. At a point in my professional music career a journalist for a magazine asked me a question, 'If you had to be a fictional character from a book or film, who would you be?' I chose the cunning trickster Brer Rabbit. The journalist asked, 'Why?' 'Well,' I said, 'Brer Rabbit always saw the opportunities others didn't see. He sees the hole in the fence others had passed, nips inside and grabs all the carrots from the farmer's field.'

I like to think I'm good at seeing an opportunity others miss, seizing it and using it to move my creativity or career onwards. Whether I'm a rascal or not remains to be seen!

2

Elbow Grease

My first music exam at secondary school scored 96% but the maths never improved and in my third year I managed 4% for the mock O level. My teacher didn't help. When she was close up to my desk, bending over my exercise book, her breath smelled of old ashtrays. For a streamed comprehensive school, I thought it was pretty good but bullying was rife. Someone fired an air rifle out of a window, there were kids dressed in *Clockwork Orange* white coats and bowlers and someone said the school had the highest rate of pregnancies of any Leeds school. Someone even stole my conker, a sixty-fiver. That meant I'd played sixty-five conker matches and smashed everyone else's conkers to smithereens.

My favourite lessons were art, English, woodwork, metal work, and domestic science. I made a pretty mean shepherd's pie and fruit salad. My friend Glenn also made a fruit salad but it ended up on the steps of the school bus when he dropped the bowl as he climbed to the top deck. My heart went out to him and I remembered the time me and others taunted him by throwing his satchel out of the third floor windows of the school. I also remembered how I had lost something I'd made. I'd spent weeks in woodwork making a fruit bowl. I was so proud of it and had to give it a final polish on the lathe. Whether it was my teacher or me who had screwed the bowl incorrectly to the lathe I don't know, but one of us managed to crack the bowl and take a huge chunk out of it. I was heartbroken. Another experience in woodwork made me look like the class idiot. We were making toast racks and had to sand the base of the rack. The teacher came round and stared at my efforts at getting the wood smooth. 'You're going to have to put more elbow grease into that,' he said.

I put down the rack and went off to search every cupboard and nook and cranny of the woodworking room before I went back to the teacher and said,

'Sir, I can't find the elbow grease.' He must have thought I was mad. I'd never heard the term, which meant to put more effort into a task.

My efforts in metalwork were better. I made a fishing stool, an enamelled ashtray and a screwdriver; all handy items that never got used. I never played sports at school. I always had to choose between going onto the field for athletics, soccer or rugby and being beaten up by the bullies or taking no kit to school and being beaten on the backside with the games teacher's trainer. In addition to the trainer beating, I had to write a few hundred lines of 'I must remember to bring my PE kit.' I taped four pens together and became a dab hand at writing the lines in sets of four, but once the games teacher spotted my device I was beaten again. Relief came when the teacher offered me and a couple of others the job of washing the school rugby team strip instead of doing games. We did the washing for a couple of years in the domestic science lab and loved overfilling the washing machines with soap powder. The only sport in which we participated was the cross country run. Once on a run, my friend pointed out a house where his grandma lived and suggested we should pop in for a drink. The front door of the terraced house opened straight from the street into the front living room. My friend casually opened the door and the three of us ran inside in our vest and shorts – only to find an elderly couple sitting and having a cuppa and who were not my friend's grandparents.

Girls were of great interest and my first girlfriend there was Gail. I splashed out on her birthday and bought her a box of chocolate Matchmakers. I even kissed her. I also fell head over heels for a girl in a church youth group and then with one who didn't return my overtures of love. For years I dismissed others in the hope the one I'd set my heart on would come to her senses! It never happened and the first of my broken hearts was a painful one. Perhaps all the emotional angst of love distracted me from school work. I know my German teacher and English teacher did. I had a crush on my German teacher and my English teacher always wore at least four or five rings. I used to sit opposite her desk and couldn't take my eyes off her hands. Finger rings have been a sexual attraction for me since then. It wasn't until my third year that I had a light-bulb moment in all the other subjects. I got better at French and my art teacher refrained from telling me to stop acting like an idiot. Once, he twisted my ear good and tight. I got the message. Physics and chemistry were unfathomable. I was more interested in short circuiting any experiments in physics and my chemistry teacher was always blowing the place up. I did have a brief 'I'm going to be a great chemist moment' though. I bought all my own chemistry equipment from a shop in Leeds and started growing crystals. One of my greatest experiments involved shaking a test tube of iron ferrous sulphide and hydrochloric acid. Hey presto – hydrogen sulphide stink bomb. The tube exploded and I burnt a hole through my jeans and nearly my leg. Biology was just about manageable except for the frog and rat dissection. The best fun was passing around Desmond Morris' book *The Naked Ape* to read the pages about sex. Who would have thought I'd be working with him as a composer many years later.

I was taking extra curricula music theory lessons at the Leeds City College of Music. My theory teacher said I'd be much better if I wasn't so careless. I felt I was doing my best. In fact I'd even made my own record— at a railway station! There was never anything to do on Sundays so me and my mates would go down to Leeds Station, buy a platform ticket and watch the trains arrive and depart. There were no shops open in the centre on a Sunday except for a newsagent in the station so we'd hang around there for a bit. But the real find in the station was a machine called the Calibre Auto Recording Booth. The booth was a coin operated recording studio and enabled one to produce a three-minute vinyl record — delivered straight into your hand — of any song you wished to sing into the machine's microphone. I recorded one of the hit songs at the time, *Gimme Dat Ding* (1970). Back in the world of formal music lessons, I was slowly improving and got my grade five in music theory and finally my grade eight. I also had to sit my O Level in Music at college because my music teacher at school was hopeless. He'd given up on the class and spent the lessons telling ghost stories. Great if you wanted to become a ghost-hunter or go home and have nightmares. The school concerts and productions, however, were a success. I produced a set design for and performed in Gilbert and Sullivan's *Trial by Jury* and performed tenor sax in a concert and community sing-a-long for Radio Leeds. Then came the blackouts!

The situation arose because of the combination of two events. In October 1973 news broke that Arab states had launched an attack on Israel. The ensuing war led to the quadrupling of oil prices. Oil supplies to the West were also reduced by the Arab states. To make matters worse, the miners union in the UK decided miners should work to rule in response to proposed caps on their wages and began an overtime ban. By the end of 1973 coal reserves were low. The government couldn't survive any prolonged period of high oil prices nor could they survive any prolonged miners' strike. They had no option except to impose restrictions on the amount of power we could use. Electricity was rationed and businesses were forced to use their power on only three days of the week. Families saw their income fall as workers (except for those in the essential services) could only bring home three days pay per week. Houses and streets in the blackout areas were plunged into darkness and candles became one of the commodities difficult to find.

The blackouts were regarded as the greatest economic crisis since World War II. Having to spend time away from school during this period was a creative godsend and fuelled a lifelong love of poetry. One of my best mates, Andrew, had a typewriter. I'd been given one for Christmas by my parents and we decided we'd use them for writing poetry. Initially, we were inspired by an album we chanced on called *The Faust Tapes*. The LP was the third album released by the German band *Faust*. It was a 'cut-and-paste' album released in the blackout year of 1973 and was somewhat Dadaist in its approach. The content consisted of spliced together segments from the band's private collection of recordings not originally intended for release. Rather than appreciate the album for its originality and creativity, Andrew and I thought the album was hilarious, wacky and we would pretend we liked it just for a laugh. Yet somehow, listening to the segmented sections of the recorded material led our brains to poetry. Perhaps it was because of the short-form segments on the album. In only a few days I found I'd written a fair number of poems and the blackout days became the times our first attempts at verse blossomed. In my first collection were poems with titles such as *When God Called Round at our House, Please Mr. President Don't Kill my Life*, *I've Lost my Whiskey at the College Fete* and *Lighthouse Lullaby*. And so it was that on creativity's evolutionary tree, my future career as a composer and poet was connected by common descent to early experimentation with music and words.

1973 was also the year of my fanaticism about fashion. I was a great fan of Elton John, saw him live around the time of his *Don't Shoot Me I'm Only the Piano Player* album and adored the flamboyant clothing he wore. I bought cravats, frilled shirts, and got my mum to make me fringed jackets. I even made a pair of ZOOM shaped spectacles. I often practised at the piano wearing the stuff! Although this was probably my favourite 'look', I went through many other fashion fads: drainpipe trousers, flares, bellbottoms, loons, Wrangler and Levi corduroy suits, two tone suits, the tartan patches that the band Bay City Rollers made all the rage and the satin jackets made popular by pop star Marc Bolan and my schoolmate Gary whom I envied as, at the age of fourteen, he was able to make his own clothes. Most of the clothing I wore was bought through advertisements in the back of music journals *New Musical Express* and *Melody Maker* otherwise I got it from stalls in Leeds Market. My other passion at the time was for comic books on horror, superheroes, monsters or the supernatural. My favourite was *Adventures into the Unknown*, one of the first American horror comic-book magazines. I believe it was this comic-book series in particular that fuelled my future fascination with narrative structure and storytelling technique.

In 1974 we had our first holiday abroad. My father wanted to return to Poland to visit family he hadn't seen since before World War II. He missed his homeland and all the land taken away from his family. I found a fragment of one of his poems written in broken English:

'I know one place I can't forget,
Where my only memory so sweet.
It was with charm and gift from God,
With sound of bees, birds always song,
Where golden fields with wheat a lot,
I used to walk all day along.
I know I lost, no more is mine again
No way today to make revenge.'

In 1974 Poland was behind the Iron Curtain and a part of the communist bloc. Getting there was a bureaucratic and logistical nightmare especially since my dad wanted to do the trip in our Hillman Imp. The Hillman Imp was a small somewhat cramped economy car. It was the first British mass-produced car with the engine in the back and with the engine block and cylinder head cast in aluminium. The car had many useful design features, which didn't appear in many cars until years later, but reliability wasn't one of them as we were to learn when travelling through West Germany. We were on the autobahn when the gear box suddenly decided to jam. It gradually became difficult for my father to change down to first gear and finally, once the car was stopped, the gearbox wouldn't function. I don't know how we got to a garage — perhaps we were towed or perhaps the car started again and we crept along until we got there. A team of mechanics looked at the engine. It was going to take time. They suggested we stay overnight in an adjoining house. It was an awful night. The three of us were crammed into a cold cellar bedroom. At one point, when the light went on in the middle of the night when one of us needed the loo, we saw the walls of the room were crawling with cockroaches. No-one could get back to sleep. In the morning we went out to see the car or rather the bits of it. The engine and gear box had been disassembled and was spread out like a mechanical jigsaw. It was shocking to see. Nowadays, with all the support networks available, it wouldn't be a problem. But for a family on their first adventure abroad, to be stuck on the road to the Iron Curtain was extremely stressful.

The following day the engine and gear box were reassembled. The gear box appeared to be working until we left and discovered the gears were playing up again. It was just possible to keep moving so we pressed on to the border between West and East Germany that divided Western Europe from the communist bloc. The Iron Curtain seemed to go on for miles. Check points, soldiers, watchtowers and document and visa checks all made for a very stressful time. After a lot of document stamping, stern looking soldiers searching the car, mirrors rolled under it and an extra helping of officialdom for good measure, we were finally allowed through. It was at that point we hit another problem. The border had a bridge above a river. On the bridge was a hut where an officer peered through an open hatch and checked our papers. It took ages. I was in the car but my mother had decided to join my father. Out of nowhere, a swarm of mosquitoes attacked my mum. She was severely bitten and ended up with well over a hundred bites. The first thing we had to do on arriving in Poland was to find a doctor. My mum was sent to hospital where she was treated and had her legs bandaged. It was some time before she could walk as her legs were so swollen. The final part of the journey from the Polish border to the village of Chobienia in Lubin County, South West Poland, where my Aunt Helena lived, was as eventful. The roads and tracks we followed weren't on our map, there were few road signs if any, and we got totally lost. Night fell and we were aimlessly driving in the dark. At one point my father reversed the car onto a railway track. A few hours later, we found the village. It was the middle of the night but we still knocked at a stranger's house and shouted to them when they leant out of their bedroom window.

'Do you know where Helena lives?'

They were happy to give directions and send us on our way. We arrived weary but elated. My father came face to face with a sister he had not seen for over forty years. The tears and hugs went on and on.

I should describe the background to my father's journey back to his roots. My father Nikodem came from a family of seven: Viktor, Fabijan, Edward, Antonina, Serafina, and Helena. Edward was taken away by the Soviets at the beginning of the war to help build an airport at Grodno. He was in his mid-twenties and was never seen again. Antonina ended up in Latvia. Serafina was taken with her children to Omsk in Siberia, 4316 km from her home. The family endured dirty train journeys, hunger and a further deportation to East Ukraine before managing to return to Poland after the war. All the brothers died before my father was able to reunite with them. He was heartbroken. They were all born in Zarudzie, (not to be confused with a village of the same name in current day Poland) a hamlet now situated in Belarus. The land had changed hands so many times. My father had a Polish passport and always identified as being Polish but at the time he was born, in 1912, there is the question of which country he was actually born in? To answer that, I need to dip a toe into the history of Poland. Poland's history began with the migration of the Western Slavs to Polish lands in the early Middle Ages. The first dynasty in the tenth century was the Piast dynasty and Duke Mieszko 1 was considered to be the creator of the Polish state. During the fourteenth to sixteenth centuries, Poland developed close ties with the Grand Duchy of Lithuania and a commonwealth was formed. This came as a result of marriage. Jogaila, the Grand Duke of Lithuania, married Queen regnant Jadwiga of Poland and he became crowned as Poland's king and was named Władysław II Jagiełło. The commonwealth ended in 1795 after Polish territory was invaded and partitioned by the Russian Empire, the Kingdom of Prussia and the Habsburg Monarchy. No independent Polish state existed between 1795 and 1918. It's extraordinary – Poland was wiped off all maps during that period.

The second Polish Republic was established in 1918 and continued until the outbreak of World War II in 1939. My father was born in a Poland that wasn't on a map. In the year he was born, that land was a part of the Russian Empire. By the age of six, however, he'd be truly Polish again when the second republic began. It wasn't until 1992 that I got to take my father back to Zarudzie to meet family he hadn't seen since before the war and visit the ruins of his family home. My grandparents Hipolit and Anna were famous for their wealth in the region. They had many hectares of land, fields and forests, and an imposing wooden house. But in 1939 the Soviet Union invaded Poland shortly after Germany invaded from the West. The Soviet government annexed the entire Polish territory and took it under their control. Their reason was that Russia had to help the Ukrainians and Byelorussians who found themselves in territory that had been supposedly illegally annexed by Poland. Everything my grandparents owned was taken by the Soviets. Only the foundations of the house are left.

Our first trip to meet all our relatives in Poland was full of revelation and emotion. My Aunt Serafina was still working in the fields with a scythe whilst her son-in-law dealt with the cows and pigs. I remember Serafina hacking off the head of a chicken a few hours before we sat down for a chicken roast. There were many meals accompanied with vodka and my father had brought gifts of *Nivea* skin cream for the men. Oddly, they were well received and the cream must have been all the rage in 1970s Poland! The women were given nylons. Aunt Helena was frail with poor eyesight. My father insisted on taking her to Lubin to buy her an eye-test and glasses. I also met my cousin Zyta, a wonderful embroiderist, and my cousin Mietek and his wife Genowefa. Mietek had been a communist official and was a dab hand at emptying bottles of spirits. I really hit it off with his daughter Elżbieta, and as a couple of teenagers, we had a wonderful couple of weeks of walks and picnics. She had wanted us to buy her a pair of Levis and the *Crazy Horses* album by pop group The Osmonds, but I think we'd bought so many presents for family that she only got the album. Elżbieta was fun, attractive and sometimes melancholic. I heard many years later that at a relatively young age she had committed suicide. There was also Janek and Danuta. Janek wrote an astonishing unpublished novella about Serafina and her family's deportation to Siberia in the Soviet reign of terror when 1,200,000 Poles were sent to the Gulag labour camps. Other relatives were my cousin Heniek a chemical engineer and his wife Jozefa and their sons Grzegorz and Piotr. Grzegorz became one of Poland's greatest natural history photographers and filmmakers and we finally got to collaborate in 2019 when I composed the score for his film *Anima Animalis*. In the lake district of Poland we got to visit my cousin Michał, his wife Basia and their children Marek, Anna, and Andrzej. It was Marek and Anna with whom I spent most time. Andrzej died as a young man in a naval accident and Marek also died in his prime. Marek came to visit us in the UK a few years after we visited Poland. I remember him taking photographs of a butcher's window stocked with meat and the aisles of supermarkets piled high with cat and dog food. He'd never seen anything like it in his own country.

My mid-teens were also challenging in terms of learning about people. One day a newspaper headline turned our world around. *The Sun* newspaper, among many others, carried a front page headline story about Stefan Kiszko, a man who had allegedly assaulted and murdered a child. That was a bad day for my mum and dad to go to work and for me to go to school. It wasn't long before everyone was asking or assuming we were connected to the murderer. It's true that our surname was unique in the UK but we had never known of any other Kiszkos. Many people, however, chose to tar us with the same brush. It wouldn't have happened if the murderer's name was Smith or Johnson. No-one seeing a headline about 'criminal Smith' would immediately blank out their neighbour also called Smith. Yet that's what happened to us. We tried to explain we didn't know of this other Kiszko and checked with our extended family. We found we were unconnected. That aside, we were still shunned by people who chose not to believe it. The turnaround came years later. It was discovered Stefan had underlying difficulties and had been coerced by a detective into giving a false confession. It was also the time when DNA testing was introduced and the DNA found on the child's clothing was found not to belong to Stefan. Eventually the DNA was traced to the actual murderer. Unfortunately Stefan died a short time after his release and so did his mother with whom he lived. The stress must have finished them off. In 1998 a feature TV movie *A Life for a Life* was made about this miscarriage of justice. For me, it was a wake-up call about how people quickly jump to conclusions and base their prejudices on assumption and hearsay.

Whilst that drama continued, I felt extremely uncomfortable at school and in social situations. I suppose slogging away at my music was a helpful distraction. Quite soon after getting to grips with the saxophone, my father insisted we buy a second-hand piano for the princely sum of £6. It even came with a free violin though I only ever got to grade one on the fiddle. I was now learning three instruments and one of my primary school teachers, David Mewis, offered to teach me piano for fifty pence a week. I became busier too with music theory lessons, rehearsals and performances with The Leeds City College of Music saxophone quartet plus all the concert band rehearsals. There were also the performances I had to give every time friends of my parents came to visit. I also had friends round to play clarinet and sax duets in the garden. This was also an opportune time to try out the practical jokes I liked to play on friends. I had a lot of tricks and gags I'd bought from the 'joke shop' in Leeds: pretend cigarettes, soap that started out as normal but then turned your hands black, nail through the finger tricks, knives with retracting blades, plastic piles of poo, joke vomit, fake scars, cuts and wounds, card tricks, masks, spiders, stink bombs and itching powder. The itching powder and stink bombs were not great laughs for those who had to endure them. Kids at school often put itching powder into clothing that was hung up whilst I was out playing games, but usually they'd get a handful of powder, sneak up on you from behind, reach down your collar and sprinkle it in. There was no way you could get rid of it and often spent the day scratching your neck and back. The stink bombs could clear a playground in seconds.

It was around this time my phobia of physical illness, as set up by the St. John Ambulance manual of injuries given to me at age five years old, took hold again. My phobia was retriggered by the death of my grandma, an aunt, and Marisia the wife of Andrej, my father's half-cousin. He'd spent years trying to get the Russians to allow his wife to join him in the UK. After many failed attempts, he finally succeeded. He was lucky to have been in the UK himself and was the only one of our relatives my father had found in England. He'd been living in Birmingham for years and we never knew. The reunion of Andrej and my father was full of tears of joy. We had a couple of happy years with Andrej and Marisia partying and dancing at our house or theirs. Sadly she very quickly got ill with cancer and died. The same happened to my aunt. She was young and it was a huge shock for me as it was for my uncle and cousins. The succession of these three deaths suddenly brought home the fragility of life and my vivid and creative imagination made me think I had or was going to acquire life threatening illnesses. Yet I sailed through those childhood and adolescent years with only the usual bumps and bruises and never broke a bone. I'd got through the measles, rubella, chicken pox and the excruciating mumps. The only things that bugged me were myopia and a strange habitual 'tic'. The tic was a movement of my right ear down to my right shoulder where I would rub the ear against the shoulder and then repeat the movement with the left ear and left shoulder. There'd be many repetitions of the sequence especially when no-one was watching. My parents were worried as it went on for well over a year. Strangely, it subsided after a visit to a church whilst on our summer vacation. I remember sitting in the church and praying about it. Sometime after that, it never happened again. The power of prayer? Or the power of positive thinking? Cue my conversion to Christianity at age fifteen.

How did it happen? My father was Roman Catholic and my mother a Protestant. I guess they both couldn't agree how I should be religiously schooled and so I went through childhood not going to church. I do remember going to Bible club classes as a five-year-old and collecting pretty stamps illustrated with Bible characters. There was also a Bible club at my second primary school. How or why I ended up there I don't know but I think it was due to the fact that a girl I fancied was in the club. Not that kind of club! I joined a church youth group at Middleton Park Baptist Church when I was around fifteen years old. I liked all the songs they sang, which were known as 'choruses' back then. I got a girlfriend there and I enjoyed the camps and walks in the Yorkshire Dales. My conversion to Christianity happened at a concert given at the church by a gospel artist Adrian Snell. Adrian was an accomplished pianist and songwriter and looked like he'd stepped out of 1960s hippiedom: faded jeans, waistcoat, headband and very long hair. I was incredibly moved by his music and lyrics and was blown away by his first album *Fireflake* (1975). I remember hearing Diana Princess of Wales had asked to meet Adrian after a performance of his song *Feed the Hungry Heart* at Peterborough Cathedral. After her death, several of Adrian's albums were found in her record collection. She must have been a fan as well as sharing his worldview about helping the oppressed. I met Adrian again in the nineties prior to his concert at Yad Vashem Holocaust Memorial in Israel.

So, I answered the call at the end of Adrian's performance to become a Christian. After that, a lot of my time was spent with my new friends or on church activities. I joined in with performing songs on piano or using basic guitar chords and discovered a very vibrant creative community. My father hated it. It was difficult for me to get out of the house to go to the youth group or see my girlfriend. He hated evangelicalism, evangelism and the arguments we had about whether one could have a personal relationship with God. He felt it was taking me away from practising my instruments. My faith, however, was strong and I took part in every church event that was going: services, youth meetings, church weekends away, door to door evangelism, children's missions, prayer meetings as dull as ditch water, and the co-writing of a musical *Happy Birthday Jesus*. I soon wanted to move on to another church in Belle Isle —West Grange Church — where I knew there was a lively young people's group, plenty of music and more girls. It was there that I met another like-minded musician and we formed a singing duo Spice of Life. We toured churches and youth groups and even performed at the Greenbelt Arts Festival. That was a big gig for two seventeen year olds! To think that years later, in my mid-forties, I would discard any truck with Christianity would have seemed heretical thinking on my part back in the day.

One thing I didn't understand at that time is how I ended up in the very small sixth form at my school. I had no idea about what it meant to stay on at school nor did my parents. On my council estate all the boys were expected to leave school at sixteen and go to work. Perhaps the fact I wanted to stick around with school friends who were going to stay on had something to do with it; or perhaps I was guided by one of my teachers. I had the requisite O levels to press on with education and found myself studying Art, English Literature, French and General Studies. I took the A level equivalent in music — the grade eight exam in music theory at Leeds City College of Music. I passed everything even though on one examination day I forgot to turn up for part of the art paper. I was astonished to pass the A Level French as I was forced into taking the subject, disliked it and struggled with translation. In the second year, my school mates were talking about applying for college or university. I had no idea how the system worked and my parents were none the wiser. My father was adamant for me not to leave home so I went ahead anyway and applied for a place at Bretton Hall College (University of Leeds). I thought the close proximity to Leeds would at least placate him. It gradually dawned on me, however, that my father's need to have me so close was an emotional reliance on me. By this time, my mum and dad were often argumentative and, as an only child, I didn't know where to turn. I felt as if I was their emotional buffer. My father often tried to emotionally blackmail me to take his side. I couldn't remember ever seeing my father cuddle my mother, kiss her or embrace her in a loving way. I grew up with them sleeping in separate bedrooms for many years. The rift was so bad that sometimes me and mum would stay up late and watch TV whilst my dad was out doing a late shift on the buses. If we timed it right, we'd flick back the curtains at the appropriate time, look across the back garden and over the fence and we'd see him walking back from the local bus station. My mum would then turn off the TV and lights and we'd make a quick getaway for bed. We later learned my father was wise to this and it had, of course, deeply upset him. It widened the rift between him and mum. My mother, who I always regarded as extremely brave, just wasn't brave enough to get out of the marriage. She'd spent years being told what to do, where to go and with whom she should be friends but still stayed in the relationship. If anyone was going to escape it was going to be me.

3

Accelerando

I was offered an interview at Bretton Hall College to do a teaching degree. I don't really know why I considered teaching but I was quickly deterred from thinking about it at my interview. The tutor interviewing me suggested I should sign up for their new BA degree course in Creative Arts. Bretton Hall is an exceptional Grade II* listed country house in West Bretton near Wakefield, West Yorkshire. The house is surrounded by parkland and woods and has two lakes. The 224 acre parkland is now the home of the Yorkshire Sculpture Park and the 100 acre Bretton Country Park has been a nature reserve since 1994. The estate housed Bretton Hall College between 1949 and 2001. The mansion house rooms have Adam style ceilings, the old dining room is decorated in Rococo style, and the old drawing room has a Baroque ceiling. The house had many different areas where students lived in their first year: Potteries, Back Landing, Bull Ring, Old Maids, and Mens Main on the top floor of the mansion where I spent my first year. What was so remarkable about the place was its idyllic location. We felt like we were in the middle of nowhere. It was a long walk down to the village to catch a bus into Wakefield or Barnsley so we seldom ventured away from the campus. It made for a very intimate setting and everyone got to know each other pretty quickly. One year when it snowed heavily, the college was cut off completely. Catering staff were unable to get in and students had to man the refectory.

New friends and the immersion in all things creative came quickly. I'd opted to divide my degree into music, visual arts and inter-arts. Inter-arts was a brand new subject area — a fusion of English, drama, filmmaking, dance, art, music and performance art. In fact, no-one really knew what inter-arts was about until we'd created it and create it we did. Some of the works I wrote or co-created during the three years of inter-arts were: *Picnic in December* and *Lord Scribble and his All-*

Musical Dinner. These were music-theatre works. The former was scored for male voice, female voice, clarinet, guitar and narrator and the latter for the protagonist Lord Scribble, two pianos, gong, and a dinner table of guests who had beaters as their cutlery and chime bars and other percussion as their plates. The large dinner gong was concealed until its entry when it was wheeled out of a cupboard behind the audience and struck hard to make them jump! At one point in the work, Lord Scribble was meant to tear up a copy of the score but unfortunately tore up the original — the only score available at the performance. The rest of the piece had to be improvised!

The Surrealist Breakfast
During one of the worst winters, we set out a table for breakfast for four in the snow. Onlookers were able to watch us dine from the comfort of the centrally heated refectory.

Room Environments
Room Environments was one of the high points in our inter-arts performance art work. Three rooms in Bretton Hall mansion were chosen: the conference room (once the breakfast room of the house), the common room (once the tapestry drawing room of the house) and the music salon, a raked modern auditorium in the music school. The conference room presentation had three characters: Past Character in eighteenth-century costume, Modern Man in contemporary costume and Transitional Character, who had the attributes of both past and present. The audience sat at a large table in the room and, since the room was once a breakfast room, they were served breakfast. The piano and harpsichord accompanied the meal, again to represent past and present. On the table we created a still life that was modelled on the images of fruit in the murals on the walls. The Modern Man character performed movements characteristic of people who might meet in a conference room. There was a simple script and poetry which connected with the history and present day usage of the room. Half way through the performance we had a student knock on the door and accidentally interrupt, apologise and step out again. This represented the world outside the room.

In the common room performance we covered the floor with newsprint and painted footprints on the paper to illustrate how crowded the room becomes. We pinned contemporary posters over what would have been the location of original tapestries. The characters in this section made entrances and exits based on how people moved through the room and adopted poses of how people sit and converse.

We were greatly inspired and influenced by Oskar Schlemmer's (1888–1943) *Triadic* Ballet (1922) and created two dances: the 'ceiling dance' and the 'wall dance' celebrating the period decoration in the room. A red lamp also created an abstract image on the walls – suggesting the room had been taken over by a new order. In terms of sound, a tape recorder played extracts of collected conversation heard in the room. Coffee was also served during the performance.

The Music Salon section was incredibly atmospheric. We blacked out the salon and placed twenty music stands in a random arrangement across the auditorium. We projected a light at these to create giant shadows of the stands. Two cassette recorders played experimental music from beneath the audience's seats. The salon had two pianos and a pianist at one played a classical work whilst the second pianist played a modern work. Both players performed simultaneously. The appearance of a conductor created patterns of movement and gesture as the baton beat time in the air. Finally, an electronic element on a Moog synthesiser suggested that music in the salon was breaking new ground in contemporary music.

Sheep Farming on the Via Dolorosa
This was a play I wrote that combined the principles of sheep husbandry with Christ's walk along the *Via Dolorosa* to Golgotha. The play sought to examine human suffering from a philosophical, theological and existential stance. It never got performed.

New Archeological Discoveries
This was an 8mm film I made with my inter-arts buddy Andrew Cartwright and our friend Dave Jones. The gripping work involved filming a train arrive at Wakefield Westgate station, dental surgery, and the burying of a sink. I think we placed it firmly in the surrealist period of our works.

The Quest of Man
This open air promenade style production journeyed around the lake. It was a ritual to cast out the evils of materialism and celebrate the riches of nature. On the journey, the audience encountered statements and challenges as they met the characters Wealth, Scientific Man, Sensuality, Politics, Philosophy, and Time. Each of the characters offered the audience different methods of cheating death. The final act of the production took place in Death's domain where materialism would be finally conquered. We used a scrapped car as a symbol of the evils of materialism and dragged the car with ropes to symbolise the pain and agony necessary to achieve purification. A fire was lit and the car was ritually sacrificed

as fulfilment of achieving a new belief system, one that rejected materialism and heralded an era of environmental consciousness.

I mention these works as they were instrumental in developing an unconventional approach to how stories could be told. We embraced different artistic disciplines, juxtaposed them and pioneered 'inter-art narratives'. Lecturers, who were as new to the course as we were as the 'guinea pigs', often looked at our productions with dropped jaw and exclaimed, 'this is what inter-arts is all about!' It was the college's focus on experimentation that gave us the freedom to allow our imaginations to play with form and content and use unusual environmental backdrops for our work. The creative flow at that time, for me and others, ran like a torrent. Luckily I was able to swim with its current and discover a highly individualistic approach to creativity.

One of my composition tutors at Bretton was Duncan Druce (1939–2015), Duncan was a viola and viola d'amore player who played in Sir Peter Maxwell Davies' (1934–2016) ensemble *The Fires of London*. Sir Peter was one of the country's most eminent contemporary music composers. I was a huge fan of his music-theatre works and decided to write a dissertation on the development of his music theatre scores. Duncan opened up the way for me to meet the great Max! Max invited me to his apartment in King's Cross, London. I'd prepared interview questions and, looking back on it, I was privileged he was willing to sit through such a long interview and offer pearls of wisdom. In one of my questions I made a comparison of musical devices Maxwell Davies employs in his works with devices the artist Stanley Spencer (1891–1959) used in his paintings. I was also writing a dissertation on the work of Stanley Spencer at the time and I mentioned to Sir Peter how I was fascinated with Spencer's war mural *The Resurrection of the Soldiers* (1929). In the mural, Spencer organises the composition of crosses held by the soldiers as if they are frames through which one is able to view intricacies and detail which at first glance may have gone unnoticed. I proposed the idea that perhaps Sir Peter deliberately constructed a similar device in his works. Did he use the structure of music in such a way that a work not only communicated as a whole but also used musical microcosms of the total work which were only visible if one penetrated the surface of the score and 'looked through the frames.' I asked whether that would be a valid interpretation. Sir Peter responded with a very lengthy and erudite answer which began with, 'It might be and I find it a very interesting point of view.'

Sir Peter went on to discuss musical complexity in Bach inventions, the late Beethoven quartets and finished his response with, 'I don't know who Beethoven discussed the complexities of his late quartets with. I suspect with nobody and when you asked about the purposes and natures of complexities that related to Spencer, which I find very interesting, I'm at a bit of a loss with knowing what to do with the question.'

Now here was the exciting bit and the rabbit that got pulled out of the hat. Sir Peter paused for a moment and then got up and walked over to a large chest. He opened a drawer and took out a few sheets of paper. As he placed them in front of me, I immediately knew what I was looking at. They were original Stanley Spencer drawings. A few of them were studies for his paintings – in particular *St. Francis and the Birds* (1935) – and one was a drawing of a plan for a Spencer exhibition. Spencer had drawn tiny miniatures of his paintings and titled them, showing in which order they were to be hung. As if that wasn't enough of a surprise, Sir Peter then offered me the drawings on loan for the rest of the year until I'd finished my dissertation. I felt as if he was handing over the crown jewels. It was a remarkable gesture of trust and generosity. After the interview finished, we talked casually for a while. Sir Peter asked me which of his scores I owned. Most of my studies had been done with scores from libraries. I told Sir Peter I had no scores of my own, they were simply too expensive to buy. Sir Peter nodded and went over to his large chest again. This time he pulled open a drawer full of his scores. He took out a selection which would have been prohibitively expensive for me to buy. He opened the cover of each one, signed them and handed the manuscripts over to me. It was a generous gift. I left the apartment gobsmacked. In my hand was a bag of Maxwell Davies scores and under my arm a set of original Stanley Spencer drawings.

As for my own skills as a fledgling composer – well I'm not sure I quite knew what I was doing. Apart from the couple of avant-garde music-theatre pieces I composed, there was no proper composition tuition such as looking at form, structure or orchestration. I took a module in 'creative musicianship' but the best I produced were a few pieces for small ensembles. I had no idea whether I could compose for brass band, string orchestra or symphony orchestra. There wasn't the opportunity to learn or the chance of trying a composition out with the college orchestra. At best, I delivered a few piano pieces, a clarinet and piano piece and a viola sonata. I never had any designs on becoming a composer. In my mind, composing was something only the privately schooled, privileged and top music scholars got to do. In any case, I loathed my clarinet lessons and didn't have the motivation to keep practising piano even though my piano teacher Jess Jameson (1928–2017) was one of the kindest people I've ever met. I wanted to please her and managed to get some Debussy arabesques under my belt but I called it a day after that. Little did I know there was a composer hiding away in me somewhere but it wasn't the right time or environment for him to emerge. To give an indication of how seriously I was taking my music studies, I organised a Music Society concert with my friend and co-organiser Andy Cartwright. We commandeered a friend who was training to be a dentist to give a short lecture on dentistry during the concert. That's how seriously I took it. One of my major *faut pas* pranks was to find Andy's score he'd written for our composition tutor. Without Andy seeing it, I quickly scribed on the bottom of it, 'Three out of ten. This sounds like an inverted version of Star Wars.'

I then scribbled a signature of the composition tutor's name under my comment. A few minutes later, Andy shot into the room, grabbed his score and ran off to see said composition tutor for a tutorial on his work. The first time they both saw my remark was when they turned over to the last page of the score. Ouch!

Andy and I also formed a punk band with our mate Dave Jones. It was called *The Lads*. We had guitars with scalpels and banana skins hanging from the tuning pegs. We also had a folk band with our friend Christine – *The Ossett Quartet*. Most of the quartet's repertoire was about the nearby town of Ossett. We had no connection with the town, chose it at random and made it a kind of spoof cultural icon. Our maxim was if music could be sent up and not taken seriously then we'd endeavour to do just that. This capacity for having a laugh at everything also permeated our takeover of running the college café – The Greedy Pig. We served fat-gunged chips in buns and our special was the orange Ossett omelette – a standard omelette with added orange juice and peas. Guess what? It wasn't a popular choice on our limited menu. We also took over the folk club and invited punk poet Dr. John Cooper Clarke to perform. We knew it wasn't folk but that's why we did it. I also managed to fit in writing a serialisation *The Exaggerated Adventures of Sir Herbert Stone and Hector Lightfoot Crab* for the college's student magazine *Orangepeel*. Perhaps this was the seed of the humorous writing that occupied me in later life.

One of my crowning performance achievements was in the college's choral society concert. This was a major event that took place at Wakefield Cathedral. It was decided the Bretton music department would perform Bach's *Christmas Oratorio* for soloists, SATB choir and orchestra. The cathedral was full. The choir waited in expectation for the instrumental introduction that would lead into the opening *Christians be Joyful* chorus of the oratorio. It was by page five, a few minutes into the score, that fun and games began. The choir had a line,
'Christians be joyful and praise your salvation, Christians, be joyful.'
After 'praise your salvation' there was a two quaver rest when the choir paused for a moment before their next big statement 'Christians'. Unfortunately, I was ahead

of myself and sang the great rousing word 'Christians' in the two quaver gap of silence. The choir then entered at the right place, straight after me, with 'Christians.' I stuck out like a sore thumb and, after weeks of rehearsal, embarrassed everyone. What made it worse was that the dress code for men was evening suit: black jacket and trousers, white shirt and dickie bow. I didn't own a suit for concerts and could ill afford to buy one. So, against the choirmaster's edict, I turned up in a brown suit. When I made my glaring vocal error, it was much easier for the audience to spot me! At the end of the music section, the singer next to me turned and whispered in my ear, 'you can write home now and tell your mum you had a solo.'

There was nothing better at Bretton than hanging out with girls and spending the evenings playing games in the mansion's cellars. The laundry rooms down there were useful 'snogging rooms'. The cellars also had entrances to tunnels which, as rumour had it, ran under the lake. We tried to venture down one but got freaked out and never tried again. The game we most often played was sardines. It's a reversal of the hide-and-seek game. One person gets to hide and all the others search. When someone finds the hider then they must hide with them too. I once remember around eight of us on top of one another jam-packed into a telephone booth in the mansion. It was a good game in terms of being in close contact with people and getting to know them. These games often became a precursor to getting together with someone for a kiss and a cuddle or a bit of intimate exploration. Although I loved being intimate with women and had a few sexual adventures, I remained a virgin at college partly due to my Christian faith and partly due to a weird guilt complex — probably linked to my father's Roman Catholicism. Perhaps I thought I'd be judged for going astray. Or perhaps I wasn't bold enough. That said, I had an enjoyable time and later in life I made up for anything I missed.

In my second year I fell in love with a beautiful fashion and textiles student who was an accomplished tennis player. I hadn't lifted a racket since bashing a ball around the streets of the council estate I grew up on, so tried to speed learn in order to impress her. My efforts were feeble. Little did I know that I would have to call on those feeble efforts at the Cannes Film Festival in 2018. The festival has a Cannes networking tennis match every year organised by film financing companies. The organiser emailed to ask if I would take part in a match. I was keen to be at the event and explained I was an absolute beginner and hadn't played tennis since university days and it was only for a few weeks. No problem said the organiser and pointed out she'd never played tennis. I responded to the email with, 'then you're the person I want to play against.' It seemed like I had a match partner, but when I turned up at the event, the organiser decided to put me in a doubles match. 'Are you crazy?' he said.

He was even more concerned when he saw me boarding what was a somewhat beat up passenger jet. The trip to Canada was tremendous with a stay with my relatives in Vancouver before we set off on a road journey that took us to San Francisco, Portland, Los Angeles, San Diego, Tijuana, Las Vegas and Reno. One night, the four of us had to sleep in the car. It was the day we arrived in LA to find all accommodation had been bought up for a world conference of Jehovah's Witnesses. I suppose they wouldn't have minded us knocking on their doors!

Getting back into the swing of things at college wasn't too difficult and the second year was one in which Andy, Dave, and me honed our best performance art pranks. We called them Basic Concepts:

1. The Unrecognised Play. We prepared a short dramatic play and performed the lines whilst in a normal conversational situation with others. The idea was that those not in the know were unaware they were in a play.
2. The Freeze Effect. We stormed into a room as two detectives and shouted 'freeze'. More disturbing was that we hid in someone's wardrobe and burst out of it shouting 'freeze'. This usually caused palpitations and got us a bad name.
3. Rearrangement. We completely rearranged the furniture in a person's room whilst they were out. Or we moved their room layout outside.
4. Minimalisation. We replaced an object with one of the same type except it would be child or doll's house size. We often created minimalisations in kitchen areas – replacing open ironing boards with miniature ones.
5. Dead People Effect. We played dead as bodies strewn on the floors around the college.
6. Hold-up. We donned gangster gear and held up the college shop.
7. Alienation Effect. We cut ourselves off from everyone else with no explanation of why.
8. Instant Party. We wore party outfits, carried ghetto blasters and beer and entered someone's room and created an instant party.
9. Goldfish Pond Scenario. We created a goldfish pond in someone's room whilst they were out.
10. Déjà vu. We persuaded someone that they were having a déjà vu by using dialogue we'd repeat in a similar conversation a day or two later

Many of the ideas were fuelled by an interest in theatre and performance art, drawing inspiration from companies such as Welfare State, Red Ladder, Pip Simmons Theatre Group, Major Road, and Phantom Captain. My second subject for two years had been visual arts and I particularly liked working with my tutor Endre Roder, a Hungarian artist. Endre encouraged me and championed my work. I almost didn't continue with art as I decided to change to drama as a second subject. I was interviewed and accepted, but eventually decided to stick with visual arts. I produced a few drawings, paintings, etchings, a large canvas titled *Pregnant Shoppers*, and designed a board game. Unfortunately I never realised the art department had a life class until I'd finished with visual arts. If I'd known, it would have been a favourite spot for me.

One of the things that kept me interested in the visual arts was a fascination with set design. I'd designed a set for one of my secondary school productions and I wondered whether this could be a future career. With that in mind, I wrote to one of the top stage designers in the UK, Michael Annals (1938–1990). Michael had designed sets for the Old Vic, the National Theatre and for Broadway. I told Michael about my interest and asked him questions about his design for the production of George Bernard Shaw's *Heartbreak House* at the Grand Theatre, Leeds. Michael replied with a beautifully hand-written seven page letter in which he discussed his set design and construction techniques. He offered to meet me but I declined the offer, probably because it meant a trip to London I could ill afford. In hindsight, perhaps I should have jumped at the opportunity.

Set design called again when we had our second year placements in creative industries. I chose to do mine at Leeds Playhouse. My job was to help with the construction of sets, take care of basic props and be a general dogsbody. One of my most laborious but important jobs was during the run of two plays: *More More* by Caribbean playwright Mustapha Matura (1939–2019) and *Equus* by Peter Shaffer (1926–2016). *Equus* is a play about a child psychiatrist who attempts to unravel why a seventeen-year-old boy blinded six horses. In the play the main characters Alan and Jill, who works at a local stables, have a notorious and controversial nude sex scene. *More More* was entirely set on a lawn tennis court. *Equus* was on every evening for its run; *More More* ran every lunchtime. Since both plays ran on the same day, the stage had to be reset each day. In the morning I'd lay the artificial grass on the stage and pin it down with hundreds of staples. After the lunchtime run, I had to remove the artificial grass so that the stage was ready for the *Equus* set. Every staple had to be found and removed from the stage because a few hours later a nude couple would be rolling about all over it for ten minutes. What a responsibility! I didn't want to carry the can for any bum injuries or worse! Then again, if I'd missed a few, I might have started up a trend for piercing in the seventies.

The Playhouse bar was a good place to hang out pre and post performances. I especially liked talking to a guy who worked on the bar. We had a lot in common:

music, visual arts, performance art, theatre and the ability to think light years outside the box. He was a student studying art at Leeds Polytechnic but was really into music. He had a fantastic presence and walked around with an air of theatricality. He often wore a cloak or gown and his eyelashes were darkened with mascara. His name was Marc and he was putting a band together. Marc was interested in my music and performance art works and suggested I might like to get involved with his group. At age twenty I wasn't as adventurous as I could have been and didn't follow up the offer but watched the young Marc Almond and his band Soft Cell go on to release the massive hit *Tainted Love*. I wonder what a collaboration might have led to?

During the final year, Andy, Dave and I rented a terraced house in the tiny village of Haigh. Haigh started out as a pit village and had its own colliery until 1968. There was nothing there except a row of houses, a chapel and a post office. The nearest place for a half decent egg and chips was Woolley Edge motorway service station where we'd nip through the back door and into the café when no-one was looking. Our house was freezing, the drain was constantly blocked and getting the coal fire started in the morning whilst shivering in your pyjamas was no fun. We usually had to walk the couple of miles into college or Dave would give us a lift in his Ford Anglia. One night four of us went into Leeds to see a show at the Playhouse. Dave parked the Anglia underneath the arches railway bridge near the station. After the show we got back to the car and Dave opened the door and we all piled in laughing and joking. Dave turned the key in the ignition and off we went. A few hundred yards along the road he turned to us.

'This isn't my car.'

We all ignored it.

'This isn't my car.'

'Course it's your car,' we all chimed in.

'I'm telling you it's not.'

We continued laughing.

'The mileage is different.'

Dave pulled over. We all got out and looked at the car. He pointed to the number plate.

'See.'

True enough it wasn't his car. What happened was this: there are two arched bridges near Leeds railway station and the Anglia had been parked half way along the road under the second bridge. But when we'd returned to the car, we'd accidentally gone to the location of the first bridge, walked half way along and found an identical Anglia that had an identical door and ignition lock. After realising the error, we all piled back into the car and drove back to where we'd found it. Luckily the same parking spot was available. We left wondering whether its owner would ever realise it had been moved and if so why?

Towards the end of a very creative and successful three years of college, I still hadn't quite decided what to do next. I'd been spoilt in sampling a fabulous smorgasbord of the arts and I couldn't decide where my future might lie. I mentioned to a tutor that I'd like a job in the media, perhaps the BBC. I was taken to one side and it was explained to me that my Yorkshire accent was so 'thick' that no-one would understand me. Even at college some students had struggled with my dialect. My tutor suggested his wife, an elocution teacher, should help me to acquire Received Pronunciation, which was essential for a BBC job. Well it was then! How ironic that I spent time having my accent doctored and spent many an hour trying to correct my weak sounding 'r' only to find local dialects became all the rage years later. However, I was still at sixes and sevens about what I would eventually do and then came my epiphany: forget about being a set designer, a musician or joining the BBC — I was going to become a film director!

4

So You Wanna Be A Film Director?

To become a film director I needed a couple of things: tuition and money. I had neither. I trawled through post-graduate film and television courses and only found one that could be done in a short period of time and had the possibility of a scholarship. The course was the one year Post Graduate Certificate in Radio, Film and Television in the Department of Drama at the University of Bristol. It was one of the most sought after and competitive courses in the world. The course had been set up in the late sixties by Professor George Brandt (1920–2007). George was born in Berlin and fled Germany with his family after the Nazis came to power in 1933. He was an accomplished film editor, director, producer and academic.

The course was also known for taking students who were more mature in their years or who had other work experience. My chances as a twenty-one-year-old were slim. Furthermore, as the course requirements included having an honours degree, I only had an ordinary degree as that was the way the 'guinea pig first timer' creative arts degree at Bretton had been set up by the University of Leeds. So, I was the wrong age and didn't have the right qualification. The course also only accepted twelve students and only four scholarships were available. Hundreds of hopefuls annually applied. Undeterred by the application criteria, I applied anyway — especially since my father didn't want me to go. Against all the odds, I was invited for an interview. I could hardly believe it and wanted to prepare as best I could. I had a grey with a light brown check three-piece suit, a fancy shirt and a large knotted brown tie — the end of the seventies fashion statement! Despite my protestations, my father insisted he was going to drive me down to the interview in Bristol. I also took examples of my work with me: paintings, poems, my play, and music scores. As soon as I arrived, I realised the interview set up was a less formal affair. It became more and more obvious to me that I looked as if I was setting out for a wedding rather than strutting my stuff as a funky up and coming film director. The department's secretary showed me into the interview room. Inside was a very large table at which sat three university big wigs and Professor George Brandt. After the formal greeting, I laid out all my work on the table. It filled the whole space and made quite an impression. It was hard to stop me talking about it.

It was a few weeks before I heard anything. When the letter arrived, I could hardly contain myself. Not only had I been offered a place but a scholarship too. I later heard Professor Brandt had argued my case with the academic board. I didn't have the necessary honours degree to meet the entrance requirements but he had fought for me to get a place. Even more amazing was I ended up as the baby, the youngest student on the course. I never lived that down. The course secretary always prided herself in telling the story of how I came to be there.

'Martin came to the interview wearing a three piece suit and his dad brought him along. Sweet!'

It was at a party in the drama department that I met the woman who was going to become my wife years later. We became friends quickly, had similar cultural interests, and also discovered we shared a Christian faith. We formed a singing duo and sang at church services, youth events and Christian mission events. Most students who arrived for the course lived close to the Drama department. I'd been offered a place in student accommodation nearby but turned it down because someone I knew in Leeds knew someone in Bristol that could give me accommodation if I was prepared to share with a family. I felt obliged to go with the offer and it was cheap at the price, but it was miles out of the centre of Bristol in a house overlooking the old Whitchurch Airport runway. The airport's heyday was from 1930 to 1957 and it was one of the few airports in Europe that remained operational during World War II. To get to university meant a long bus journey, a walk across town, a short cut via the NCP car park lift to the eighth floor and then crossing the road to the Department of Drama.

If one believes in synchronicity, destiny, the universe setting up events or God intervening in personal affairs — and I must confess to believing in all of those at certain times in my life before chucking them out of the window — then one might speculate there was a reason for me ending up miles out of the centre. First, the old runway became the perfect location for the short film I made in Bristol, *Biggles Learns to Fly*. Second, I would never have got to meet a fifteen-year-old schoolboy who was sitting behind me on the bus one day and interrupted a conversation I was having about film. He was a film aficionado and had ambitions to get into the film industry. We became lifelong friends. Since that time, Vadim Jean has directed many successful feature films and TV dramas and is credited along with Gary Sinyor of producing and directing one of the first truly independent movies in the UK – *Leon the Pig Farmer* (1992). We worked together as co-writers on screenplays and I also ended up scoring a few of Vadim's TV projects: the ITV drama *Just Desserts*, the Channel 4 documentary series with Anita Roddick, *Skin Deep*, and the animated film *The Nutter Tales*. Whenever we got interviewed and were asked how we got together, we'd always say we met on a bus. The third opportunity that arose from living in Whitchurch came from sharing a house with a couple called Derek and Marilyn. I'd mentioned to them I had an interest in lighthouses and was keen to make a film about one. Coincidentally, Marilyn's brother-in-law Richard Lambert was a lighthouse keeper on Skokholm Island lighthouse off the coast of Pembrokeshire. Richard was a Bible believing born again Christian and his conversion happened as a result of mistuning his radio whilst searching for Radio Luxembourg. He landed instead on a programme by Christian broadcaster Trans World Radio. Initially, I got to speak to his wife Rose about an idea to make a documentary about the life of a lighthouse keeper. Once Richard had heard about the proposal and agreed to do it, there was only one thing I needed to do: sell the project to everyone on my course and get to Skokholm Island to meet Richard.

Every year on the university film course, one student got the opportunity to have their story idea made into a short film. There was a session where everyone had to pitch their movie, discuss the pros and cons of getting it made, garner interest and win supporters. You might imagine how embarrassed I felt pitching a film about a born again Christian to a room full of atheists, intellectuals, alternative thinkers and the revered Professor George Brandt. George, however, expressed interest and took my side in the flurry of negative comments my colleagues dished out. In no time at all, George was steering the conversation towards an in-depth discussion of the project and, before I knew it, it looked like the film was going to be green-lit. Students often found George a challenging person. His standards were high and he expected commitment, intellectual rigour and outstanding practical skills. Occasionally, if something went amiss in the department or he got annoyed, he would shout 'Shit and corruption', at which point everyone would dive for cover or would be well advised to. I always found him a wonderful person for intellectual sparring. As a result of his experience in the UK as an immigrant and his left wing politics, he completely understood my family background was similar to his own. I think this connected us in a special way. I was especially impressed when he invited my mum and dad for tea. They couldn't believe it – a bus conductor and a shop assistant being invited round by a professor. They were so worried about what kind of conversation they would be engaged in but George and his wife were accommodating and made them feel welcome and comfortable.

Getting the go ahead for the film meant arranging a recce of Skokholm Island and meeting Richard Lambert. During Easter, when I had a few days off to go back to Leeds and visit my parents, I announced it was great to see them but I was going to head off for Skokholm Island. I had nothing set up for the visit and they both stared at me incredulously. Before they could say anything, I insisted I was going and left the next day. I bought a ticket at Leeds Station and took the train to Haverfordwest in Wales. I then hitched the twelve miles to Dale, a small village located on the peninsula which forms the northern side of the entrance to the Milford Haven waterway. Looking out to sea, 2.5 miles from Dale, was Skokholm Island. I'd asked my driver whether there were bed and breakfasts in Dale and heard there were a few. He dropped me near the first one and luckily they could accommodate me. The next day I headed into the village and started doorknocking.

'Does anyone know of a boatman who could take me out to Skokholm Island?' A few people said no, a few said boats wouldn't go out due to the weather and a few directed me to other houses in the village. One house had a promising result: one of the boatmen a few houses up might be prepared to take me. I knocked on his door.

'Hello. I'm Martin. Sorry to disturb you. I'm going to make a film on Skokholm Island and need to get out there to do a recce for a couple of hours and meet the lighthouse keepers.'

The guy gave one of those looks that workmen give when they think it's going to be a difficult call even if it isn't.

'Skokholm. Can be tricky with currents at the moment.'

He looked me up and down.

'I only need a couple of hours.'

He thought about it. At that moment I thought it was my last chance — I'd never get there and there would be no film.

He nodded.

'Thirty-five quid.'

Half an hour later we were on our way.

Landing at Skokholm was like taking the first step into a new world. The island truly belonged to birds. Skokholm has the third largest Manx shearwater colony: fifteen percent of the world population of the species. It has twenty percent of Europe's population of storm petrels, several species of gulls and thousands of guillemots, puffins and razorbills. This cacophony of sound, along with the sea and wind, was perfect for the film's soundtrack as were the pink thrift and white sea campion for camera. Skokholm is only a mile long and half a mile wide so my walk to the lighthouse wasn't far. Inside, I was able to visit the radio transmitting room, the kitchen diner and climb the steps to the lamp. Outside, I checked the shed where I wanted to show Richard at work on his hobby of wood carving.

The recce was a success and even better was the boatman still waiting for me back at the landing. I returned to university with photographs of the recce and a structure for the film's narrative which I sketched out as a storyboard. There were four of us who went out to film on the island: Martin Kiszko (director and composer of the titles and end credit music), Susannah Shaw (camera), Mark Goertz (sound) and John Lavender (location manager). Michele Ryan edited the film and *Skokholm Light* turned out to be a unique lyrical portrait of the work of a lighthouse keeper prior to Trinity House (the official authority for lighthouses) switching over from manned lights to automatic ones. The film followed Richard's daily routine on the light as well as his contemplative thoughts about his faith and isolation. In the first scene, Richard finds a small block of wood floating near the landing. Throughout the film, the carving of the wood into what finally becomes a beautifully polished fish becomes a metaphor for the character building attributes a keeper develops during his solitary watches. But we couldn't leave the island without any drama. In fact, we couldn't leave at all. The weather turned. We had a laugh about it at first with lots of nautical jargon such as 'there's a squall coming in,' but we were actually stranded. The currents were now too dangerous for a boat to come in. Lighthouse keeper Richard to the rescue! There happened to be a Trinity House ship in the area. Richard was able to radio the ship and it headed for the island. Someway out, the ship sent out a zodiac to pick us up, return us to the ship and take us to Milford Haven.

Skokholm Light the film was released in 1980 and was screened at the National Film Theatre. It was also screened in the first half of an event at the Arts Centre Group, London. The ACG was a national organisation set up to support and encourage artists from all disciplines who also had a faith. On the evening I showed my film, there was another filmmaker who was projecting his student film. That filmmaker was the four times Oscar winning director Nick Park, the creator of *Wallace and Gromit*. Although that was the night we first met, it wasn't until Nick moved to Bristol after finishing his studies at the National Film School that we became life-long friends. The making of my film whetted an appetite for film direction. When the course ended, I went out in the big wide world to look for work to keep me going until I found a break into directing.

One of the first paid projects I was offered was to compose a music score for a new play at the Little Theatre in the Bristol Beacon (formerly known as the

Colston Hall). The play *The Man from Glasgow* was a ridiculous farce written by Jack Mariott and with song lyrics by poet and playwright Tony Connor. Dick Penny, who later spent twenty years as CEO of Bristol's Watershed arts venue, was working on the show as its administrator. Dick phoned me and said they had a musical in rehearsal which would open for a run in two weeks time. The composer had dropped out and Dick wanted to know if I could compose the music for ten songs, teach the songs to the cast and perform piano on stage during the performances. I gave it a few seconds thought. I had no reputation to lose so I said yes and set to work on creating arrangements for the songs. The schedule was demanding but the music was a success. The experience taught me to say yes when offered a demanding job and worry about how I would get through it once I'd put the phone down. Fortunately, I made enough money to stay on at my shared accommodation with four other guys, but I knew it would require all my effort to find work which would enable me to stay in Bristol.

I'd been carrying around a phone number in my wallet for nearly a year. Dave Lambert, my inter-arts tutor at Bretton, kept telling me he had a film composer friend in Bristol who I should meet. I phoned but he was in hospital having an appendectomy. I almost didn't bother to call again, but as persistence was something I felt I was a bit of a master at, I rang a few weeks later. The composer was Edward Williams (1921–2013). Edward had studied with eminent British conductor Muir Matheson (1911–1975) and one of England's greatest composers Vaughan Williams (1872–1958). Since the 1940s, Edward had composed many documentary film scores with British Transport Films and the Shell Documentary Film Unit. He was not only one of the greatest of UK film composers but one of the fathers of British electronic music along with composer Tristram Cary (1943-1998) who I met a few years later in Australia. Edward had a brilliant mind when it came to raising the bar in producing new ways of making music. At the point he invited me to visit his studio, he was completing the music for the landmark BBC David Attenborough series *Life on Earth*. It was a meeting that changed my life.

Edward's studio was behind a Chinese restaurant close to the BBC on Whiteladies Road in Bristol. The studio was above the kitchens and we often heard the staff playing Mahjong or chopping meat. I enjoyed conversation with Edward about music of all styles: electronic, orchestral and contemporary. We really got on especially in our discussions about electronic music. Edward was the owner of twelve EMS VCS3 synthesisers — the first affordable modular synthesisers in the UK — and I was a great aficionado of the instrument. Although he composed many scores using electronic analogue sources, such as VCS3 oscillators, he'd grown dissatisfied with the palette. Instead, he developed methods for electronically storing, modifying and transforming the sounds made by conventional musical instruments or the human voice. It was this remarkable approach he embedded in the soundtrack of the *Life on Earth* series. Edward mentioned he had copies of the *Life on Earth* programmes on a Philips VCR format and wanted them transferring to the brand new VHS (Video Home System) format. Did I know anyone who could do it? I adopted the same approach I'd used with accepting the work at the Little Theatre. I thought 'no I don't' but said 'yes I can do it'.

I took the tapes to technicians in the university Drama department. One of them said they'd be willing to do it. The tapes got transferred and I proudly took the copies to Edward and was paid a princely sum for my efforts. From this point, a working relationship developed. At first, Edward offered me menial jobs: opening up the studio and getting coffee brewed up ready for his arrival, sorting out the bookshelves, mopping the floor and toilet, preparing a salad lunch, carrying equipment around. Bit by bit I gained promotion and contacts. Edward introduced me to actress and dancer Deborah Cranston with whom he was working. Every month, over one weekend, they put on a music workshop and performance for children. After assisting Edward on a couple of the weekends, he handed over the baton and I worked with Deborah on many workshops, performances and children's opera camps. Deborah also introduced me to her husband Dennis Marks. Dennis was a leviathan in arts and social documentary films and with Barrie Gavin, another maven of arts filmmaking, they both worked out of the BBC arts unit in Bristol. I was in awe of their work.

Dennis was intellectually formidable, well read, erudite, and didn't suffer fools gladly. I felt I always needed to be up to speed on the arts before I could risk a conversation with him. I think I just about managed to hold my own the very first time Deborah and Dennis invited me for a meal. The starter was gazpacho followed by a main course with an avocado salad. At the age of twenty-two I'd never ever eaten gazpacho or avocado. Funnily enough, they weren't foods seen on the tables of working class northern families. Both the cold gazpacho and the texture of the avocado made me retch but I knew I had to politely get it down. It wasn't easy having a discussion about Kandinsky whilst trying to block out the taste of the food. A few years later my taste buds must have got gentrified as I couldn't get enough avocados. As for the gazpacho, I managed to handle it at dinner parties but still disliked every single spoonful. Dennis became especially instrumental in helping to kick start my music career. After hearing my 1985 score for the C4 drama series *Zastrozzi – a Romance*, he recommended me to World Wide Pictures director Martin Rosenbaum to compose an orchestral score for a Total Oil Marine film about oil rigs. *A Pattern of Energy* was all about the erection and maintenance of oil platforms. Not that jaw dropping until the music was added! My job was to emotionally connect the viewer with oil rigs and make them look sexy and dramatic. The success of the score landed me my first major BBC natural history series, the eight part *Land of the Eagle* produced by the BBC's Peter Crawford.

But that first connection with Edward and Deborah's children's music workshops also led me to Barrie Gavin. I'd always wanted to meet Barrie but it seemed like it would never happen. He was always directing abroad, in the US, in Asia, in Africa or working with celebrity musicians, artists and opera singers. How could one possibly meet such a stellar director? Well, one Saturday I was setting up chairs and percussion for the children's workshop. I also had to move a piano from one end of the hall to the other. As I struggled with moving it, a guy wearing a grey mackintosh and sporting a scruffy beard and long scarf came through the door.

'Want a hand with that?'

'Yes please.'

We moved the piano across the room.

'My son's taking part in a music workshop here. Just checking the performance is here too?'

'Yes,' I said, 'it would be good to see you.'

And then he left.

After the children gave their performance on Sunday, the same man stepped out of the audience to collect his son. He then came up to me and told me how much he'd enjoyed the performance.

'I'm Barrie. Barrie Gavin.'

I was speechless.

In those days when there was no internet, it wasn't possible to simply look a name up and see what someone looked like. I was stunned to find myself chatting with one of the world's greatest arts film directors and to think I'd thought he was just a guy from the street helping me to move a piano! Like Dennis, Barrie also recommended me for work in BBC arts. That experience taught me never to judge anyone by appearance. I still tell the story to my film music composition students: remember, the person you least expect to help or connect you because of a judgment you've made about appearance, dress, personality or education is often the one that will change your life. The chain reaction from a Bretton tutor, to a phone call and meeting with Edward, an introduction to Deborah, a meal with Dennis, and a chance meeting with Barrie whilst moving a piano all led to me having a group of well respected arts practitioners who helped to forge my path.

Around this time Edward promoted me! I found myself in the studio cleaning tape machine heads, tidying and checking cables, filling in his logbook of music compositions, labelling ten-inch spools of audio tape and beginning to help with the mix of music tracks. Much of Edward's creation of music involved the use of electronic transformation techniques. It would be normal to see audio tape travelling around the studio to create a tape delay effect or watch Edward twiddling the knobs of a VCS3 to manipulate the output of music from a tape recorder. The studio was cram-packed with Revox A77 tape recorders, EMS random voltage generators, pitch to voltage converters, filter banks and an EMS sequencer. The new mixing desk Edward had commissioned as a custom built piece of gear regularly started smoking, had gaps in the mixing board and we were always waiting for new faders or parts. We used it anyway and lived to tell the tale.

My first major project with Edward was to try my hand at co-producing and mixing an album of his music. His idea was to release an album of his *Life on Earth* soundtrack. This meant using the completed music tracks on quarter-inch audio tape and mixing the end of one track into the start of another to create longer music tracks for the album. Often, four tracks would be joined in this way to create one piece. It wasn't easy as we didn't have a multi-track machine. It all had to be done with two-track tape recorders. So, for a track that required three mixes to join four different pieces, we would line the start of each piece up on a separate tape recorder. For the incoming sections on each tape recorder we would have to calculate a pre-roll that would start at a pre-determined point of the outgoing section on the tape recorder that had played before the incoming one. My precarious job was to make the required mix from section to section as one tape recorder completed its section and another began its music section. It was like building a house of cards. Sometimes the first mix across went well, often the second too, but perhaps the third didn't work. Start again from the top! The outputs of all four tape recorders in a four section music piece set up would go via the mixing desk to a fifth tape recorder which would record all the mixed sections as a complete piece. The endeavour was always fraught with frustration and the air could turn blue if one of us missed starting a tape recorder at an appropriate point or stopping a tape recorder that had played back its section. To add insult to injury, an electronic glitch of the tape recorder turning on or off could often be heard on the final master track.

With much trial and error we finally achieved a final edited mix for the *Life on Earth* album. I was also proud to have suggested we introduce 'waves' of Sir David Attenborough's voice on the final track *Man — A Choice for the Future of Life on Earth*. This was achieved by putting David's voice through the envelope shaper of a VCS3 synthesiser and allowing a random voltage generator to trigger the release of a phrase or part of a sentence. I didn't get to play around with Sir David's voice again until the 1990s when along with singer Maddy Prior we created a soundtrack made up entirely of songs for Steve Nicholl's BBC natural history film *Shadow of the Hare*. This was probably the first natural history film to deliver a large portion of the narrative through song rather than rely on David's narration. In a letter from David in 1993, he remarks how well he remembered the music from the hare film and was pleased to receive a copy of the soundtrack. There were many David Attenborough films especially in the BBC *The Natural World* series, *Wildlife on One*, and *Wildlife on Two* that I scored during my career. It was always a privilege to work with him and sometimes I even got to hear his response to the soundtrack. This message was passed to me during a dubbing session when David was recording narration for the film *Watervoles, A Life on the Edge*. 'Everyone is happy with your watervole composition. David Attenborough apparently went around whistling the tune!'

During the early eighties I was making some kind of a living from part-time work for Edward and managed to pay my rent. I supplemented my income by getting a few commissions. Through contacts in the university drama department, I ended up scoring the films *Radiotherapy* and *Stuart Devlin Master Goldsmith*. At that time, the instruments I had were a clarinet, saxophone, guitar, and electric piano. I chose to score the film on radiotherapy for two clarinets and the film about the goldsmith on electric piano. Another short film about vaccinations, *The Cold Chain*, I composed in downtime at Edward's studio. I think each film paid around £50 but every little helped. My break into the BBC came in 1982. I'd started to send out information and examples of my work on audio cassette tapes and had a call to go in to the BBC and meet writer and producer Barry Paine, one of the great wildlife film narrators who was working with executive producer Peter Jones on the film *Forest in the Sea* for the series *The World About Us*. It was a tall order for such a young composer to be asked to produce music for one of the BBC's landmark series. The film required twelve music cues totalling 16'50" of music.

One of most difficult demands on a film composer is always the post production schedule for the delivery of music. Music is usually left to the end of the production process and everyone is keen to get the soundtrack wrapped up as quickly as possible. A composer often has to work at speed and under stress and it was more so with this film as a first ever BBC project. I had to get it right. Edward kindly agreed to allow me to record the score in his studio and I began to compose the music for piano. After recording the piano, I put it through various tape manipulative procedures such as tape delay, playing the music back in reverse, creating tape echo and putting the music through electronic processing with a VCS3 synthesiser. One of the challenges that put me on my knees in the studio was coming up with enough quality thematic material for the production. I can remember going through a crisis of writer's block. It finally took Edward to come to the studio and say, 'for God's sake just write it!' It was an important rite of passage. From that day on I composed music without ever allowing writer's block to get a grip on me again. I also remembered the words of author Jane Austen who said 'I am not at all in a humor for writing; I must write on until I am.'

If I am a composer, there is no answer to not being able to compose except to press on and compose.

I was also making a few more contacts. My music workshop colleague Deborah got me involved in a production of *King of the Coast*, a children's opera by composer Wilfred Josephs (1927–1997). She asked me whether I'd be interested in rehearsing and conducting the score. I'd first met Wilfred at The Association of Professional Composers meetings in London. He was a prolific composer. As well as his twelve symphonies, twenty-two concertos, ballets, operas and chamber works, he was also a composer of music for film and television. I greatly admired his music for *I, Claudius* (1976) and *The Voyage of Charles Darwin* (1978). Although having conducted quite a few of my own film music recording sessions, I've never regarded myself as a competent conductor. Conducting the opera was one of my first attempts and a baptism of fire. It all went well and I especially remember the accommodation I stayed in during the weekend of performances. Whilst I was taking a bath, the woman who owned the house insisted on entering the bathroom without knocking.

'Hello! I've brought you a gin and tonic. Don't worry. I've got three boys. Nothing I haven't seen before.'

I began to assist Edward more and more with the track-laying and mixing of his scores. It became easier once Edward acquired a multi-track tape recorder. Our mornings in the studio were often full of discussion about electronic music techniques and how electronics could be used to transform the sound of instruments in real time performances. The conversation would sometimes continue over lunch at the Thai restaurant next door and then we'd be back in the studio for the afternoon. Edward would create more wonderful sonic combinations and I would track-lay or mix the material. We'd also discuss our plans for Uncle Jambo's Pendular Vibrations a touring group that would collaborate with writers, painters and sculptors, theatre directors, designers, dancers and choreographers, film, video, lighting and projection artists. The aim was to explore new ways of making music using live real time electronic modifications and transformations of the sounds of conventional musical instruments. We also sought to use these modifications to control musically related visual events such as the control of images or text generated on a computer. The choice of name for the group always led to a heated discussion. Edward finally insisted the name was apposite since he saw himself as the 'uncle' figure, Jambo meant 'hello' in Swahili, and 'pendular vibrations' related to the core of what music and sound is all about. During our times together, he often quoted Georg Ohm's (1789–1854) Law of Acoustics as if it was a daily mantra: 'Pendular vibrations in the air are the only vibrations perceived as pure tones; and all varieties of quality in different sounds are the result of the combination of pure tones.' In fact, the name of the group didn't stop there. The full name added The Electron Ice Dream Pleasure Drome. I never quite got on with it and would usually refer to the group as Pendular Vibrations.

The group we formed brought together a diverse collection of performers and we gave our first concert at Bretton Hall College in 1983 and another at the Huddersfield Contemporary Music Festival in 1984. Our programme of pieces incorporated most of the performing and visual arts. A piece I composed for trombone, live electronics and video was performed by trombonist and composer James Fulkerson. The piece, *The Stratagem of Nauplius*, was a modern adaptation of the myth of Nauplius who wrecked the argonauts' boats in revenge for the death of his son. The rest of the set included *Supreme Fictions* by James and Mary Fulkerson, *The Vision of Victor Frankenstein* by writer Nick Otty and performed by actor Sir Tony Robinson, *The Last Post* by composer Duncan Druce, *Showdown* by composer and Led Zeppelin bassist John-Paul Jones, *Talking Head* by videographers Brian Johnson's and Rick Cocker, and *Sunpiece* by composer Edward Williams. Computer programmer, cameraman and technician Mark Newbold assisted with the complicated technical requirements of the performances.

All these works required an elaborate rig which Edward designed. Each instrument had its own microphone and the signal could be directed via a foot pedal to any of the devices on a trolley at the side of the musician. One of my jobs was to cut hollow steel bars into appropriate lengths and construct the trolley. The trolley's devices included a VCS3, a pitch transposer, a random voltage generator, a pitch to voltage converter, a filter bank, and eventually one of the very early sampling modules which allowed us to store a maximum of 1.6 seconds of performed material which could then be looped or modified for playback. The rig for our concerts also required numerous cables. Back in the studio, there were so many that they had to run upwards on poles and above our heads. The signal would often disappear and we'd spend ages trying to find the fault. Then we'd get super frustrated, pull all the cables out of the mixer with one massive yank and end up with a knotted spaghetti heap of wires at our feet. My task was to check them and re-plug one cable at a time. I'd spend hours unplugging and testing cables or replacing them with new ones. The rigs at the concerts usually required all of the studio gear (fortunately not the grand piano) to go into the back of a large truck which I drove to the venues. We needed a lot of devices, pedals, and cables just to create one single video effect that could be achieved today by pressing one key on a laptop.

The festival concert was also the launch pad for an instrument Edward had been thinking about designing for many years; an instrument that would detect movement, translate the movements into sounds, and put control of the transformation of performed material (whether musical or visual) into the player's or audience's hands. A similar device, the theremin, had been invented by Leon Theremin (1896–1993) in the 1920s. The theremin used two metal antennas to sense the position of the thereminist's hands in the air within the vicinity of the antennas. The antennas responded to the hand positions by controlling oscillators. One hand's movement controlled amplitude (volume) whilst the other controlled frequency (pitch). Edward's vision was for a similar instrument but with an ultrasonic sensor rather than antennas. The prototype we used at the festival was named The Lone Ranger and later became known as the Soundbeam. We first used the prototype in workshops with disabled children. The device was very basic in those days but the children had fun moving their wheelchairs through the invisible beams. The closer they got to the sensor, they could affect a rise in pitch of a synthesiser oscillator. As they moved away from the sensor, the pitch descended. With the development of MIDI (Musical Instrument Digital Interface), which enabled music devices to communicate with each other, Soundbeam went from strength to strength and is now in its sixth incarnation. The instrument has been demonstrated in many countries by Soundbeam's Adrian Price and Tim Swingler. It has sold worldwide and has been an enormous success with individuals who have profound physical or learning impairments.

In our early discussions about Soundbeam, Edward and I always planned for the device to be used by dancers to create the music which accompanies their body movements. We produced a few successful pieces including my work *Inua*, which told the story of a shaman's journey to find healing for a community, and my work *Vi-Spy* (2008) for Soundbeam, dancer, and violin with spycam. *Inua* won me the Ivors Academy (formerly The British Academy of Songwriters, Composers and Authors) 2004 Composer of the Year Award in the community and educational category. In 2011, I also performed the Soundbeam in the performance of

Edward's *Music for Life on Earth Suite* at the Bristol Beacon and with Charles Hazlewood and the BBC Concert Orchestra at a concert presented by Jarvis Cocker at the Queen Elizabeth Hall, London. As I moved my hands through the invisible ultrasonic beams, I was able to articulate and control elements of electronic music extracts from Edward's original electronic cues from the *Life on Earth* series. It brought Soundbeam to the attention of a concert going audience.

The first few years out of university felt as if I had landed in a magical world of exploring the electronic arts: electronic music, videographics, multi-media, and experimental performance techniques. I was firmly embedded in a world of inter-arts. On the one hand I was courting a future in electronic music and thought I'd study in New York or at the Groupe de Recherches Musicales (GRM) in Paris where I went for a speculative interview. On the other hand, I'd spent time on a couple of Barrie Gavin's film shoots to gain experience of the director's craft. Yet with all this immersion in the creative pursuits I adored, I couldn't decide whether to become a film director, a film sound recordist, a sound mixer or a composer. Nice to be spoiled for choice.

5

Big Break

The indecision about a career path led to circumstances my friend Steve Fairnie (1951–1993) called 'art as fairground', a state in which a creative wants go on all the rides. Steve had successful bands: Fish Company, Writz, Famous Names. He was an accomplished artist, fashion model, games designer, pop video director and starred in the thirteen-part TV drama series *The Kid*. He also made a living as a Charlie Chaplin lookalike. It felt natural for our paths to cross – we were both polymaths, embraced the interaction of different artistic disciplines, thought outside the box and we spent many an hour dreaming up narratives for TV programmes, performance art ideas and parties. One Christmas we threw a Narnia party. We attached a wardrobe of coats to the front door of Steve's house. Guests had to enter through the wardrobe, find their way through the coats and hangers and exit into a corridor deep in artificial snow. We had a wind machine going and everyone had to fight their way through a blizzard. After that, they could choose from having their photograph taken at the fireplace in a pose lifted from the film *White Christmas*, visit the grotto of working gnomes we'd created in the cellar or take a tour of stalactites growing down there. I've always regarded the capacity for play as not only an intrinsic part of what it means to be an artist, but essential for how we approach life. So many adults have managed to kill off the gift of the 'inner child' in exchange for becoming highly focused, rigid and with little capacity for imagination or invention. Without allowing my inner child to flourish and remain active throughout my adult life, I would never have taken the steps to develop new approaches to my primary disciplines of music and poetry. Keeping the inner child active gives the creative mind freedom – the kind of playful freedom a child enjoys moving from one activity to another: I'll play this game, now I'll draw a picture, now I'll ride my bike. The inner child's playground is the artist's workshop space for art as fairground.

Other themed parties I set up at my place were as imaginative: a Russian soirée, an event based on drumming and an airport party. The airport party was a joy to set up. I built a model X-ray machine for scanning handbags. All the party hosts were in pilot and cabin crew costume and miniature cans of drinks and airline meal trays were served to guests from silver trolleys. The hallway had projections of the updates of arrival and departure times of flights leaving from Bristol Airport. I also built a large Airfix model of a 747 and erected this on a short pole in the garden to make the plane look as if it was preparing to land. I laid blue fairy lights along the garden to create the landing strip. As darkness fell and guests glanced out of the window, they were taken aback by the effect. Whilst the passion for art as fairground is a tremendous blessing, it can also be a curse. In those days, I felt the pressure to choose one fairground ride on which I should remain. To that end, I began to write letters to see what kind of work might come my way in music or film. I wrote to directors whose work I admired. In terms of film work, I contacted the producer David Putnam at Enigma Films. David had produced the box office success *Midnight Express* (1978), the Academy Award winning best picture *Chariots of Fire* (1981) and the movie *Local Hero* (1983). He fixed up for me to meet his production manager Robin Douet for an informal interview. I showed Robin my lighthouse film and he offered me the opportunity of becoming a runner on their productions. This would have been the first stepping stone to becoming a third assistant director and then moving upwards from there. I should have jumped at the chance, but I didn't want to risk a move to the big city. My opportunities for any film direction in the South West were on the wane so I began to focus my attention on looking for film music composition work.

My next letter was to one of the twentieth century icons of cinema, the film director Fred Zinnemann (1907–1997). I'd sent him a sample of my work on audio cassette, which he liked. It took another letter or two over the following years to get him to agree to meet. Fred graciously arranged some time even though he had been recovering from a serious illness. It was a tremendous honour to spend an hour with him. Zinnemann had won four Academy Awards. Amongst his twenty-five feature films are *High Noon* (1952), *From Here to Eternity* (1953), *Oklahoma* (1955), *A Man for All Seasons* (1966) and *The Day of the Jackal* (1973). He directed Marlon Brando in his film debut *The Men* (1950) and Meryl Streep in her film debut *Julia* (1978). I met with Fred at his apartment in Mayfair. We got on really well and there was a connection that resonated in a similar way to the one I had with Professor George Brandt at Bristol University — a connection to Poland

and WWII. I was able to tell Fred all about my father and my family's displacement during the war. Fred described his family history too. He was born in Rzeszów, Poland, and after studying in France and working in Germany, he emigrated to the USA. His parents were tragically killed in the Holocaust. We also discussed the role of music in film. Although he wasn't planning on making any more films and couldn't offer any opportunities for me, he kindly wrote a testimonial:

'I was strongly impressed by the quality of his work which I have heard on TV on several occasions...I believe the man has remarkable talent and that even a brief audition of his work would be convincing proof of his potential.'

Whilst such a testimonial was like precious stones in my hand, it didn't go anywhere to landing me my debut feature film score. It's often the case that directors don't want to accept a recommendation from others; they prefer to discover the composer themselves. I continued, however, to be prolific in terms of letter writing. I still have a box file of the rejections! An artist is always subject to rejection and it can hurt. One's work goes in and out of vogue, there are fads and fashions and so many different opinions about what the market is looking for. The rejection of work is often a bitter pill to chew but I remained resilient, highly motivated and kept my rhino suit tightly zipped up. There was always my pillow to cry on when no-one was looking. A handful of rejections ran like this:

'We listened to your work with interest with, as you can imagine, many others.'

'The director decided to use a composer with whom he's worked before.'

'Please find enclosed your tapes which I am returning to you.'

This one from the multi award winning filmmaker Sir Alan Parker (1944–2020) who directed *Bugsy Malone* (1976), *Fame* (1980), *Pink Floyd – The Wall* (1982), *Midnight Express* (1978) and *Mississippi Burning* (1988):

'As before, I found it most interesting and at the risk of repeating myself – will bear it in mind for the future.'

I think I may have sent one letter too many! I also collected replies from directors Richard Attenborough, Michael Apted, and a plethora of TV directors. Most of these letters had similar narratives:

'We will definitely bear you in mind.'

'I will certainly keep your biography and letter on file.'

'I will stash it away in the appropriate cardboard box that the producers ferret in when they are looking for musical ideas.'

Must have been a big box as I never received anything back from the ferreting producers. One big box I did manage to break into was Pinewood Studios where I got to meet Iain Smith OBE several times over a period of a few years. Iain was an associate producer on *Local Hero* (1983), *The Killing Fields* (1984) and *The*

Mission (1986) and worked as a producer on *The Fifth Element* (1997), *Children of Men* (2006) and *Mad Max: Fury Road* (2015). Again, I got on well with Iain and enjoyed discussing music and film with him. Unfortunately he couldn't lever an opening for me into features and I ended up coming out with another glowing reference other directors took little notice of:

'It seems that confronted with almost any kind of subject matter, Martin is intuitively able to detect, and unlock, the finest musical opportunities lying dormant within the rough cut of a film. Martin has never once lost sight of his ultimate objective: to excel as a major feature film composer. In my opinion, he is certainly a significantly gifted composer who will be more than a match for the big screen challenges he craves for.'

It's extraordinary that I looked outside my own patch for the big break when actually it was slowly growing on home turf. Through my mentor composer Edward Williams, I'd met other filmmakers: David Sproxton and Peter Lord of Aardman Animations and filmmaker Colin Thomas. David and Peter asked me whether I would create music for a Duracell battery commercial they were animating. I composed a track but it didn't make the final cut. My track was too sound effects based and it appeared the advertising agency was looking for something song based. I was disappointed and felt I hadn't produced a good calling card for any future work with Aardman. In later years, however, I did get a shot at composing a pitch recorded with the City of Prague Philharmonic for the movie *Chicken Run* (2000). I was also employed as a music consultant on the video game *Wallace and Gromit: The Curse of the Wererabbit* (2005). My next meet was with independent film director and producer Colin Thomas. Colin's documentary and drama work was radical, rebellious and provocative. He was also involved with the ACTT (Association of Cinematograph, Television and Allied Technicians) the union one had to be a member of in order to work in the film and television industry. To obtain a union card allowing you to work was akin to a mysterious alchemy that one day might produce a miraculous result and place the elusive elixir into your hand. Along with Colin's backing and the support of others, I was given a union card to work as an assistant sound recordist.

I began sound work as a boom operator on dramas and news and current affairs programmes. I wasn't that well built and holding a boom pole in the air for hours is hard work on the shoulders and biceps. Poor me! The longer one holds the pole the more one has to control the ensuing shakes, trembles and wobbles as weakness sets in and this can affect sound quality and, worse still, drop the boom into shot. The work was, however, well paid and got me trips abroad. I worked on a series in Russia, one in Australia and Singapore following the tour of a Welsh male voice choir, seven films in Turkey about the New Testament churches of Asia Minor and a film about the international harp festival on the Isle of Man. The trip to Russia involved picking up money for expenses on arrival in Moscow. I was taken to a room in which was a large grey metal cabinet. The official opened the doors. The cabinet was stacked from top to bottom with rouble notes. He took out several wads of notes and handed them over.

'Here, these are your daily expenses for the next two weeks aside from your accommodation and food which is all taken care of.'

So off I went on the two week shoot. On the last day I returned to the office and said, 'Here's all your money I'm returning. There wasn't anything for me to buy in Moscow.'

Closer to home, I sound assisted on several film dramas in Wales for the newly formed channel S4C. On one production location in deep caves, I had to retrieve a Nagra tape recorder from the cave entrance. The route back down to the location deep in the cave's system involved a precarious descent with only a handrail rope to hang on to with one hand whilst the weight of the Nagra kept pulling me over towards a sheer drop at the other side. It freaked me out and I couldn't finish the shoot. I was also given work by Graham Edgar, a well seasoned cameraman and producer. He was a kind and generous man who gave me a break as a fully fledged film sound recordist. One of my first jobs was to go to Wales and record a news item for BBC national news. Unfortunately, complaints came back from the newsroom in London to say I had the interviewee on microphone but hadn't turned the microphone to pick up the interviewer's questions. Graham looked a little annoyed but was gracious enough to understand the learning curve I was on and employed me again. All these opportunities led to income. I also wanted independence so decided it was time to leave the shared accommodation I was in and use the money I'd saved to get a mortgage for a house.

The manager at the building society looked me up and down.

'So you're a composer, a filmmaker, a sound recordist?' I nodded.

'And a film director. Just starting.'

'Have you got any kind of financial security?'

'No.'

'Have you got any big projects that you think might provide financial security?'

'No, but I'm meeting a guy in a pub every week who is going to employ me if he gets his project off the ground.' The manager smiled.

'I like you. I'm going to give you a mortgage. You'll need an accountant to provide me with evidence that you're likely to earn.' And that's exactly what my friendly accountant did.

It now depended on the guy I was meeting in the pub to come up with the goods. That guy was David G. Hopkins (1940–2004). David had been based at BBC Bristol as a documentary director working under the head of unit John Boorman who went on to become a five times Academy Award nominated director. After working as a filmmaker in West Africa, David came back to Bristol and set up the film company *Occam* with his wife Jane. My girlfriend and I got to know them well. Many an evening, if we weren't doing up the wreck of a Victorian terraced house I'd bought in Southville, Bristol, we'd be with David and Jane discussing religion, politics, philosophy, film, and the arts. David's atheism always led to a challenging discussion and I held on to my belief system for dear life. Yet, our evenings together had balanced discussion and posed many questions often with very ambitious sounding answers. 'You are simply stardust!' he once exclaimed whilst banging his fist on the table. David had also been turning over two projects in his mind for a couple of years. He liked to meet every couple of weeks in the pub to pitch them. His idea was to make my girlfriend the researcher on the projects and I would be the composer. He also brought in costume designer Maggie Hayes. The three of us would encourage, support and endeavour to grow our own belief in David's pipe dream. He was a maverick in the realm of film narrative and waxed lyrical for week after week about a four-part film adaptation he wished to make of Percy Bysshe Shelley's (1792—1822) bad but inspired gothic novel *Zastrozzi – a Romance* (1810). He described his proposed adaptation of the novel as, 'money and desire passing each other in the night – a comedy for bailiffs and stockbrokers set in the unknown landscapes of England.' The script would be a scathing commentary on contemporary England. He also wanted to make an animated five-part apocalyptic post nuclear satire: *Sweet Disaster* in which each film would use a different experimental animation technique.

The weekly meetings and readings of David's storylines went on for such a long time that our belief began to wane. Yet David never lost his vision. He produced sample synopses and scripts and asked me to come up with music themes based on the characters, narrative themes and plot. He also asked Maggie to come up with preliminary costume designs. We went ahead on a wing and a secular prayer. One evening David arrived at the pub with news. He had been talking with Channel 4's founding chief executive Jeremy Isaacs. Jeremy was interested in both *Zastrozzi* and *Sweet Disaster*. We hesitated before raising our glasses with a cheer. How interested? We were all too familiar with wading through mountains of bullshit in the film and television industry. David looked us in the eye as if we were pirates sitting round the table in the Admiral Benbow Inn in Stephenson's *Treasure Island.*

Martin on the streets of Chapeltown, Leeds 1963

Martin and his mother Edith, Belle Isle, Leeds

My dad was a great conductor!

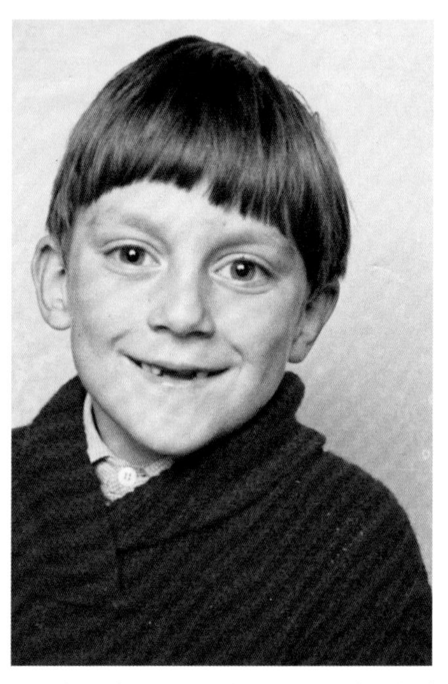

The photo that got wind-creased and soaked

Martin and his father Nikodem

Performing in *The Quest of Man* at Bretton Hall

Martin directs his film *Skokholm Light*

On the film course in Bristol

With my mentor Edward Williams

Working on my piece *Cairoglyph*
with Sir Tony Robinson

Working on *Land of the Eagle* with Dick Lewzey

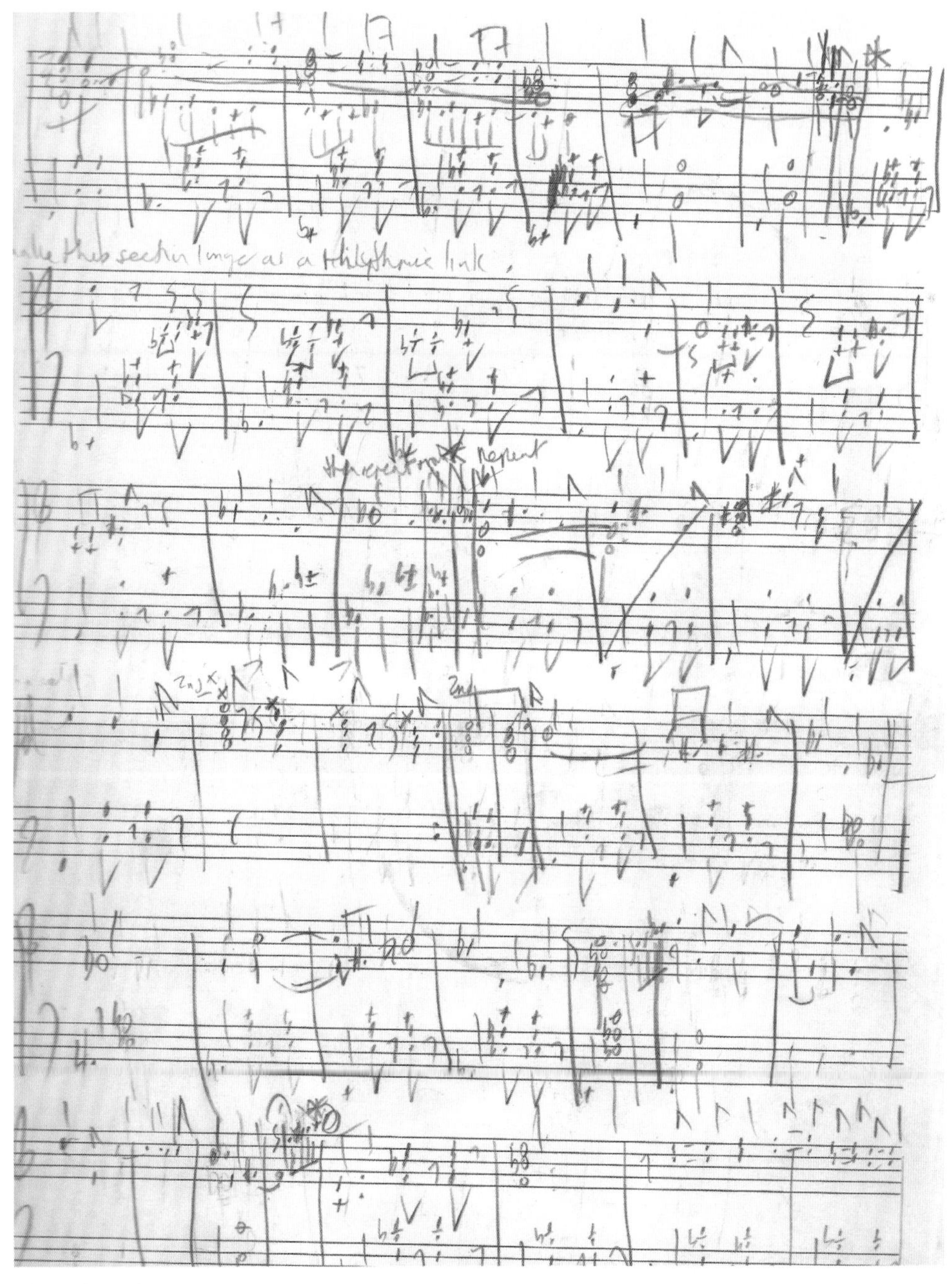

Sketch from the TV series *Zastrozzi – a Romance*

Conducting myself!

Land of the Eagle session at CTS Studios, Wembley

'*Zastrozzi* and *Sweet Disaster* have been commissioned.'

We were knocked out by the news and it took more than a few rounds to sink in. *Zastrozzi* had been commissioned for £1.3 million — more than C4 had ever spent on a drama production; *Sweet Disaster* for approximately half a million. David also went on to secure a stellar cast which included Tilda Swinton, Geff Francis, Mark McGann, Hilary Trott, Yvonne Bryceland, Maxine Audley, Chris Barrie and the veteran comedian Max Wall. I left the pub with three thoughts haunting me. My first thought was about vision. I was reassured that vision, especially when held on to, can produce results. David's dogged determination to realise his vision had paid off. My second thought was that my mortgage lender would at least be happy for a while. My third thought was about the music score. I was now the composer on a £1.3 million television drama. Could I do it? Self doubt set in. Ten years previously I was a kid leaving a council estate with little vision at all. I now had to have the vision to be a successful film composer and, like David, I had to hold on to it.

In our numerous discussions about the approach to the music score, David and I decided the score and script should develop side by side, a somewhat unorthodox approach to film scoring. Usually, music is composed during the post-production part of the schedule when the film shoot has been completed. At that point the director and composer 'spot' the music. The spotting session is the process of identifying where the music should go in the film. The decisions made in the spotting session might cover mood, atmosphere, style and the palette of the score. More crucially, decisions are made on where a music cue should start and where it should stop. This is based on an entry or exit on a fraction of one twenty-fifth of a second since film runs through a movie camera at twenty-five frames per second for UK TV transmission. Our approach threw all that convention out of the window. David wanted the score to convey meaning and emotion not only to the viewer but to how he approached the script — he wanted to play my music sketches as he penned ideas. As our working relationship developed, we decided it was essential to use the music as choreography for the camera. Camera moves on location would be dictated by the flow and rhythm of the music. This was the approach the composer Ennio Morricone (1928–2020) and the director Sergio Leone (1929–1989) used in their collaborations.

Another approach we agreed on was to use the music as an emotional template which would be played to the actors prior to their scene. We also decided the music should have an operatic feel to highlight the gothic elements of the original novel. This was especially the case in the composition of many of the harpsichord recitative cues. In opera, recitative is a narrative song in which a singer uses the rhythms of ordinary speech. The song may describe emotion or actions and the singer's voice is usually accompanied by harpsichord or a few instruments rather than the orchestra. In *Zastrozzi*, I used solo harpsichord to create recitative style melodic statements which heralded the arrival of a character, highlighted narrative, accented a caption on screen or connected a gap between dialogue statements. In contrast to these solo moments, the music also had to play a featured role in scenes where it made its own comment on the narrative rather than being simply placed as 'mood filler' alongside dialogue and sound effects.

Up to this point in my career, I'd never approached a score of this size. The big question I kept asking myself was whether I'd be able to bring it off. Although I'd composed a few music-theatre works and pieces for a handful of players on my degree course, I'd never composed for classical quartets, quintets, octets and other chamber groupings. In addition to the operatic feel the director required, *Zastrozzi* also featured the main characters dancing a waltz and the waltz had to become an essential part of any score. I first set to work on choosing a palette for the drama: flute, clarinet doubling soprano saxophone, French horn, harpsichord doubling piano, violin, viola, cello and double bass. I concentrated on the waltz and composed eight music cues based on Straussian waltz structure. I felt very insecure during this first part of the composition process and was totally reliant on my mind's ear. What did a melodic line on horn sound like against a light accompaniment on strings? How would it sound against a piano? How would it sound if the clarinet played part of a melody and then passed it on to the soprano saxophone? The process of choosing the sound colours (known as 'timbres') of instruments and determining how these timbres will sound if they are combined is an essential tool in the composer's toolbox. The choice of timbres alongside melody, rhythm and harmony also communicate emotion to the viewer so decisions must be made about how certain sound colours and harmony can create an emotional response.

A pressing problem, however, was that I had no multi-track tape machine or sequencer to lay down all the instrumental parts and try them out. I called a friend to come round and play the flute part I'd written whilst I played the clarinet part. To my ears it sounded terrible but my friend thought it was fine. I wasn't convinced. It got closer and closer to the day the director would be coming to my home studio. The studio was a small bedroom in the house I'd bought. I had a couple of synthesisers: a Korg Poly 61 and a Yamaha DX7. I also had an electric piano and a tape recorder. On the day David turned up to listen to the first sketches for the waltzes, I was wondering whether I was completely out of my depth. He sat down and listened to me playing through my compositions on the piano and seemed to like what he heard. He then looked at my overflowing waste basket of manuscript paper.

'What's all this?'

'Stuff I tried out but didn't like.'

David picked a couple of sheets out of the bin.

'Can I hear them?'

I reluctantly played one of the pieces.

'That's wonderful. Let's put that one in the use pile.'

He picked out another and I played through the next one.

'That has exactly the ironic feel I'm looking for. It could even work as the title music.'

Very soon my bin was empty and David had reinstated all the work I'd trashed. I realised I'd set my bar high and was being hard on myself. From that first day I promised to play David any pieces I discarded as well as those with which I was happy.

It was going to be a long hard road. A four part drama series requiring music as operatic gesture throughout was going to need a lot of music. I ended up composing one hundred and fourteen music cues, around ninety minutes of music. In my mind I could hear every note of it but the proof of the pudding wouldn't happen until it got played by an ensemble of professional musicians. As for the prospect of conducting such a group, I had no experience. I also knew from watching my mentor Edward at his recording sessions that there was no way I was going to risk it. In the back of my mind was the story Edward told me of his conducting experience with his mentor conductor Muir Mathieson and the British composer Ralph Vaughan Williams. Edward mentioned the story again when I interviewed him for the Wildscreen Archive in 2007:

'When I got the job with Muir, I was eighteen or nineteen I suppose, and although I had conducted student orchestras, I'd certainly never conducted professionals. Muir had said to me, 'when can you start?'

'As soon as you like.'

'Right well come to Denham Studios Monday morning, we've got a recording for a film called *49th Parallel.*'

It turned out that they were recording the music by Vaughan Williams, my great god at the time. I was absolutely thrilled to bits, sitting in there, actually paying me. I had no idea what Muir wanted me to do but I took it for granted he wanted me to bring his coat or bring a glass of water. Anyhow, Muir had some beautiful title music for *49th Parallel* and played it two or three times through. He said, 'Edward'.

So I went to him thinking he wanted a glass of water or something. And he said, 'Just run this through for me will you?'

And I was absolutely appalled. I mean I'd never ever conducted a commercial orchestra in my life and never ever conducted any orchestra without seeing the score first of all. So white and pale and trembling I stood up there in front of all these old chaps. Anyway, I waved my way through this piece, just managed to negotiate a five-four bar, just in time somehow. And, when it was all over, they could see I was sweating and there was a certain murmur. The leader, dear old George Stretton, leant forward and said to me, 'Well done my boy, you followed us really well.'

To be a competent film conductor requires years of experience. When a film music conductor stands on the podium, he or she is expected to perform an act that is akin to rubbing your tummy, tapping your head and juggling at the same time. The conductor has to be able to read the score, interact with the orchestra, watch the elapsing picture and timecode and often listen to the studio mix in one ear of headphones whilst using the other ear to listen to the live music coming from the orchestra. I'd heard about a conductor called Harry Rabinowitz (1916 –2016). The film's production company approached Harry and asked whether he'd be interested in conducting my score. Harry came with an amazing pedigree. He had been music director for BBC television light entertainment and had conducted at the Hollywood Bowl. Later in his career he conducted the Boston Pops Orchestra and conducted many scores for feature films including *Chariots of Fire* (1981), *The Remains of the Day* (1993), *The English Patient* (1996), and *Cold Mountain* (2003). At the point I got to meet him, he was head of music for London Weekend Television. Harry asked to see the score and invited me to London. It was nerve-racking as I watched him flick through the pages of my manuscript. His pencil circled a few notes here and there, added a question mark or inserted a sharp or a flat. He was an incredible stickler for detail and his questions were as sharp as a needle.

'Is this bar fourteen harmony with an E flat in the cello really what you mean?'

I survived that first meet and I must have done well as he contacted the production company to congratulate them on finding such a new talent! Well, little did he know that I still didn't have the confidence to believe the performance of my music would sound identical to how I heard it in my head. It was a massive risk for me and if it didn't come off, the production company would be on my back big time and the beginning of my career would come to an abrupt end.

Harry suggested a line up of players. They were all of celebrity status in the classical and session music world. Many of the music cues were for harpsichord and I decided to brush up my knowledge of the instrument by spending time with the harpsichordist Lesley Pearson. Lesley introduced me to the different registers of the harpsichord. The registers produce different qualities – for example, a register may be an octave above or below the normal sounding register of the instrument. The next step was to find a recording studio. Edward had always recorded his sessions at CTS Wembley. CTS studios had seen many European and Hollywood movies come through its doors and, during my time there assisting Edward, I was able to get to know the senior recording engineer Dick Lewzey who had music mixed *The Mission* (1986) and the Bond movies *A View to a Kill* (1985), *The Living Daylights* (1987) and *License to Kill* (1989). We were privileged to have him on board *Zastrozzi – a Romance.*

Watching Harry at the first session and at future recording sessions of my scores was extraordinary. He was a master of his art. Often, after the first rehearsal of a music cue, he would immediately point his baton at the musicians.

'Violins bar twenty-two should be an F sharp, clarinet your entry was a tad late, horn observe the dynamic at bar thirty-two and everyone wait for my lead for the accelerando at bar sixty-five.'

In addition to all that, Harry was able to conduct a piece at exactly the metronome tempo marking the composer dictated: eighty beats per minute, one hundred and twenty, or any other tempo without using an electronic click-track in his headphones. Click-tracks can be useful but Harry seemed to know every tempo by heart. I asked him how he was able to multi-task so quickly and how he'd perfected his craft. Harry told me that every morning he performed three tasks simultaneously: rode his exercise bike, listened to his metronome beating out a new daily tempo, and brushed up his languages by listening to a foreign language tape at the same time. It was a way of teaching the brain to handle simultaneous channels of information. I was blown away.

The beginning of a music recording session always gets the adrenalin going and no more so than on your very first professional session. The instrumentalists turned up and I introduced myself. Since Harry was conducting, I spent some of the time on the studio floor but most of the time in the control room assessing the quality of the take of each music cue. I listened in for any spurious clicks, accidental scrapes or knocks, any problems with intonation (tuning) and for whether the performance created the necessary emotional effect I'd intended. Once the ensemble had tuned up, we started rehearsing the first music cue. The first few minutes made my heart pound. The music sounded awful. I took a deep breath and looked at my score. I think Dick Lewzey noticed I was somewhat uncomfortable and very encouragingly said, 'It's okay. Don't worry. We're just playing around with levels at this point.'

I hadn't realised that was how a session started and expected the whole score to sound perfect immediately. By the second take, once the levels had been set, the music mix sounded wonderful. I was thrilled by what I heard – and for the very first time – I realised I was hearing exactly what I'd heard in my head whilst composing. I didn't require hours and hours of lessons to become a composer, I appeared to have a natural ability for orchestration. A few weeks later we'd completed all the sessions and the location shoot began. The recorded session music was used on location for the featured dance scenes, to create an emotional template for the actors and to be a tempo map for camera moves. In the post-production period editor David McCormick began to place music with picture to create the 'operatic gestures' the director required.

Zastrozzi had a very mixed reception on its first broadcast on C4 Television on April 13th 1986. Commentators described it as 'surreal', 'totally irreverent', 'provocative,' 'confusing', and 'an attempt to push television in an experimental direction.' I was over the moon with the one liner from the *New York Times* which described the music as 'splendidly haunting.' The series commissioner Jeremy Isaacs, when interviewed years later, mentioned the series as one of the ten he was most proud of during his tenure as Channel 4's chief executive:

'The main thing was to get it made. It was such an extraordinary idea. *Zastrozzi – a Romance* was Channel 4 at its risk-taking best. Martin Kiszko's music was crucial to its success.'

It wasn't until 2017 that I released the *Zastrozzi – a Romance* album. The original master tapes hadn't been played since 1985 and were on ten-inch reels of quarter inch tape. It was touch and go whether the tapes would still play. Tape can often stick together or break after it has been in storage for a long time. I was advised to have the tapes baked – a process which assists the playing back of the tape on a tape recorder. Even then, tape can break. I handed all the master tapes over for transfer to digital and waited for the telephone call. A few days later an audio engineer called up to say not only did they go through the machine without a glitch, but they also sounded amazing. The next step was a very long detective style search to find the musicians who played on the 1985 session so they could be properly credited. I also had to contact actors Tilda Swinton and Mark McGann to get clearance permission to use their photographs in the album booklet. It wasn't only *Zastrozzi*, however, that required my efforts back in 1985. David Hopkins was also setting up the production of his *Sweet Disaster* series. I had to come up with the title music for the series, a music score for two of the films *Dreamless Sleep* and *Conversations by a Californian Swimming Pool*, and provide sound effects for the film *Babylon*. For the series title music, David asked me to arrange the hymn *The Day Thou Gavest, Lord, Is Ended* alongside the sound of an 'apocalyptic wind'. My girlfriend had a suitable soprano voice and performed the track. The film *Dreamless Sleep* was made by BAFTA winning animator David Anderson (1952-2015) who also animated the pioneering pop video *Sledgehammer* for Peter Gabriel. *Dreamless Sleep* won the 1987 Hiroshima International Animation Festival Peace Prize. David remarked that the title for the film came to him as a result of 'going to a carol concert in Bristol with the composer Martin Kiszko and listening to *Oh Little Town of Bethlehem*.'

6

Fusion

It was in 1986 that I cast my net wider and into the ITV television network. There were thriving ITV production centres in Bristol and Cardiff. It was at HTV Bristol where I met Sidney Sager (1917–2002), the director of music for HTV. Sidney was born into a Jewish family in London's East End and joined the British Army at the age of fourteen as a band boy. As a young man, he studied at the Royal College of Music and played trombone for the Royal Opera at Covent Garden. He became a composer and conductor of film and television scores including the landmark children's series *Children of the Stones* (1987). Sidney was a gentle and quiet man with a perspicacious and exacting mind. The first job he offered me was to copy out instrumental parts for one of his film score compositions. Copying wasn't my forte. Before the advent of computer software which prints out professional looking music parts, the industry had dedicated music copyists who were masters of music calligraphy. My first attempt didn't make the grade but Sidney was gracious, took the parts and paid me. I don't know whether he used them or got the parts re-copied but thankfully he recognised the stature of my composition for *Zastrozzi* and put the word around the producers and directors at HTV that they could commission me if I approached them and approach them I did.

One of my first commissioned scores for HTV was a short piece called *Bristol Bells*. The piece was part of a live Friday night show *The Weekend Starts Here*. I was not the most confident musician in the world when it came to performing music on live TV and was certainly having a few nervous gulps and a racing heart before going on. I was also thinking I must stop saying yes to things and then considering the consequences of the decision. I was also overheating in the gear I was wearing. It didn't help. As I waited in the wings, I could feel the tingle of an emerging cold sore on my lip. Not now I thought. The hotter I got the more it seemed as if it was growing at a remarkable speed perhaps as a result of heat and nerves. When my cue came to go on set, I walked to the two synthesisers I was going to play: a Sequential Circuits Prophet 2000 and a Yamaha DX7. The presenter did a short interview with me at the synths and the floor was then mine. As I started the piece, all I could think of was the cold sore and the fact that the studio lights, to my mind, seemed to be accelerating its growth. Next, cue the camera that comes gliding midway over the synths and swoops in for a big close up. Now my face was flushed with embarrassment by the thought of the viewing audience getting a massive close up of the sore. I took a deep breath of relief when I got to the end of the piece. I couldn't wait to get off the studio floor. In the wings waiting for their interviews were artist and conservationist David Shepherd CBE (1931–2017) and Jim Davidson the comedian. They both congratulated me on the performance and Jim even asked whether I'd like to join one of his shows as a musician. I declined and couldn't wait to get out of there.

Luckily the cold sore didn't interrupt any other musical offerings. HTV commissions for series music came thick and fast: *A New Way of Living*, *The Countryside in Question. Busting the Block, Hand in Hand, Problems, Channel Traders, The Kennet and Avon Canal* and the game show *Hazard a Guess*. I really had my eye on many of the dramas being made out of HTV Bristol and Cardiff but I couldn't seem to get my hands on one. All I could do is continue to pitch for projects over and over again. Pitching to directors was a whole different (and to some extent preferable) ball game back in the 1980s. Nowadays, when directors are looking for music for a production, they simply open up an mp3 file on their phone or computer. It was normal practice back in the day that once a director expressed an interest in a composer, the composer would go away and compose a pitch demo. This might be a piano sketch, a rough mix or a polished mix of a thirty second piece of programme titles music or a pitch indicating the style of the incidental music for a production. The final master recording of the pitch demo would usually be on audio cassette tape. To my mind this was a perfect medium. I had a ghetto blaster I used to carry into the BBC and other TV studios. I'd enter the director's office, explain my approach to the music and press play on the cassette recorder. The music was immediately heard by the director — job done! Often, in this extremely sophisticated digital age in which we now live, it isn't as straight forward. When I'm working with film music students, I can wait several minutes to hear a completed music track or demo pitch if at all. There's often a problem with, 'well it was there when I composed it on my laptop,' or 'I don't know what's happened,' or 'maybe I didn't correctly transfer the audio.' In a face to face pitch to a very busy director, any such hitch would be a waste of time and potentially lose the opportunity of getting heard and on board a production. I always insist my students carry their final mixed work around on several formats so if one fails in a pitch session there is an immediate back up. Like a ghetto blaster!

Another element of those early pitching sessions was a director's request to hear the music alongside the appropriate film section it accompanied. To do this an elaborate system of transfers was necessary. The composer delivered the music on a 15ips (inches per second) audio reel which was transferred to audio magnetic track. The magnetic track had sprocket holes along the edges and was laid in accurate synchronisation alongside the film on a pic-sync or a flatbed Steenbeck machine. To pitch music locked with picture was time consuming, had costs and therefore seldom happened. Instead, my approach in all my pitching sessions was to ask the director to set up the picture on a monitor. The picture would have (but sometimes didn't) a timecode in vision. I'd ask the director to roll back the picture five seconds before the start of the picture sequence and I'd roll back my cassette tape to approximately the same number of seconds. I'd then count out three, two, one...go! Yes, very professional! We'd hopefully press our respective buttons at the same time. On most attempts we'd get a pretty good synchronisation and we'd be able to determine how the picture sequence worked with music. Crude and not perfectly synchronised, but it got me the commissions in those days. I often went through this pitching process with producer Dilys Breese (1932–2007). Dilys was the series producer of the BBC wildlife strand *Wildlife on One*. She was kind, down to earth, very supportive and always great to talk to about birds and British wildlife. The *Wildlife on One* series was narrated by Sir David Attenborough and a few of the early programmes I got to score were *Who Really Killed Cock Robin?*, *The Tale of the Pregnant Male*, *Trivial Pursuits*: *The Natural Mystery of Play*, *Blubber Lovers*, and *Kingdom of the Crabs*.

Pitching music in Lah Lah Land has certainly changed a lot since then. A few years ago, I was part of a group of composers on a UK trade mission to LA and I got to pitch to music executives at Universal Studios. Twelve of us were sent there to hear what kind of music the executives were looking to commission. The studios had *First Man* (2018) and *Fifty Shades Freed* (2018) in pre-production. The idea was that we'd each be able to give a two minute pitch about who we were and what we'd composed and so on. On returning to the UK to lecture my MA film music students, they were keen to ask the question, 'So how did you manage to make your pitch more appealing and different to everyone else?' They gathered round as if I was about to tell a wonderful story.

'This is how I did it. On entering the board room I first looked at the seating arrangement and where the executives were standing. I chose a place at the table where I knew I would be the last person to pitch. In my opinion, it's often the first pitch or the last that is remembered and my position also gave me the benefit of listening to everyone else's pitch so I could work out what I'd say that would be entirely different. The pitches began and everyone talked about their experience and the music they'd composed. No-one talked about the two movies the executives had mentioned. When it got to my turn I simply said I wished to pitch for the movies, briefly discussed my approach and promptly thrust two of my albums into their hands. No-one else could get in there quick enough with samples of their work as the executives left a couple of seconds later!' Suffice to say, one is always up against big Hollywood names in the pitch arena but I was pleased to have had the opportunity to cut to the chase with my music proposal.

The house I'd bought in South Bristol was still in dire need of more work to get it up and running. Everything needed doing to the property and the interior hadn't had a makeover since well before the war. My girlfriend and I became experts at stripping back the newel post, banister, spindles, architraves and doors. Who would have thought so many hours of joy could be spent with a toothbrush, scrapers and paint stripper? There were layers and layers of old wallpaper to be steam stripped, timber and damp treatments to put in place and fireplaces requiring restoration. The inner front door had a large piece of cracked Muranese glass. After a long search I located a replacement and drove from Bristol to Twickenham to collect it. We were also able to afford our first car: a banged up old Ford Escort. We tried to sort out the rust but in our attempt to repaint the bodywork, where we masked off the bits for re-spraying, we ended up with a car with large patches all over it. We also had a go at dealing with the passenger side rear window which wouldn't stay in its frame and flapped in the wind. We made a suitable repair with parcel tape and gaffer tape. One day, conductor Harry Rabinowitz arrived in Bristol to take part in the HTV game show *Gallery*. It was a very windy and rainy day. As I picked up Harry at the station, the rear window of the car was noisily flapping away. I apologised profusely for driving one of the world's greatest film conductors around in our banger but Harry simply gave a wry smile and said, 'No Martin. That's just the way it should be.'

I think I've been lucky to have worked with great professionals who were down to earth and hadn't forgotten the roots from which they came or their struggle to make it to the top. Looking back on those early days of finding my feet, I realise connections I made were often with those who had also experienced separation from their homeland or family in much the same way as my father's family. They all had common denominators of East European and Jewish heritage: George Brandt, Dennis Marks, Wilfred Josephs, Harry Rabinowitz, Martin Rosenbaum, Sidney Sager, Fred Zinnemann and Oscar nominated actor Ron Moody who I worked with in 2000. During my early years at HTV I met a Jewish lady who was curious about my surname. She knew quite a bit about the roots of surnames in Hebrew and told me my surname had Hebraic roots. Whether I had a Jewish heritage somewhere down a long ancestral line I don't know, but it has always made me wonder how those early relationships fell into place in such a wonderful way. Was it common heritage and a shared experience of our ancestry or was it coincidence and mutual contacts. Whichever, there was certainly a lot of hard slog required too.

The big event of 1986 was my marriage. We'd both been members of the same community church in Bristol – Fellowship of the King. From the name of the church, I think many non-Christians felt we were part of some kind of 'Tokienesque' cult. It was, however, a happy charismatic community of young people. We decided to hold the wedding and reception at a venue the church often used for worship. It was the building where balloonist Don Cameron MBE manufactured many of the world's hot air balloons including Britain's first modern hot air balloon the *Bristol Belle*. The venue therefore seemed appropriate for the ceremony of another *belle* launching herself into married life.

We didn't have the money, nor did our families, to put on a lavish wedding and reception. We saw the rings we wanted in a jeweller's shop but they were too expensive so we found out the name of the goldsmith and pleaded for a hefty discount to which he kindly agreed. The bride's dress was 1930s style ivory lace decorated with tiny seed pearls. I wore a white brocade jacket made by a young Iraqi tailor who was finding his feet as an up and coming designer in Bristol. I'm pleased to say it still fits me! Friends provided cars for the wedding day and many members of our church agreed to donate food and prepare, cook, and serve on the day for one hundred and twenty guests. Rather than using a conventional wedding march, my mentor Edward Williams composed a piece for viola and live electronics. It created an ethereal dream-like sound-world for the bride's entrance. The service was filled with music we usually sang in church and a performance of my piece *Acclaim This Day* for violin, piano, electric bass, and choir with Latin hand percussion. After all the photographs had been taken, we donned our going away gear and headed for our car, now covered in foam, tin cans, balloons and spools of film which trailed from the bumper. The roof was topped with a traffic cone. To waves and cheers we set off for our honeymoon in Venice. Venice in March was beautiful – crisp cold air, sunshine and blue skies. One day we headed for the islands and came back wind-chapped, sea-kissed, and sun-burned. We'd booked seats for a *commedia dell'arte* at the *Teatro La Fenice* opera house and arrived there weary from the day's outing. It was a full house and we had good seats in the centre of the stalls, but within a few minutes our heads were dropping and nodding towards each other. The next thing we heard was the end of the production applause and a group of German opera aficionados, who were seated behind us, shouting at us in disgust, 'sie schlafen, sie schlafen!'

Back home our careers got into full swing again and the demand for music for television kept me on my toes. One of the attributes a film composer must have is the capacity to turn a score around quickly and one of my fastest turnarounds was for the BBC arts documentary series *Omnibus*. I was an avid viewer of the series and leapt at the opportunity to compose the new title music. The series producer rang me on a Friday evening to offer the job and explain the brief. The signature tune music, albeit a title sequence of only seven seconds duration, had to be ready the following day for broadcast that same Saturday evening. In the days of no internet we used the British Rail courier service Red Star Parcels. The video tape would be biked to Paddington Station in London and sent by train to Bristol. At Bristol, I could either pick up the package myself or have a biker deliver it to my studio. The *Omnibus* titles tape arrived by lunchtime on Saturday and I got straight to work with coming up with an idea for the music. If the project's director wanted to hear the music, it was done over the phone and any adjustments were made on the basis of playback over telephone. I completed the music within a couple of hours, had it biked back to the station, and on to London where it was picked up by the BBC ready for broadcast the same evening. There were many scores which required this kind of speed-composition. On the score *The Natural History of an Alien* for BBC director Mark Jacobs, I had to compose forty-eight minutes of electronic music in three days. Requests for new cues came in thick and fast and I was often taking music brief instructions via fax machine whilst composing!

Keeping up with the competition from other composers in the UK was always a challenge. The ongoing development of new technology meant keeping abreast of new synthesisers, tape recorders, mixing desks and emerging sampling devices. In terms of writing for acoustic instruments and the orchestra, I had very little competition. There were perhaps five film music composers in the South West of England who could write for orchestra. My only disadvantage was being the youngest and least experienced of the group. I'd proved my worth with the *Zastrozzi* and *A Pattern of Energy* chamber and orchestral scores but film directors still went for the most experienced composers first. It would often be composers who had composed for a big BBC drama series or for feature films. It was different with the electronic palette. There were many composers, keyboardists and bands with no experience of orchestral composition but who had the ability to compose with synthesisers, electric guitars and drum machines. They flooded the market and created more competition when it came to pitching electronic scores. To match them meant spending a lot of money on equipping one's own recording studio. I knew I was lagging behind in not having a state-of-the-art studio but it was a chance commission that changed all that.

One day a director from HTV phoned me and asked whether I'd like to work on a forty-five episode game show called *Keynotes*. The premise was a music game show based on the recognition of popular tunes. Each contestant had to guess the title of a well known tune by hearing up to nine notes of the tune. If correct, a fifteen second arrangement of that tune was played back. The offer was for me to compose one hundred and eighty-five tune arrangements and learn how to program an animated bouncing ball that played notes selected by a contestant. A composer from Los Angeles, Fred Lapides, who had worked on *Keynotes* and knew all about the programming, would teach me how to do it. When I look back now, I don't know how I had the stamina.

'Is there anything else you'd like to know?' asked the director.

'Not sure it's my type of thing.' I replied. 'What do you think?'

'Yes you should do it.'

'When does it start?'

'You need to be learning how to program the computer's bouncing ball and then we start filming in studio in three weeks time.'

I hesitated. I wasn't sure.

'What's the budget?'

The director mentioned the budget for each programme. It sounded like too little, but multiplied by forty-five episodes it was a small fortune.

'Do you know how much that adds up to?'

'Well yes,' said the director. 'The production company know what it's going to cost. You decide. Give them a call.'

I did. I found myself speaking to Reg Grundy Productions. Grundy produced hit shows such as *Celebrity Squares, Going for Gold, Fort Boyard, The Price Is Right, Lily Savage's Blankety Blank, Blockbusters*, as well as re-edited versions of soap opera *Neighbours*.

The producers asked me to meet them at their Kensington apartment in London. I was there the next day. The meeting was short. They ran though how the game worked and discussed the schedule. I mentioned, from the budget they'd given my director colleague, just how much they'd be spending.

'That's right,' they said.

'Anything else?'

'There would be consulting fees for any information required about which music tracks to use for the show.'

'That's fine.'

As I left the apartment, I felt like I was walking on air. I realised the income from *Keynotes* would enable me to equip my home studio with everything I required to compete with my peers — fine composers like Hans Zimmer, George Fenton, Rachel Portman, and Bristol composing team Nigel Beaham-Powell and Bella Russell.

A week later I was at HTV studios with the producer and Fred Lapides. Fred took me through the procedure for programming the bouncing ball that would sound out the music notes in the nine note sequence. Once I'd got that under my belt, my next job was to liaise with the producers about which songs would be suitable for the episodes. Songs usually came through as faxes of each song's manuscript. Sometimes ten or more songs totalling perhaps sixty pages would come through. But there was only one fax machine available to receive them at HTV and it was in the office of the top executive at HTV, Director of Programmes Derek Clark (1932–2007). Derek often entered his office in the morning to find rolls and rolls of music manuscript scrolling across his desk and carpet. Given we had to assess hundreds of songs, his office soon looked like my own personal fax room. Once I had the songs and we'd chosen suitable ones, I'd write the first nine notes on music manuscript with a diagram of how the computer's bouncing ball would create the rhythm and pitch of those notes at the required tempo. Once that was in the bag, I'd play the show's producer the first nine notes of each chosen song over the telephone to ensure the tune was guessable.

Finally, I had the one hundred and eighty-five fifteen second arrangements to compose. It was a back breaking task but I could now afford the equipment necessary to deliver it and any other scores. I ordered a Soundtracs 16-8-16 mixing desk, a Fostex E16 sixteen track reel to reel with a Fostex 4035 synchroniser controller. All my tracks got mixed down to a Revox B77 or a Fostex E2 reel to reel tape recorder. I used a Quad 405 Amplifier and Tannoy Little Gold speakers. The jewel in the crown was adding one of the latest but super expensive keyboard sampling instruments. The choice was between the Fairlight, the Kurzweil, and the Emulator III. I remember sitting next to Godley and Creme, the duo that split off from British rockband 10cc. They were going in for a demo of the Fairlight and I was next on the list. I knew I was out of my league even sitting next to them. I had the demo but baulked at the fifty thousand pounds price tag. My next demo was with the Kurzweil. I knew that a composer I admired, Michael Kamen (1948–2003), used the instrument to create expansive orchestral soundtracks on movies such as *Highlander* (1986), *License to Kill* (1989) and *Lethal Weapon* (1987), but

I didn't find the programming of the instrument user friendly.

I decided, instead, to check out one of the newest kids on the block: the E-Mu Systems' Emulator III. Emulators became popular with many musicians such as David Bowie, Genesis, Jean Michel-Jarre, Pet Shop Boys, Stevie Wonder and film composers Brad Fiedel and Vangelis. I'd heard many good reports about the EIII and preferred it, because of its high quality components, to the Akai S1000 a popular Japanese sampler. I had a demo of the EIII in London and found myself alongside composer, singer and songwriter Gary Numan who had created a cult following after his single *Cars* (1979) reached number one in several countries. We both exchanged a few words about the merits of the EIII and the quality of its samples. I don't know whether Gary bought one or not, but I spent £14500 on one with an external removable disk drive. That's enough money for a young composer to buy a complete start up studio these days and demonstrates how prices dropped in the era of the democratisation of music technology. For a few thousand, anyone could try their hand at becoming a composer!

One day the phone rang and it was a nurse on the end of the line. My father-in-law had suffered a heart attack and was in hospital. It meant a quick dash up the motorway and luckily we arrived in time to spend some moments with him before he passed away. It was an exceptionally difficult time as we had also planned to take my parents back to Poland for a family reunion. The departure date for the trip fell not long after the funeral and amidst incredibly sad circumstances we decided to go ahead with the visit. Emotionally, it was a difficult trip set against a backdrop of grief and loss. Our Polish family, however, welcomed us with open arms. At the home of each of my relatives was the ubiquitous table of cold meats, pork cutlets, herring, eggs, tomatoes, sauerkraut, boiled potatoes with parsley, cabbage rolls, cucumbers in cream, bread, lots of Polish beer and the forever flowing fountain of vodka. Our whistle stop tour took us to Kraków, Szczecin, Wrocław, Warsaw and Zakopane at the base of the Tatra mountains. We made a stop at Oświęcim, site of the Auschwitz concentration camp. Nothing can prepare one for standing on the ground on which the horrors of the Holocaust took place. Due to my father's wartime experiences, he couldn't even face stepping through the main gate. In Warsaw we visited the Stare Miasto (old town) which was meticulously rebuilt from its ruins after German invasions and bombings. Especially moving and indicative of the many incursions the Poles have had on their land, was the statue *Mały Powstaniec* (the Little Insurrectionist). The statue commemorates the child soldiers who fought and died during the 1944 Warsaw Uprising. My father and I were also keen to make a stop west of Warsaw at the village of Żelazowa Wola, the birthplace of composer Frédéric Chopin (1810–1849). It seemed appropriate after my father's insistence on me playing Chopin waltzes throughout my teens.

It was back in Warsaw, however, that we all got embroiled in a confrontation with the Polish army and police. We were staying at a hotel in Warsaw adjacent to a large public square. We'd parked our car close to the square but hadn't been around when the police put up notices about events happening on the following day. It was the day we were supposed to be leaving for the airport to fly back to the UK. As we got our luggage ready to take to the car, we were stopped outside the hotel by police. The square opposite us now looked completely different. The streets had been emptied — including the removal of our car — and hundreds of Polish troops were marching amidst posters and banners heralding the arrival of Soviet leader Mikhail S. Gorbachev. Gorbachev was to address a mass gathering in the square and our car had become a security risk. At that moment, my father went into panic mode and it brought on an angina attack. We all tried to calm him down whilst trying to negotiate with the police who kept telling us we had to wait until the event was over. I insisted we had no time to spare and needed our hire car to get to the airport. It was finally agreed we'd be allowed to go by foot across the square, waving passports at one security checkpoint to another, until we could exit the security perimeter at the other side. It was an extremely stressful higgledy-piggledy pathway though the jostling crowd with my mum worrying we'd all be getting locked up somewhere down the line or dad would have a massive heart attack and we'd never make the flight home. For someone who was terrified of flying, she couldn't wait to get to the plane! We left my father at the hotel — he was in pain and unable to walk the distance. The plan was to return for him once we located our impounded car. Luckily, we were able to trace where the police had taken the car and, once we'd argued and paid the fine, we headed back to a place where we were allowed to pick up my father — now tanked up on heart pills. I never expected our final relaxing afternoon before leaving Poland to be compounded by dealing with a sick father, truculent hotel staff, the leader of the Soviet Union, the Polish army and the police. Moral of the tale: never park in the president's spot.

Phew! Glad to have got back home. What next? Buy a new house! The house we had was a terrace and the students who rented the house next door kept us awake with all night parties most weeks. No amount of complaining to the landlord made any difference. The 'five go mad in a student house' also decided to keep an Alsatian dog that was unfortunately left to bark all day in an outside toilet whilst the students were out. Coupled with the fact we were in a housing boom and it was a seller's market, we decided to go. A few people came to look at our house but weren't interested. One day an architect from London came for a viewing. He had a good look at the house and appeared to like it. Things were looking positive. He then wanted to get a better view of the roof and stood on the garden party wall. He was standing about three feet away from where the dog was locked away in the neighbours' toilet. I kept praying he wouldn't see the dog and the dog would stay quiet. About a second later, the toilet door opened and the dog leapt out, barking and leaping up against the wall to try and take a chunk out of the architect's ankle. The architect got himself a look at the 'woof' rather than the 'roof'! I was convinced it was the end of any sale but the great god of property must have been watching over us and the architect bought the house.

Our plan was to move north of the river, Clifton, Redland, Cotham or Kingsdown. One house we looked at had a basement like the Leeds and Liverpool canal with water that had almost reached the ground floor. Every room had a folding commode, a toileting sling, safety rails and everything you might need if you were over ninety or wanted to sit on the loo all day. We chose instead a house in Clifton that had been used for multiple-occupancy. The conversion of it to a family home took many years of painstaking reconstruction. Even the basement floor had to be lowered by a foot to create enough headroom for what was going to become my new music studio. As we completely renovated the interior and put the final coat of paint on an architrave in the hall, we spotted a strand of what looked like a web. Our builder Roy decided to take off a piece of architrave. One piece led to another and, bit by bit, as floor boards were removed in the bathroom above, we discovered the mother of all dry rot fruiting bodies. Dry rot had been covered up by the previous owners and it had spread to four rooms in the house. We had to move out of the house and into our neighbour's spare bedroom whilst half of the house was taken apart and rebuilt.

Doubly challenging was that this happened at a time when wonderful news arrived which required all hands on deck to complete the house and studio. Our first child was on the way and I had been offered my first major BBC Natural History series — an eight-part documentary series about the social and natural history of North America, *Land of the Eagle*. There have been a few times in my career when big career breaks or opportunities have arrived hand in hand with a major positive or negative life event. Is there anything in that I wonder? It feels as if someone is playing a game where one is tested on how many balls can be juggled at any one time. It's been during those times of challenge, when one is stretched in all directions and demands are made on one's stamina, that I believe I've produced some of my best work.

7

Powwow

The income from the music I'd composed for the game show series *Keynotes* provided enough money to equip my studio with essential gear I required for the composition of a score that changed the course of my music career. *Land of the Eagle* was an eight-part BBC/WNET series about the natural history of North America. To successfully compose for the series, my studio required picture and audio synchronisation. Film runs at twenty-five frames per second for UK TV transmission and the music needed to be locked to that frame rate for accurate synchronisation. To do this, the videotape required the recording of a timecode on one of its audio tracks. The other track carried commentary and sound effects. The video also had burnt-in timecode displayed as an elapsing clock at the bottom of the screen. The clock ran in hours, minutes, seconds and frames (twenty-fifths of a second). My sixteen-track tape recorder also had a timecode recorded onto one of its tracks. The video machine was commonly known as the 'master' and the audio recording machine as the 'slave'. Although the video and the tape recorder both had timecodes, they didn't necessarily both begin at the same point in time. The video might start at the number 00.00.00.00 but the tape recorder timecode for the first piece of music recorded on the tape might start at 00.00.01.15. In order for the sound to start exactly where the picture started, an offset time (the difference between the video and the audio timecode starts) had to be entered into a synchronisation controller device. Once the device calculated the offset and went into lock, the music slavishly followed the picture in strict synchronisation. With everything technically now under my fingertips and with the challenge of one foot in the analogue world and one foot in a new digital era, I was ready to compose one of the biggest scores in my oeuvre.

When it comes to working on music scores with directors, not all of them are able to accurately and succinctly tell you what it is they require. I always believed directors came in three categories: first, those who knew nothing about the different genres of music. Their listening experience was limited to a preferred choice of listening and any ability to articulate their wishes using music vocabulary didn't exist. On the whole, this category of filmmakers was easy to work with since they would be happy to trust the composer to deliver a great score. The second category of directors was extremely rare. In it were directors who had educated their ear. They had a comprehensive overview of music history, were avid listeners, conversant with a variety of music genres, and had developed a vocabulary of music terms useful in discussions about the choice of instrumental palette or stylistic approach to the score. For example, would the palette be mainly strings based and would the style favour flowing mellifluous melodic material or strident rhythmic figures? The third category of directors was always the most problematic. A director from that group would say, 'I'll know what I like when I hear it.' This phrase made my heart sink. I knew I'd be working on endless versions of a score for such a director until I came up with something he or she eventually liked, if ever! They would also have no grasp of music vocabulary to aid communication of what it was they required or what they wanted changing at a music session. It wasn't unusual for a director to point out that a music cue was 'an octave too loud' or confused the style of 'minimalism' for 'minimalist'— the former meaning a score with slowly developing repetitive melodic and rhythmic patterns and the latter a score with a simple and sparse texture. On occasions the briefs given to me by directors were nonsensical. I was once asked to score a thirty second title music cue and was given a page of contradictory information and requests. There was no way I could incorporate all the requests into such a short piece of music. In that case I broke ranks. I ignored the brief and did my own thing. Fortunately, the director was very happy with what he heard at the recording session. On another project for a big series, the music brief was based on the wishes of a group of people: a director, producer, co-producer, executive producer and a film editor. In that scenario of 'commission by committee', the composer can get truly cornered when the producer doesn't like brass, the director only likes rock, the co-producer hates flutes and the editor has suggested a piece she heard two nights ago in a pub!

Luckily on *Land of the Eagle*, my big break into international natural history television, the producer and his team of directors were all extremely music savvy. The series producer Peter Crawford had heard a good selection of my work and was very impressed with my score for the film *A Pattern of Energy*. Peter loved the expansive orchestration and asked me to pitch for his series. The brief he gave was articulate, succinct, and perfectly summed up what he was looking for:

Time warp element – going back in time.
Native American versus European view of the land.
Phenomenal landscapes.
Creatures doing their thing.
The whole lot coming together to produce something American.

The series graphic designer also provided a storyboard of the proposed titles sequence. The storyboard depicted an eagle launching into flight and soaring across changing American landscapes until the title *Land of the Eagle* filled the screen. Approximate timings were given for the changes from one shot to another on the storyboard. I'm a great believer in doing in- depth research prior to composing for films and, to respond to Peter's brief, I immersed myself in the music of America: the psalmody of the New England pilgrims, music of the Spanish renaissance, early French folksong, whaling shanties, southern folk hymns, minstrel music, jazz, the works of American composers of the nineteenth and twentieth centuries, American minimalism, and most importantly the rich compendium of Native American songs and dances. There is no personal experience in Native American life where music does not play a part. The rich variety of their music includes songs of animals and birds, songs of beavers and buffaloes, skunks and fireflies, eagles and caribous. There are songs about canoeing, love, travel, war and death. I knew I'd be delving into a rich collection of material with which I resonated – music that embraced and celebrated the natural world and spawned a spiritual connection to the land.

To begin the process of composition of the titles music, I chose to base the opening and closing of the cue on the song *Mata No-otz*, a song of the Mescal Rite given by Mowihaiz (Magpie), leader of the Mescal religion found among the Southern Cheyennes. The song describes an eagle in flight, 'breathing deep with the joy of well being'. To this day I try to speak that line to myself whenever I am in a stressful situation or whenever I wish to celebrate the world around me. I found the song in Natalie Curtis' book *The Indians' Book – Songs and Legends of the American Indians* (1907). It's astonishing to think that when Natalie Curtis first started collecting Native American songs, they were absolutely forbidden in government schools in the USA. It was only through her appeal to President Theodore Roosevelt (1858–1919) and his personal interest in her work that the singing of Native American songs in Native American schools was not only permitted but encouraged. In 1906 Roosevelt said:

'These songs cast a wholly new light on the depth and dignity of Indian thought, the simple beauty and strange charm – the charm of a vanished elder world of Indian poetry.'

I also chose the folk song *Ho! For California* (1849) to blend into the melodic line of the title music and I decided to base the orchestration on one of my favourite American composers Aaron Copland (1900–1990). As well as preparing an electronic 'mock up', sometimes known as a 'polaroid' of the title music, I also provided information to support my composition:

Mowihaiz's song of the eagle provides the backbone of the musical language for the title music for *Land of the Eagle*. Not only is the eagle the 'national bird of America', but it is also a symbol of spiritual importance to Native Americans. The use of my adaptation of Mowihaiz's song is featured in the opening sequence and in the last two bars. The main body of the title music is given over to a theme which reflects contemporary American music language found in composers such as Copland. In this way, the music aims to combine the Indian view of the continent with that of the Europeans. The breakdown of musical elements in the title music is as follows:

Opening close-up of eagle: Native American feel based on *Mata Na-Otz* song (clarinet and drum). As eagle takes off, move into strings/cymbal crescendo. Eagle soars over changing landscapes – entry of a contemporary theme on trumpets and horns, conveying the spirit of exploration. Landscapes: plains, desert, Rockies – theme moves into a few adapted phrases from *Ho! For California* played on clarinet. Strings and brass hover above with a theme evoking Copland. A choral woodwind accompaniment serves to follow the two wing beat pattern of the eagle. Eagle's ascent: a series of dramatic trumpet/orchestral build-ups moving to a climactic titles chord (full orchestra) and giving way to a short recapitulation of the opening *Mata No-otz* theme (again on clarinet) as the eagle flies across the screen. Final chord for title, sub-title and fade through.

Once the demo theme had been played to all the directors on the series and the budget and schedule had been discussed, the go ahead was given to begin composition. The stage at which one is waiting for approval of a signature tune can be a stressful and challenging time. In my experience, the tune is not only played to the commissioning producer or director but to co-producers and directors, their partners, crew members, the crew's brothers and sisters, and their cats and dogs! My theme for the BBC series *Realms of the Russian Bear*, which drew one of the largest postbags of positive responses from viewers, was even played to cleaners in a BBC building before receiving its final approval. At this point of approval, I was already thinking about making adjustments to my demo. I made a very minimal reference to the original song, removed the *Ho! For California* folk song, and decided to add Native American instrumental timbres to the opening and closing. Luckily after many calls to the US, and via the ethnomusicologist at the Smithsonian Institute, I came across the Indian Pueblo Cultural Center in Albuquerque and managed to purchase a Native American drum and a Navajo flute.

Conceptually and thematically, the ideas that emerged from the title music had to permeate what was going to be a leviathan of a score: one hundred and sixty minutes. It's one thing composing a thirty second or fifty second signature tune , but the skill, creativity, and invention of the film composer — as I often mention to my film music students — is this: 'Are you able to develop thirty seconds into a hundred minutes of music?'

The development of thematic material is one of the challenges fledgling film composers find most difficult. Why is this? I believe it's because young musicians have grown up in a music environment where the digital sampler's loop is king. I've listened to many compositions in which a young composer has selected a loop of a few bars of drums, bass or synthesiser and presented that loop, often a few minutes long, as finished work. Lifestyle programmes on TV are a usual culprit where composers attempt to jolly along the programme with repeating loops of pizzicato strings every time there's a cute creature or someone relocating to Spain. This isn't a development of thematic material. Creating strong thematic material is all about the contours of melodic statements, the intervals used, how they rise or fall, how the melody modulates from one key to another and finally how the phrases of melody are structured — for example, as 'question' and 'answer' phrases. Many successful signature tunes are also based on classical music structures or song structures such as AABA and variations which include introductions, link sections and codas.

Throughout the series it was important to maintain authenticity and integrity in the composition of the Native American element of the score. It would have been too easy to have resorted to the romantic notion bred by film westerns about how the music of the Native Americans should sound. In order to avoid that pitfall, I spent three months studying the music and instruments of Native American tribes. Native American music is one of the most specialised types of world music. It is almost entirely composed of percussive accompaniments to voice using drums, rattles or rasps of various kinds. Songs can tell a story or may be made up of 'vocables' such as 'hi-hi-yo-wah'— syllables with no specific meaning, but which are inserted into a song for expressive or rhythmic purposes. In order to ensure the Native American element in the music was relevant to Native American viewers, I often made references to songs that would be familiar to their tribes. It was like a secret code included in the music specifically for them. No other viewers would recognise the significance. For example, in an Ojibwa wall painting sequence in Episode 2: *Confronting the Wilderness*, I based a flute melody on an Ojibwa beaver song which tells of a hunter setting up camp and waiting for a beaver to arrive. It is only at the end of the sequence, when we cut to the next sequence of the beaver dams, that the true significance of the music is realised — that is, if you are familiar with the beaver songs of the Ojibwa! I also used the call of a White-throated sparrow as thematic material in the programme. The same episode also required detailed research into the music the first French settlers might have brought to 'Nouvelle France.' I enhanced the French content of the narrative by basing cues on some of the most beautiful early French songs: *Nanette*, *La Plainte du Coureur des Bois*, and *En Roulant ma Boule*. These were songs sung by pioneering canoe-men, the *coureurs-de-bois*, as they paddled the river-ways of Canada. Even strains of the unofficial French Canadian anthem *A la Claire Fontaine* were orchestrated for shawm, bagpipes, hurdy-gurdy and string orchestra to remind us of the roots of those first settlers.

Choosing a timbral palette, the different 'sound colours' of instruments, is also essential in creating a successful score. Although I'd decided on writing the score for a symphony orchestra, a group of singers, and a group of period folk instruments (bagpipes, hurdy gurdys and shawms), much of the score was realised electronically, especially the Native American element. In terms of creating the Native American feel for the films, I wanted the timbres to be as authentic as possible. I created my own samples of Native American sounds rather than relying on samples from sample libraries. An essential timbre for the score was the Navajo flute, which I performed and recorded into my Emulator ready for playback on the keyboard. The Native American flute is peculiar to several tribes and was used by young men to woo, express inner feelings or even provide background music during times of relaxation. I felt the flute could do the same for the series music. It could express the inner feelings and spiritual character of the Native Americans and reflect a love relationship between the Native American (and thus hopefully emotionally for the programme viewer) and the land. I was also asked to perform the Navajo flute on the album *Flying Kites* (1991) by Scottish band Lies Damned Lies.

The Plains frame drum became another significant timbre in my palette and I also used simple methods used by the Native Americans to create percussion. I made shakers by sewing patches of leather together to form a bag I filled with seeds. I also filled coconut shells or tin cans with small pebbles. The sounds of the shakers were again recorded into the Emulator. One of the most featured elements of the score was Native American voice. I decided to use my own voice and based my performance on recordings I'd heard of Native American songs and dances. I recorded myself singing a series of single notes as well as phrases, rhythmic chanting, expressive shouts, and vocables. I pitch shifted my vocal samples once they were recorded into the Emulator, creating a deeper more resonant voice and bathed this sound in reverberation. The voice, alongside the rattles and shakers, the plains drum and the Navajo flute, created an authentic and magical sound-world.

It was on Episode Three: *Conquering the Swamps* that I got to work with producer and director Steve Nicholls. Steve and I seemed to resonate. We were both fascinated with the use of ethnomusicological research to assist the natural history score and our collaboration on *Land of the Eagle* led to many future collaborations where we broke the mould in terms of the relationship between music and film narrative structure. Steve's episode was set in Florida and it required inspired guesswork as to what instruments were played by the Calusa tribe in that region. Unlike other tribes, there was little information about their music activities. We knew beachcombing was part of the Calusa's life and so we assumed they must have had percussion. Instrument makers probably collected shells or any other *objet trouvé* to make rattles and shakers. Perhaps they even fashioned wind instruments such as ocarinas from stones and shells. Eventually, in-depth research unearthed information about an archeological dig on which strange copper pipes were found. We decided these ancient copper 'panpipes' could provide us with the timbre for the melodic and rhythmic content of the Florida score. I set to work blowing across and electronically sampling all types and lengths of copper pipes. Luckily my bathroom had enough piping left at the end of the project!

Students and those interested in film music often ask me what my approach is when composing music for pictures. For many composers, sitting at a keyboard and composing as the film is running is a preferable option. This is a lot easier nowadays as numerous takes of music sketches and ideas can be recorded on computer software. The composition process I used on *Land of the Eagle* is one I still use today in conjunction with sitting at the keyboard and playing to picture. Step one was to use a metronome. I would choose a tempo I thought suitable for the picture sequence, set the metronome into motion and watch how the beats fell in relationship to the picture. If the metronome tempo suited the pace of the editing and worked well with the speed of any commentary or dialogue then that tempo would be a contender. For example, a tempo of one hundred beats per minute. I would then check to see where the stronger beats of the bar fell. If I'd decided on a time signature of four beats in a bar then the strong beats in a four-

four bar would be beats one and three. I'd see whether these strong beats fell on any narrative or visual moments in the picture sequence that required enhancing through music. Such moments in a film music cue are known as 'hit' points, 'highlights' or 'accents'. If most of the strong beats fell on moments I wished to emphasise then I would normally go with that tempo. I'd then take a sheet of manuscript paper and draw the number of bar lines the cue required based on the tempo I'd chosen. I'd also write descriptions of any of the major narrative and visual moments I wished to highlight. This was a helpful guide as I turned my attention to expressing these hit points through the use of instrumental colour, harmonic language, the start or end of a melodic phrase, dynamics, modulation or changes in the flow of the rhythmic spine of the music. The same method can be used with the music software available today. Suitable markers for hit points can be marked on the empty score ready for the composer to introduce musical effects as he or she performs to picture.

Equally important for any composer's approach to a score is how the music works with dialogue and sound effects. In this respect it's essential to ensure chosen instruments for the score aren't in a similar frequency range to the narrator's voice in a documentary. The entrance and exit of music also requires careful attention. Music can enter on a dramatic hit point in the narrative, a few frames or seconds before it to create anticipation of what is to happen in the narrative or the music can enter immediately after the narrative hit point and create a comment on what the viewer has just seen. There's no doubt there are a few viewers who would prefer it if there was no music at all, especially in natural history documentaries. That's a shame when I am showing off my film music composition prowess and doing my very best to create emotion, dramatic anticipation and impact, character leitmotif, and a sense of location whilst staying out of the way of the commentary. The best way I can reply to the objections any such viewers have is in the words of a popular Ojibwa song: 'better stand further away or you will crush my feathers.'

The sessions at CTS Studios Wembley featured the London Film Orchestra led by violinist Pat Halling, with Harry Rabinowitz conducting and Dick Lewzey mixing. The orchestra had a stellar line up of distinguished principals from all the major orchestras around at the time. Amongst them were flautist Susan Milan, clarinettist Nick Bucknall, trumpeter Crispian Steele-Perkins, harpist Skaila Kanga and keyboardist Dave Arch who went on to become the music director of the BBC's *Strictly Come Dancing*. The recording session is the 'golden moment' for the composer. Never will he or she hear the music in all its unadulterated glory again unless there is an album release or concert. Many seven-day weeks were spent composing the score and there was a mountain of part copying for each instrument that was hand written by my copyist Oliver Ledbury. The opportunity of writing such a large scale score enabled me to spread my wings in terms of the timbral palette for the orchestra. In case the reader wishes to write a major score for a film about the natural history of North America, here's the line up I used:

2 flutes
2 oboes
Shawm
2 clarinets in Bb
Alto Saxophone
2 bassoons
Bagpipe
Trumpet in D
2 trumpets in C
4 horns
2 tenor trombones
Tuba

Harp
Spanish guitar
2 hurdy gurdys
Piano accordion
Vocals (tenor/baritone/bass)

Percussion: timpani, bass drum, Native American framedrum, field drum, tom-toms, rototoms, suspended cymbals, hand cymbals, tam-tam, thundersheet, cabasa, claves, crotales, glockenspiel, guiro, sleigh rattle, triangle, vibraslap.

8 1st violins
6 2nd violins
4 violas
3 cellos
2 double basses

Emulator III digital sampling instrument with the following samples:
Native American voice, Navajo flute and rattles which were samples of my own performance and chimes, breath effect, piano, strings which were samples from the Emulator's library.

TV and film viewers are often unfamiliar with how orchestras are assembled on the sound stage in a studio. In the concert hall the orchestra is heard as a cohesive whole with the conductor controlling the dynamics of each section of players as dictated by the score. In the studio, the orchestra's sections must be separated with players often situated behind screens or in booths. On *Land of the Eagle* the string section and harp were immediately in front of the conductor and the woodwind section was behind the strings. The brass was screened off to one side and the folk instruments group was behind screens at the opposite side. The vocalists were in a booth and the percussion was screened off and behind the conductor. The reason this is done is to ensure that when the orchestra is playing, the recording engineer can record each section without any spill over of sound from one section to another section's microphones. This is essential for the mix down stage so that the engineer has control over each section. The session layout again exemplifies the challenging job of the film conductor. It's often difficult to hear the full blend of orchestral sound coming off the studio floor when instrumentalists are so separated. The conductor must therefore often rely on the mix the engineer is feeding him or her via headphones.

In addition to the twists and turns of musically highlighting locations, creatures, stories and factual content in *Land of the Eagle,* the series presented me with a psychological challenge — one from the past that suddenly washed ashore again. The whole compositional process spawned a stumbling block that became an anxiety and a laborious time waster. It was an obsession with achieving perfection in the composition, recording and mixing of the music. The issue came to the fore in a music cue in which two horses were galloping. I'd created a rhythmic track to accompany the scene, which was only a couple of minutes long, but I couldn't quite get a successful mix from one track to another at a point where there was a picture cut. I laboured over the section for hours and hours and was constantly displeased with how it sounded. I didn't want to risk performing the whole track again as I was pleased with most of it and thought another performance might make it worse. I also couldn't double up the track to try out another take as I had no spare tracks left on my multi-track tape recorder. To put this into context, we are talking about a point on the track lasting no more than a third to a half of one second, but my ears were very finely attuned to hearing even the slightest glitch. It was at that moment my doorbell rang. It was my parents. My father wanted to know what I was working on. I took him into the studio and showed him the sequence with which I was struggling. He came up with complimentary comments.

'But it's no good,' I said.

My father looked perplexed.

'No good? What do you mean?'

I rewound the picture to thirty seconds before the section with which I was unhappy, pressed play and the tape recorder spun into action to synchronise with the picture.

'Listen to this bit coming up now.'

The section played back and my father said nothing.

'Can't you hear?' I said. 'It's not a smooth enough transition there. It sounds uncomfortable to me.'

My father shook his head.

'I don't know what you're talking about.'

I replayed the track back and forth over the spot until he understood. He began to laugh.

'Are you crazy? Forget it. Who can hear that?'

He was right. In the flow of the music, commentary and effects, it was virtually inaudible, but it bugged me. The obsession with perfection not only hampered my work but it also bled into my life — for example, the choosing of paints, furniture or clothes. I once turned down the purchase of a suit because one stitch was out of alignment. The obsession also permeated relationships with women later in life — a preoccupation with finding the perfect look, gait, eyes, smile or character trait. In terms of friends, I was fine if I felt I was receiving perfect loyalty in exchange for my friendship. If that high standard of loyalty and love from the other person wasn't reciprocated, it was easy for me to become unhappy and pull away from the relationship — ultimately discarding the person. In my neediness as an only child wanting a sibling, I would often expect my friends to become that missing piece. I so desperately wanted the loyalty Muhammad achieved when he sent a herd of his horses to race to an oasis to drink. Midway, he called them back, but only five returned. These were the selfless loyal ones known as *Al Khamsa* — 'the five'. I even had great disappointment in my own physical and mental blemishes. I remember the first time the preoccupation with imperfection kicked in. I was six years old and on my way home from school with a school photograph. It was a very windy day and the photograph was an unflattering portrait of me with no front teeth, a small crescent moon birthmark on my forehead, a bright red jumper my mum had knitted, and a pudding bowl haircut thanks to my father's attempts to cut my hair. As gusts of wind strengthened, I found it difficult to keep the photo in perfect condition. As I began to run to escape the onset of rain, the photo got more windblown and wet. I became angry. Instead of trying to protect it more, I shook it and intentionally damaged it. Rather than keep the photograph I would rather have got rid of it.

The photo survived. When I look at it now, I can barely see where the image got wind-creased and rain-spotted. What I was dealing with at age six was dissatisfaction with the tiniest of blemishes. Was there a time prior to six years old when this obsession was born out of another event? I've no idea. I realised, however, the more I became a slave to this way of looking at things, the more I had to drill into my head that the stuff of life, whether physical, mental, material or interpersonal, gets a bit bent and creased here and there but it is still worth having. It's important that such experiences are anecdotally passed on to fledgling composers. So little has been discussed in colleges and universities about the mental health issues connected with what is a demanding and solitary profession. My own students are always eager to ask many questions relating to what it means to be an artist. To become a film composer, any young musician must realise the job isn't simply about composing music. It is about developing a robust psychology to deal with rejection. It's also about understanding the psychology of those with whom you are working, having a good business mind, being a good publicist, being personable, a good communicator, and having the ability to create an original 'voice'. Unless one is commissioned to compose a pastiche, it's important to develop a voice unlike any other. As an artist, there is little point in being like someone else. One must carve a niche, become distinctive, desirable, and therefore indispensable.

My immersion in all things Native American for *Land of the Eagle* was a pivotal moment in a first step towards modifying and refining parts of my belief system. I cherry-picked from pantheism, panentheism, animism, and shamanism which had certain similarities to Native American spirituality. Strands of these beliefs became interwoven with my Christianity. The fusion of isms was not always palatable to my Christian friends. I also strongly believed in biophilia: an innate attraction and connection to nature. I knew such an attraction could be alive from an early age and it certainly had been the case for me. I was ancestrally rooted in forests, marshes and the lakes of my family's land in Belarus. Fields, meadows, ponds and woodland had been big pulls in my childhood and my later involvement with natural history filmmaking became another stepping stone towards intimately understanding and celebrating the natural world. It was the Native American relationship with Earth, however, that became a preamble to what would later become a full conversion to becoming an active environmentalist – a trajectory that led to the birth of my environmental campaign *Green Poems for a Blue Planet*. There's no way I could have imagined how those first encounters with the natural world would end up with the green buds of change down the line. More importantly, when I renounced my faith due to events in later life, I sought solace in nature and headed for wilderness.

One year, I was especially happy when visiting my friend singer and songwriter Steve Cooke in Los Angeles. On arriving, Steve and his wife Sandra suggested we should spend a week in Palm Springs. I loved being in the desert and hiking the sacred Tahquitz Canyon — the ancestral home of the Agua Caliente Band of Cahuilla Indians. Whilst on one of the trails, we stopped to take photographs. I sat on a rock and posed. Steve eyed up the shot.

'Who's the guy behind you?'

'Behind me? What do you mean?

I turned round. There was no-one there.

'Come and take a look.'

He held the camera out.

On the image, directly behind me, was what looked like the shadow of a Native American warrior in a headdress and fringed shirt. It was difficult to ascertain where the shadow had come from but I assumed it had been made by the leaves of tall palm trees. I like to think that chancing on this image was a reminder from the Native Americans that in the words of conservationist Grey Owl, 'You belong to Nature, not it to you.'

Land of the Eagle was a huge success. It launched my career as a major composer of orchestral music for natural history films and it became a rolling snowball in terms of picking up new commissions. Work poured in as a result of word of mouth, reviews and peer approval. The score was lauded by film directors and producers as 'unique', 'inventive' and 'a super blend of conventional and unconventional instruments' — even TV presenter Noel Edmonds asked me to compose a pop single about saving the planet. I composed the song *Blue Planet's Blue* but it never got further than a demo. I also got interviewed about my approach to the music score by presenter Eamonn Holmes on BBC's daily live programme *Open Air*. On the back of such positive feedback, it was important to publicise the success of the score. I'd employed photographer Pat Aithie to shoot the music sessions and she came up with dramatic images which were ideal for publicity purposes. Prior to sending a few of the photos out, my wife and I were heading to visit my parents in Leeds for Christmas. I'd decided to take all the photos to show my parents. They were all neatly filed in a briefcase along with the original negatives. We packed the car with our luggage and put the Christmas presents we'd bought on the back seat along with my briefcase. En route to Leeds we had to drop off a Christmas present near Birmingham. We knew our friend was involved with a church Christmas party at the time we were passing, so we decided to drop it off with her.

We pulled into the car park, got out and went into the church, exchanged our

Christmas greetings and handed over the present. It was no more than a couple of minutes spent inside. On leaving the church we were shocked to see our car windows had been smashed and my briefcase of photographs had been taken. The loss of the photographs and negatives totally gutted me. Somehow, probably from years of experience in taping up the windows of our banged up old Ford Escort, we managed to secure the windows and make our way up to Leeds. The loss of the photos put a cloud over my Christmas but deep inside I believed they would come back to me. This feeling has often been with me at times in my life when I have lost or wanted something. We reported the theft to the police but there was no likelihood of any witnesses or leads or returned property. Weeks went by. I held on to a crazy belief the photographs would be returned. As another couple of weeks passed, I was almost about to resign myself to the loss when the phone rang. It was the landlord of a pub in the Midlands. They'd found a rain-sodden briefcase in their car park with one of my business cards inside. It was extraordinary to hear all the photos and negatives were still in the case but soaked. A few days later I received the photos and negatives and pegged them out on lines of string in the basement of our house. Fortunately, the only damage was to the borders of a couple of images. Whether one can connect the return of the briefcase to the notion of visualisation — mentally focusing positively on something desired — or to some supernatural helper or simply to luck and chance who knows? I've certainly lost things and people in life that I wanted to retrieve but never got them back.

8

Back in the USSR

At the beginning of the nineties I felt as if I was launching on eagle's wings. My professional and personal life was soaring on high as the result of two life changing events: the final programme in the *Land of the Eagle* series was broadcast within a few days of the birth of our first child Serafina. Named after my Aunt Serafina, who was deported by the Soviets to Siberia during the 'reign of terror' in World War II, baby Serafina was reluctant to appear and had to be induced after going three weeks over term. She certainly gave the obstetrician and the hospital's first male midwife a run for their money as her heart rate dropped to a worrying low level at one point during delivery. She surprised us by emerging with a head of red hair. A flurry of BBC and ITV commissions for series title music followed these wonderful events. It was an extremely prolific period of my career and resulted in series signature tunes for BBC current affairs programmes *Newsround*, *Assignment*, *Europe on the Brink*, and *Public Eye*, as well as the natural history series *The Natural World*, *Wildlife on Two* and *Wildworld*. I also scored incidental music for programmes in *The Natural World* and *Wildlife on Two* series. The music for *Newsround* was especially exciting to score not only because it was such a well known current affairs programme, but because the icing on the cake was to have the show's presenter Juliet Morris turn up on my doorstep to do an interview about how I composed the theme.

Public Eye was a lesson in keeping any signature tune simple and memorable for the viewer. The director of *Public Eye* heard and liked my work and wanted the music delivered in a week. My first and second attempts at the music weren't approved by the production team in London. I had other projects running at the same time so I suggested that since I hadn't nailed the signature tune then perhaps a different composer should be approached. I thought it somewhat strange when the director insisted I should be the composer and no-one else. Running short of time, I made my third attempt at the music in a somewhat lackadaisical manner. I played a few banal repetitive phrases, added a simple conventional ascending figure to the last melodic statement and ended with a closing cadence familiar to any listener. I also added a few musical effects to synchronise with elements of the picture. It took no more than a few minutes and I packaged it off to London thinking it would be my worst attempt to date. Ironically, it was my best and was hailed as a great title music theme. The experience brought to mind the approach of composer John Philip Sousa (1854–1932), the king of marches, who believed melodies must be written for the 'musical and unmusical ear' alike. Perhaps this is why his march *The Liberty Bell* was so popular and memorable as the signature tune for the anarchic comedy series *Monty Python's Flying Circus*. For future scores I reminded myself of Sousa's maxim and relaxed a bit more in an attempt to keep it simple stupid!

One of my most intellectually stimulating collaborations came as a result of meeting maverick film producer Peter Symes, an innovative filmmaker who was instrumental in setting up the first documentary film festival in the UK, the Sheffield Documentary Film Festival. Peter invited me to provide music for a film poem *The Gaze of the Gorgon* written by Tony Harrison, one of the UK's foremost poets and playwrights. I was over the moon! I greatly admired Tony's work and it was a once in a lifetime experience to create music to accompany his epic poem about the politics of conflict in the twentieth century. This astonishing piece of work used the idea of introducing the petrifying gaze of the gorgon of Greek myth as a metaphor for the modern gorgons of wars: dictators, leaders, and the elite who have the power to 'petrify' the masses. A potent image Tony mentions in the poem is that of a 'barbed-wire lyre'. One of my many tasks was to record samples of plucked barbed wire and combine these timbres with library samples to produce the sound of such an instrument. Amidst the BBC projects, I managed to fit in the composition of title music for ITV documentary series *Murder Squad* and a score for a four-part series about the Kennet and Avon Canal, *The K & A*. There were also projects offered that I would have given my eye teeth to have won. I didn't manage to come up with an acceptable demo theme for BBC's landmark series *Blue Peter*, *Tomorrow's World*, and *Question Time*. Whilst I failed to win these particular projects on the suitability of my signature tune, I often warn my students that any music they pitch, albeit well composed, may come up against other agendas in any selection process such as which school or university you went to, who you know, what you're prepared to concede in terms of intellectual property rights, and how much you charge.

In 1991 I was approached by producer John Sparks to compose the music for a six-part series *Realms of the Russian Bear*. The series was presented by Nikolay Drozdov, one of Russia's greatest natural history commentators and writers. I'd met John when he was working on David Attenborough's *Life on Earth* series and later during his time as head of the BBC Natural History Unit when he suggested to filmmakers Jan Aldenhoven and Glen Carruthers that I should score their film *Kingdom of the Crabs* – a remarkable story tracing the migration of one hundred and twenty million Red land crabs on Christmas Island. The score won a music award at the Missoula Film Festival, USA. John was wonderful to work with and I liked him from the moment we met. His natural history knowledge was breathtaking, but more importantly he was an authentic person devoid of the 'look at me' egos or 'games playing' in our industry. He called a spade a spade and I always knew where I was with him. This is what made our collaboration so successful. John agreed it was important that before embarking on any compositional sketches for *Realms of the Russian Bear*, I should engage in a research period in which I studied the native instruments of what was in 1991 still the USSR (Union of Soviet Socialist Republics). I came away from one meeting with John knowing we were going to do something pioneering with the music for the six films. I'd asked him whether he and the Natural History Unit would be willing to send a composer to Russia to collect samples of indigenous music. John saw the benefits of such an approach and agreed to it. I was grateful he trusted me to deliver a score that fulfilled his personal vision of music which blended indigenous instruments with an accessible theme that aurally branded the series.

If you ask anyone what they know of the music of Russia, it won't be long before they come up with balalaikas, the Red Army Choir, and composer Maurice Jarre's soundtrack for the film *Dr. Zhivago* (1965). Russia covers a sixth of Earth's surface, spans eleven time zones and in 1991 the combined republics had a population of 293 million. It is surprising that the variety of its instruments and repertoire was relatively unexplored by musicians and scholars in the West. At the start of my research I'd expected to discover some of the most common instruments: balalaikas, bayans, dulcimers, shepherds' horns, flutes, domras and guslis. What I didn't expect to find was a palette of over a thousand folk instruments. My initial introduction to this palette came via K.A.Vertkov's book *Atlas of the Folk Instruments of the USSR* (1963). I used the book to trace references to Russian folk instruments in other dictionaries, music books or articles. After many weeks of research, I ended up producing my own English language compendium of the indigenous instruments of the USSR – four box files of snippets, cuttings, music manuscript and illustrations. I chose around a hundred of the instruments from my do-it-yourself dictionary as instruments that could fit with the locations in which the films were set. I also chose instruments that would be aurally accessible to any viewer. It was also important to locate recordings of these instruments so I could introduce my producer and programme directors to a potential timbral palette for the series. Once these had been listened to, we edited our palette and came up with a selection of instruments which would work well across the films. But the pioneering part of the process was about to happen.

We arranged to fly all the musicians we required from the Soviet republics into Moscow and digitally sample and record their instruments at the famous Melodia recording studio. The BBC provided me with sound recordist David Tombs who assisted me in recording the music on DAT (Digital Audio Tape) a state-of-the-art format at the time. This meant the recording would be of the highest quality for my Emulator sampling instrument back in the UK. The music was also recorded on ten-inch reels of audio tape by Melodia's studio engineer. Those tapes would also act as a back-up for my digital recordings and were also the master tapes the BBC used for transferring the music. I was also assisted in Moscow by Duncan Balfour Thomson an interpreter and assistant producer from the BBC natural history unit. My session recording plan was to first record all the ensemble pieces I'd composed back in the UK. These were for balalaika ensemble or a small ensemble of folk instruments. I next recorded duets or solo instruments for which I had composed themes. Finally, I recorded individual samples from every instrument: single notes, chords, motifs and phrases. With the stringed instruments I also recorded individual samples of bowing, strumming or plucking. This meant that once back in the UK, I could choose a music cue I'd recorded in its entirety, use that cue and overlay samples I'd loaded into the Emulator or completely compose a score from scratch by using the individual samples of each instrument.

As I travelled to the Office of the Folklore Department in Moscow, someone at the BBC must have had friends in high places or was it a coincidence that all the traffic lights were on green! At the department I worked with Eugenia Andreyeva on the scheduling and organisation of the music sessions. I thought the office was very representative of the state of the country. The electric element used for heating water for a cuppa was plugged into a stray electrical socket which trailed over a heap of manuscripts, across a video recorder and over a pile of books on top of the old writing desk of one of Russia's greatest composers: Dimitri Shostakovich (1906–1975). There were many conversations related to my score that I could never have envisaged. One day Andrei Kabanov, the leader of the vocal group I'd booked, came in for a meeting. During our conversation he asked me to explain two things: why would his group be singing indoors and why did I expect them to sing at a level less than *forte* (loud)? Whether he was joking or not, he said he was only able to sing *forte* or *fortissimo* (very loud)! I reminded myself that Andrei's reservations were well founded. His group was traditionally used to singing in the open air, in fields and festivals linked to the agricultural cycle. Their voices could normally carry a distance of kilometres.

Another extraordinary meeting on the first day of recording the thirty-five musicians was with Jurij Illich Sheikin, a Siberian ethnomusicologist whose collection of Siberian instruments probably caused fellow passengers on the four-hour flight from Novosibirsk some discomfort. Jurij's first session performance on the kingula, a ten-foot long hollow plant stem, raised a few eyebrows as well as the sound recordist's headphones! Lifting the long twig into the air, which had to be supported at the other end by my assistant, he placed the end of the stem in his mouth and produced the most incredible piercing tones. The instrument was commonly used by the Chukchi tribe to call reindeer, but in the Melodia studios it only called rain! During a normal studio session environmental factors rarely cause an interruption, but Melodia Studios was based in an old Anglican church and recording couldn't take place when rain pitter-pattered on the roof. An additional problem was the ongoing roadworks outside. It was impossible to pay the workmen to go away as they were laying essential new telephone lines to the studio. Once the rain and roadworks ceased, Jurij continued the session with a rendition of *The Seagull Song* from the Chukchi Peninsula. The song is to date one of the most astonishing pieces of music I've ever heard. The sounds emanating from Jurij were a combination of animal cries and calls, hyperventilation and expressive grunts similar to the male orgasm. Even though the song seemed to have very few different timbres in it, the piece actually had forty-one different vocables which were not distinguishable by the impoverished ears of those of us in the Western hemisphere. Jurij had learned this vocabulary of vocables as a received oral tradition from a Siberian shaman and he entertained us further by dancing around the studio while singing into a buben, a shaman's drum. At one point during the recording of this dance, the microphone was rubbing against his clothing. Jurij was prepared to undress to create a clearer recording but what would the lapel microphone attach to? Let's not go there and we didn't! The songs fuelled my interest in shamanism and influenced my later work especially my Soundbeam multi-media work *Inua* (2004).

The Soviet Central Asian instrumentalists in my sessions presented challenges in the recording of their instruments. I would often ask them to perform short improvisations of around forty-five seconds to a minute's duration. These would be useful to lay on any film sequences. On one occasion, once the dutar (two-stringed lute) player had started his improvisation, it was impossible to stop it!

All my arm-waving was in vain. These musicians were used to performing epic songs in their homeland — songs which can last for hours if not days. One final challenge was our resident Soviet recording engineer who, following a jobsworth's rule, switched off the studio power every evening at six o' clock even if we were in the middle of a take!

Once I was back home in my studio, I started the task of loading all the Moscow samples into my Emulator. I employed programmer Ian Steele to assist with the loading, editing and looping of samples as well as layering the samples to create multi-timbral sounds. Ian had worked as a programmer all over the world with musicians Joan Armtrading, The Bee Gees and 10,000 Maniacs. He was a wizard with synthesisers and samplers and he became my regular programmer on my natural history and drama scores. The title music for the series was recorded at CTS Studios, Wembley. Dick Lewzey mixed the score and Harry Rabinowitz conducted. The line up included a small orchestra with woodwind, brass, strings four balalaikas, dulcimer, and two bayan accordions. The title music sequence depicted a brown bear padding through different regional landscapes of the USSR. I often show this signature tune sequence to my students when teaching the composition of featured titles music. After playing the sequence, I mention that the most difficult part of the studio recording session was to get the bear to walk exactly in time to the orchestra playing my music. It's always wonderful to see the astonishment on their faces as they contemplate the difficulties of manoeuvring a bear in a music studio. A couple of seconds later they collapse into laughter as they get the joke.

There was such a large amount of research for *Realms of the Russian Bear* and I decided it mustn't go to waste. I applied to the University of Bristol to pursue a part-time MLitt on Russian folk music. As my research developed, I discovered that rather than focusing my dissertation on the lesser known folk instruments of Russia and its former republics, I would concentrate on the balalaika, the most well known Russian instrument. I'd initially rejected writing about the instrument because of its popularity until I realised that no-one had written an in-depth article or academic paper on it in the West since 1900. I was determined to be the first to do it. As my research progressed, I had to learn basic Russian to read articles written about the balalaika. The result was the completion of my first major academic paper *The Balalaika — A Reappraisal.* The paper was subsequently published in one of the world's leading musicological journals *The Galpin Society Journal* in March 1995. I was also asked by *The New Grove Dictionary of Music and Musicians* to write the entry on the balalaika for the dictionary. The University of Bristol recognised this as a significant achievement and I was upgraded from my MLitt to a course of study for a PhD. I decided to write the first PhD about the balalaika and I wished to explore how the instrument had migrated from Russia to the USA. The title for my PhD was one of the longest the music department had seen: *The Origins and Place of the Balalaika in Russian Culture, its Migration to the USA, and the Dissemination of Balalaika Orchestras in America with Particular Reference to the Kasura and Kutin Collections at the University of Illinois.*

The PhD was going to take me a number of years of part-time study and was completed in 1999. One of the Sisyphean tasks was the compilation of text, graphs, tables, illustrations and music manuscript examples. These were the early years of computing software and although I managed to find someone to properly format my word document text, the importing or design of graphs and tables was a nightmare. All the illustrations had to be cut and pasted into the document and I mean cut and glued in! I was lucky to have had one of the finest PhD supervisors around: Wyndham Thomas. Wyndham fired perspicacious questions and often made me wonder whether I was up to the mark to pursue a PhD. I could easily have chosen to research an area of film music composition, but that would have been too easy. I wanted to set myself an academic challenge by tackling a PhD in ethnomusicology. Thankfully, the intense supervision sessions were often defused by Wyndham's anecdotes. One of my favourites was the time he was asked to play piano for a contemporary dance group rehearsal. Wyndham improvised the whole score on the spot, introducing inventive atonal motifs, plucking the piano strings, banging his fist on the keys to make random cluster chords or haphazardly gliding his hands up and down the keyboard to create dramatic glissandi. His final flourish was to grab hold of the piano's lid and slam it shut. The dancers held their final poise and the choreographer turned to Wyndham,

'That was wonderful. Don't change a note of it!'

The PhD also required visits to the USA. I interviewed a balalaika player in Los Angeles and members of the Balalaika and Domra Association of America, but I spent most of my time in the Kutin and Kasura collections at the University of Illinois at Urbana-Champaign. The collection houses the largest collection of Russian-American balalaika arrangements in the USA. Russian émigré Alexander Kutin (1899–1985) and Walter J. Kasura (1919–1983) were the two most prolific performers of balalaika music in America. It was amazing to page-turn through Kasura's handwritten arrangements – stained with mustard from his lunchtime sandwiches. Here was a man who was arranging at every available minute he could steal from his desk job at an insurance company. My research also examined the question of the balalaika's origin, construction technique, the rise of the balalaika in Russian society, its emergence in the Western hemisphere, the balalaika and the American recording industry, the balalaika's role in the Hollywood soundtrack and the effect of McCarthyism on the instrument. The balalaika went underground in the USA during the 1950s period of McCarthyism when all things Russian were outlawed. It wasn't until the early sixties with the release of the film *Dr.Zhivago* (1965) and Maurice Jarre's soundtrack replete with balalaikas that the instrument enjoyed a renaissance. Another research coup on my project was the acquisition of an image from Anya Titova whose husband Grisha played balalaika in vision on many films including Charlie Chaplin's film *City Lights* (1931). Chaplin was a balalaika aficionado who also employed Titov to perform for him during shooting, lunch breaks, and at production parties.

A portion of my research had already been done as part of my work for the *Realms of the Russian Bear* series. I'd made notes at a visit to the Glinka Museum of Musical Culture which boasts over three thousand musical instruments in its collection. I also planned to visit my ancestral land in Belarus and record indigenous music. This visit, in 1992 was also an opportunity to take my father, at age eighty, back to his roots to meet family he hadn't seen for fifty-six years. It was a challenging task since my father had already had two heart attacks and suffered from angina. His slow pace and shortness of breath made it difficult for him to move around. We spent the first day in Vilnius, Lithuania. My father had spent time there in the first year of World War II. The next day I hired a car and driver to take us into Belarus and on to the village of Volkolata where some of our family were based.

The journey from Vilnius to Volkolata took a couple of hours on roads lined with pine and silver birch forest. The trees eventually petered out to reveal the village. We were to stay at my cousin Edmund's house, a beautifully quaint blue building with outbuildings, farmland, a horse, and a well in the yard. The usual full table of food and vodka was set out to greet us. The kitchen had a sink unit obstructing the oven's door, a large wardrobe with a mirrored door, a fridge, and two chairs on which were buckets and large steel pots used for cooking or for taking water into the tiny birch sauna. On one chair was an enamel cup used for scooping up water to pour on the hot coals. The best part of the sauna experience was the scrubber: a handful of birch twigs. The village was small. It had an impressive church, a village hall, a shop, post office, and a couple of 'vodkaholics' lying on the pavement. The cemetery was the most dramatic feature in the area. Set on a hill overlooking the village, it seemed to proclaim 'we are the dead living above the living.' Valera my half cousin, who normally drove an old ambulance around the region, was going to be our taxi driver and guide for our time in Belarus. One of our first visits was to Zarudzie, the village where my father was born. It was heart-wrenching to watch him stare at the spot that was once his house and land, a place where he had such fun playing music with his brothers. Across the fields, a path led into woodland and deep in the middle, somewhat unexpected, was a tiny cemetery. As I looked around, the one word that stood out most was my surname. I realised I was standing in a place where more of my relatives were beneath the land than above it. My father stood with his jacket slung around his shoulders, hands in pockets and head down. Three headstones stood tall and proud: Hipolit my grandfather and my uncles Viktor and Fabijan.

Such a reunion of the dead and the living took its toll. There was endless family conversation about those lost in the war and late nights spent with copious amounts of vodka, herring, cold meats, and more vodka. There was, however, time for me to get a bit of research time in for my PhD. A group of women came to tell me their life stories and sing songs they remembered. I also interviewed the village priest, a meeting which proved to be one of the most informative and inspiring. During our conversation, the priest told me a story about the village people of Volkolata. It was about the Nazi invasion in World War II. What the Nazis wanted most from the villages and towns they ransacked was refined metal they could melt down and use to make weapons. Much of the metal was found in door knobs but mostly in church bells. The port of Hamburg in Germany was piled high with over one hundred thousand bells ready to be melted down. The villagers of Volkolata knew the Nazis were approaching and what they were looking for. So, the villagers took down the two bells from the village church and buried them. After the war, they searched for the bells but could only find one. The story struck me as a great narrative for a film. Where was the missing bell? What would happen if someone set out to find it? My story *The Bell* was to become one of the projects closest to my heart but the road to its realisation was a rocky one full of dashed hopes and disappointment. It was one of the projects that drove me to utter despair in later life at a time I could barely function due to depression.

Back in the UK life was hectic. I was full on with my PhD and film music composition and my wife was busy setting up film productions at home and abroad. In terms of a work-life balance, it was a demanding time. Despite our workaholic dispositions, there was respite. We decided to treat ourselves to a vacation in Kauai in the Hawaiian Islands. At eighteen months old our daughter Serafina managed to scream for the nineteen-hour flight but our arrival in paradise was well worth the effort. The tropical climes even settled a spot on her nose that no-one in the UK could sort. In successive years, no matter how many children or the demands of workload, we learned to prioritise making the time to take a break whether it ended up as a week of rain on the Pembrokeshire coast or a sun-baked beach in Majorca. It sure got a lot crazier when our son Luka was born in 1993. He was born in the back bedroom at home, a big baby with broad shoulders. It was the quick action of one of the midwives who saved complications for both mum and baby as she wrestled him out. I got to cut the cord and cradle Luka in my arms. I was wearing my Hawaiian shirt and later wrote a poem *Hawaiian Arms* to celebrate his birth.

Despite the demands of a second child, work kept pouring in. Sometimes I wonder where I got my motivation, drive and stamina, but I'm so lucky to have been blessed with a great amount of energy. I like to believe that when it was given out, I was first in line, asked for a double portion, and later went back for an extra one! It's certainly essential for a freelance musician to make hay whilst the sun shines. You never know when markets will change or when life chooses to throw its googlies. Then, before you know it, as I learned in my fifties, the unexpected grabs you by the balls. So whilst the going was good I kept going, always in the hope of avoiding burn out. Whatever I was running on must have been high octane and I was more than ready for the next big challenge: the eight-part series *The Nineties*, a BBC documentary series looking back at the lives of nonagenarians. The series required a seventy-nine minute chamber score and the usual quick turnaround. The composition of the score is especially memorable for me as there were moments when the music seemed to emerge from the air rather than the head. I remember one sequence in which I improvised music to picture. On completion of the cue I had no idea what harmony, rhythm or melody I'd put in place. It was as if I'd received the music rather than planned the cue's music structure. Executive producer Annie Paul sent me a letter of thanks:

'I have experienced a real sense of pleasure from the delicacy, sensitivity and atmosphere created in the textured layers of the music – often transforming some fairly ordinary scenes into something very special.'

This is the power of music! Music is able to lift a statement or action in such a way that viewers can be transported to an emotional or even transcendental realm. I often wonder whether it's possible for young composers to successfully score films when their range of emotions and life experiences is limited. There are methods I've developed for teaching film scoring but it is the collection of and memory of the emotional responses to life's knocks, bruises, break-ups, sadness and loss which are essential in translating such responses into melody, harmony, timbres and textures. This is an indispensable requisite for any composer who truly wishes to resonate with and interpret screen narrative. I especially enjoy learning about how my students interpret screen narrative in order to help them get the most out of the marriage of music and picture. On a visit to give lectures at the Eastern Mediterranean University in Northern Cyprus, a student announced that when she watched a man and woman kissing in a TV drama, the accompanying music made her feel more emotionally engaged than when she kissed her *own* boyfriend in real life. She asked what I thought of that. My answer,

'Perhaps you need a new boyfriend?'

There were two films in my career that were most enjoyable to score as they allowed me to explore new ways of working with music and narrative in wildlife programmes. These were the BBC *Wildlife on One* projects *They Came from the Sea,* a film about crabs, and *Shadow of the Hare*, a film about hares. Both films were directed by Steve Nicholls with whom I'd forged a great collaboration on the *Land of the Eagle* series. Steve was open to exploring new approaches to the timbral palette of scores or new ways of applying music to narrative and images. In *They Came from the Sea* I suggested, because of the very mechanistic way in which the crabs moved, we might explore the use of prepared piano. Prepared piano turns what is already a percussive instrument into a more percussive one. It involves placing objects known as *preparations* in between or on the piano strings. The preparations alter the sound of the piano when the keys are pressed. Amongst the objects that can be used are pencil erasers, nuts and bolts, bits of plastic, keys, paper clips, combs, and clothes pegs. The invention of prepared piano is attributed to the avant-garde composer John Cage (1912–1992) who believed it was possible to place the equivalent of a percussion orchestra into the hands of the pianist. I played extracts of Cage's works to the director and he immediately expressed an interest to experiment with the sound palette.

Our next collaboration was even bolder. Steve and I had discussed the role music could play in being a featured part of a film narrative rather than its role as an underscore or secondary voice in film. I had once heard the great jazz pianist and composer Michel Legrand (1932–2019) speak at an event where he described film music as 'the second conversation in a movie.' Steve and I wondered whether we could elevate this conversation to first place and decided to replace parts of Sir David Attenborough's commentary with song! That didn't mean David would be singing, although that would be a remarkable first for natural history programming and I would definitely be the conductor! My director and I loved the music of folk rock group *Steeleye Span* and their lead singer Maddy Prior. The band had chart hits with *Gaudete* (1973) and *All Around my Hat* (1975). The production approached Maddy to collaborate on the film's score and she accepted.

Maddy began composition by sketching out lyrics based on the mythological story of the hare. Alongside her, I worked on scoring the arrangements for her melodic material. I also contributed one of my own: *Winter Wakeneth* which ended up on Maddy's album *Year* (1993). The use of song in natural history films was a pioneering first at a time when commissioners and producers were still somewhat reluctant to take risks with their soundtracks. That didn't stop me from practising my powers of persuasion to take producers on unexpected musical journeys. *The Natural World – Ytene's Ancient Forest* used tin whistle, recorder, hurdy gurdy, framedrum, Baroque flute and guitars to evoke ghostly figures of the forest's past; *Pandas of the Sleeping Dragon* featured internationally acclaimed Chinese multi-instrumentalist Zhao Ben playing traditional Chinese instruments; *The Natural World* signature tune used a tam-tam suspended in a bath of water. As it was struck and pulled out of the bath, a wonderful metallic shimmering glissando sounded to mark the programme's title. *Taming the Iron Monster* in the *Locomotion* series used a choir performing extended vocal techniques to create the idea of ghost trains travelling a disused railway track, whilst in Mark Harrison's innovative series *Magic Animals* I experimented with a palette of electronic and vocal timbres.

One of my concert career highlights at this time was my composition *Hearts of Earth and Fire*. The piece was a collaboration with Anne Ridler OBE (1912–2001) one of my favourite poets. Anne, regarded as one of the best poets of her generation, had published ten collections of poetry, libretti, verse plays, and was for a time assistant to T.S Eliot (1888–1965). I'd first become aware of Anne's work in 1988 when my wife inherited a library of well-thumbed plays and poetry collections from her father. Amongst these were two pencil-marked poems for reading aloud. We'd decided to use one of the poems *For a Child Expected* as part of a service of dedication for the birth of our first daughter. I then came across Anne's republished *New and Selected Poems* and really resonated with the metaphysical content and themes in the collection: birth, death, resurrection, natural history and cosmology. I wrote to Anne's publisher to ask whether she would be interested in collaborating on a short musical work. At the ripe age of eighty-two, Anne not only agreed but turned up at the premiere.

After the performance we made plans to create a large scale piece we called *Sea Star*. The embryonic themes of what became a cantata were based on a journey from sea to space, a list of types of ice in a geology textbook and the link between the Virgin Mary and the sea. In the Roman Catholic Church, Mary is known as the 'star of the sea'. The Latin office used on feast days of the Virgin Mary is the *Ave Maris Stella* (Hail! Star of the sea). Furthermore, the call to prayer for the devotion commemorating the angel's announcement to Mary, her acceptance of her vocation and the incarnation, is accompanied by the ringing of the Angelus bell. In *Sea Star*, the bell relates to the nautical theme of the work both as a sound colour permeating the score and as the 'floating buoy' referred to in the words of the cantata's penultimate section. Although Anne began writing the words soon after *Hearts of Earth and Fire*, the score only existed as sketches for a few years. Initially, I'd envisaged the work as a multi-media piece; a version even existed for a performance in a swimming pool for 'goggled tenors' and soprano synchro swimmers! It was a concert version, however, that finally took precedence.

A turning point leading to the completion of *Sea Star* came in 2001 when I visited Antarctica. For the first time, many of the images Anne created in her libretto came to life first-hand: ice covered worlds, floes and hummocks, the slow bubbling of ice thawing and cracking and the sound of ice shelves calving. The narrative of *Sea Star* travelled from the depths of the oceans with their nascent aquatic life-forms, through land and sky, to the far reaches of space where other water-worlds exist in the icecaps of Mars and ice-belts of Saturn. As the characters in the texts ascend these levels, it is as if they are on a quest to understand their destiny. The forty-four minute work and subsequent album release was scored for tenor Mark Cunningham, symphony orchestra, and a choir of one hundred and twenty singers conducted by David Ogden. The world premiere of the cantata was premiered as part of a gala concert at the 2001 Spiritual Sounds Festival at Clifton Cathedral, Bristol. *Sea Star* was an exhausting feat of composition: eighty-six pages of hand-written score on A1 size manuscript paper. A gargantuan task.

An opportunity that might have U-turned my career to film directing came via my friend graphic designer Richard Higgs. We were offered the opportunity to pitch to make a video for a new song by Tony Banks, the keyboardist from rock band Genesis. He was making a new album with band Wang Chung and asked us to come up with a concept and designs for his song *Only Seventeen*. After meeting Tony for a briefing and submitting our pitch, which would use state-of-the-art videographic techniques and a highly stylised main character, we didn't get the gig. Could have been a whole new life for us making videos for rock stars and being followed around by groupies but it wasn't to be. Also disappointing was the failure of my fledgling film company Wild Idea. It either had its ideas nicked or was regarded as being too low profile because it didn't have a shed load of money behind it! I told myself there would be better things ahead. Somehow I also managed to eke out time to co-found the MA in the Composition of Music for Film and Television at the University of Bristol. I taught two modules in scoring for film and television, and with the music department's technician Jonathan Scott, I also introduced live recording sessions to picture so students could experience how a professional recording session is set up and run in the real world. The teaching of my craft is a passion of mine and I teach a group of international fledgling film composers every year.

I also squeezed in a trip to the University of Illinois, USA for my PhD research and to give a talk: *The Art of the Score*. Getting back from Champaign airport to Chicago for my flight to London was an adrenalin run. Champaign is a very small airport with a runway almost adjacent to the flight terminal. I sat with a coffee in the café and waited for the announcement to board. Unfortunately I hadn't noticed there was no public address system. Nor did I know the flight departure time had been moved ten minutes earlier than scheduled. I looked at my watch and thought I'd pop next door to the tiny departure lounge. It was empty. I rushed to the window. Down below was my plane with the door closing and the steps being taken away. Oops, my luggage was on board for Chicago and onward to London but not me. Given I've always operated with the belief everything is possible even against the odds, I ran for the steps down to the ground floor but the gate had been closed. That didn't stop me. I pushed the gate door open with the shouts of 'hey you, where do you think you're going?' somewhere behind me. I sidestepped two airport personnel on their way up the stairs before I confronted an emergency door and pushed it open. Only metres away were the tarmac and the plane. I ran towards the cockpit and waved at the pilot. Extraordinarily, he waved back and the steps were reinstated to allow me on board. Moral of the tale: no harm in trying or rather, in today's world, lots of harm in trying! Doesn't bear thinking about. The flight home and the whirlwind of projects I'd taken on that year, however, was nothing compared to the next big thing: the composition of music for the BBC's six-part series *Alien Empire: A Journey into the World of Insects*. And what a journey it turned out to be.

9

Alien Abduction

Alien Empire's producer Steve Nicholls and directors Rupert Barrington and Peter Bassett wanted to shoot the series as if it were a feature film! Their ambition was to create a magnificent drama rather than a straightforward factual series concentrating on the behavioural aspects of insects. The films used state-of-the-art computer animation and boasted a selection of tongue-in-cheek visual references to well known sci-fi and horror movies. Steve and I discussed the approach to the music early on in pre-production. We decided the score would be composed before the series was edited and Steve asked me to produce orchestral sketches which suggested the 'alien empire' of the insect world. The sketches pencilled in the mood and texture of the music and indicated the duration and tempo of each piece. This skeletal score was composed on my Emulator III and Emulator XS samplers using Mark of the Unicorn's Performer 5.02 sequencing software on a Macintosh computer. I composed seventy-two music cues, around a hundred and twelve minutes of music. Picture editors Martin Elsbury and Tim Coope were able to use these temporary cues as guide tracks for the editing.

Conceptually, it was important to find a stylistic approach that would not paint a banal portrait of the insect world. I required an instrumental palette to reinforce the drama of insect birth, death, survival, flight, conflict and invasion. In terms of structure, the cues were based on American minimalist music in which short melodic, rhythmic and harmonic motifs evolve slowly throughout a piece and often build to a consuming climax. So what made this approach to the images so different? As in my *Zastrozzi* score, the music was composed before the edit. The difference, however, was in how the sketches were used in relationship to picture. Normally when a music cue is laid to picture, the editor and director will make picture cuts and then return a new version of the amended picture to the composer. The composer then has to re-tailor the music to fit the new cut. When this happens, the editor might have snipped out a second here, a third of a second somewhere else, five twenty-fifths of a second at another place, a couple of frames here and there and so on. These picture adjustments can make the composer's rewrite of his or her music track quite tricky. It's like snipping random bits of cloth out of a well tailored suit and hoping you can make an even a better suit once you've patched it up again. It can alter the original integrity and feel of a piece first composed very intuitively to picture. In *Alien Empire*, however, the team were flexible and agreed any cuts in the picture would be exact whole number durations corresponding with whole numbers in the beats of the music. For example, one whole bar or two whole beats or a four bar section. This meant the music cue could maintain, for the most part, its structural integrity.

As the editing progressed and the music cues were locked to picture, I moved on to the orchestration stage. For me, this is where the real craft of composition takes place. Each piece of melodic material or rhythmic unit is meticulously honed and distributed to an instrumental palette. It's all in the composer's mind's ear. In terms of the orchestration, I wanted to choose an unusual palette to add a distinctive aural signature to the series, one that would avoid the conventional orchestral line up one is familiar with in the concert hall. In my head I was hearing sixteen horns interacting with six alto flutes, six timpani and a bass drum accompanying a piano or thirty strings. Imagine the sound of eight horns on a close-up of a butterfly's wing flap or a cockroach scurry. As I developed my approach to the orchestration, I wanted to build on the dark but romantic themes which characterised my previous scores. I also recalled the melodic writing of composer Bernard Herrmann (1911–1975) who composed for many of Alfred Hitchcock's films and I immersed myself in the powerful instrumental palettes Gustav Mahler (1860–1911) used in his symphonies. These references became the building blocks of my material. I was especially influenced by Hermann's rejected score for Hitchcock's movie *Torn Curtain* (1966), a score with large groups of only one instrumental colour: sixteen horns, twelve flutes (all doubling on piccolo, alto and bass flute), nine trombones, two tubas, two sets of timpani, eight cellos and eight double basses. The instrumentation for my score was two piccolos, six flutes doubling alto flute, two clarinets, two bassoons, two trumpets, sixteen horns, two trombones, tuba, piano, harp, Emulator sampler, electric guitar, six timpani, bass drum, side drum, suspended cymbals, belltrees, crotales, thundersheet, ten 1st violins, eight 2nd Violins, six violas, four cellos and three double basses. The clarinets were only used in the title music.

I believe the real craft of composing lies in the orchestration. Bernard Herrmann said that the thumbprint of the composer is the orchestration. There is no better way for the composer to express his or her response to picture than through a personal distribution of melody, harmony and the selection of timbral colour. Many feature films use teams of orchestrators. In those movies the composer has often only written the melodies and perhaps sketched the cues in 'short score', which is a condensed shorthand intention of how the final score might look. When I watch a film's credits roll and see a team of orchestrators has been employed, I applaud them! In my opinion it is their personalities permeating the music score and not the thumbprint of the composer.

One of the orchestration devices I borrowed from Mahler's symphonies was the idea of taking a full section and dividing it so that a pair or more of the same instrument articulated a different sound colour. In *Alien Empire* the horns are divided so that their overall effect as a section is multi-timbral. For example, in a section of eight horns, two horns may play open, two with mutes, two hand-muted and two cuivré, an effect which gives an exaggerated brassy timbre. In the same way, the flutes and alto flutes were combined to create a hybrid of breathy brooding tones and sweeter velvety ones. I also wanted the orchestration to underpin the notion of a world on the edge by using repetitive harmonic material which slid back and forth in tones and semitones. I used the piano as well as four cellos and three double basses to depict 'flow' or 'drive' in many of the cues. In contrast to the incidental score, the titles and end credits music had conventional orchestration. As well as keeping the sixteen horns, there was doubling in the woodwind (two flutes, two clarinets and two bassoons) and in the brass (two trumpets and two trombones with an additional tuba). This extended palette of timbres was required to create sufficient timbral variation in the title music statements.

The structure of the titles music was A, B, A1, C, A2. Section A has a fanfare statement. Initially on horns, it is passed to trumpets in section B, recapping on horns in section A1. Section C has the main strings and flute theme soaring high to meet and celebrate the Earthrise in the pictures. Here the string theme, string divisi accompaniment, trumpet fanfares, the driving force of the lower strings, piano and trombones all connect. They are cut across by bars of crotchet triplets on the horns which provide a descending motif as the picture depicts a descent from space through the atmosphere and cloud cover to the surface of Earth. Section A2 recapitulates the horn fanfare of the opening to create the idea of a powerful alien empire colonising the planet. The titles conclude with a closing tutti flourish.

We chose to record the score with our usual team at our usual studio, but I didn't envisage the choppy waters we were about to navigate. CTS studios and the London Film Orchestra had been booked and everything was about to go ahead when the producers of the series discovered the clearance of the American rights for the series music would cost extra thousands to the £50000 we were already spending on studio staff and orchestral sessions. The problem was due to the series being a UK/USA co-production. In co-production deals, American companies invest in BBC films and series but they want to buy all the rights to the music up front before they take delivery. On no account do they wish to pay again for any element of the music for repeat transmissions. But the multiplier for American usage on the player's basic session rate often becomes prohibitive for a UK production to accommodate. This is why the scores for many films and television programmes are recorded abroad rather than in the UK. The predicament we found ourselves in was devastating for UK musicians who had no power to negotiate as rates were set by the Musicians' Union. After many discussions with the MU we drew a blank. We didn't have the extra money to pay British musicians the required fee to use their performances in America. Our only option, which would cause chagrin to the MU, was to record abroad. I contacted orchestral contractor and music supervisor Paul Talkington to check out which European orchestras and studios might be able to take the project. We chose the Munich Symphony Orchestra and recorded at the Bavaria Film Studios. I was disappointed with losing the opportunity to work with our top class musicians in the UK, but the project became a pioneering one as I introduced European orchestras to the BBC Natural History Unit for the very first time.

The next step was to choose my team. I needed a recording engineer who was available to work in Munich. Keith Grant (1941–2012) was one of the most highly regarded engineers in the business. BAFTA award-winning Keith had worked with The Beatles, David Bowie, Jimi Hendrix, Queen, Led Zeppelin, Eric Clapton and many other popular performers. We met at his studio in Sunbury-on-Thames where he sketched a diagram of how he planned to place the microphones for our recording session. The score would be recorded on the modular thirty-six track Alesis A-DAT digital multi-track recorder. I also invited pianist Mark Marshall to join us in Munich. The piano featured prominently in the score and there was one piano solo I wanted us to work on before we started the sessions. Mark put in some dedicated rehearsal time and delivered a sterling performance. My music copyist Oliver Ledbury joined us too. Oliver had handwritten the seven hundred and fifty pages of orchestral parts for the sessions. It's always useful to have a copyist or assistant around at a session in case major rewrites of parts are required on the spot. It happens. Once, in a session for *Land of the Eagle*, I had to dismiss a player on whom I'd taken a risk. The player wasn't a reader but was prepared to learn the part by ear. At the session, the player's solo with orchestral backing fell to pieces. It was partly my fault for taking the risk with a non-reader. It meant I had to rewrite the part for a different player and instrument which resulted in a loss of valuable minutes of recording time. In terms of booking a conductor for *Alien Empire*, I again booked Harry Rabinowitz as a pair of safe hands to conduct my sessions. This powerhouse of a man, eighty years old, arrived in Munich raring to go. His first words to me were:

'Right Martin, let's get to the galleries and find any post impressionist work I haven't seen.'

He even kept me up drinking in a bar till 2am. Indefatigable, he then conducted two days of sessions. The team for the Munich sessions also included Paul Talkington, producer Steve Nicholls and the series film editor Martin Elsbury.

On the day of the team making their way to Heathrow from various parts of the UK, my copyist and I were on our way from Bristol to Heathrow. Along with our luggage, we were carrying the score, instrumental parts and the master U-matic video tape which had the timecoded programme episodes on it. The tape was an essential item as it would be used at the studios in Munich to synchronise the pictures with the orchestra's performance. When our cab pulled up at departures, we offloaded our things from the boot and continued on to check in. By this time, other members of the team were also checking in. As we moved on through security, we became aware something was missing: the videotape. My heart sank into my boots. The video had been left in the back of the taxi. This was a huge problem. Nowadays, the media would simply be sent over the net but we needed the physical tape and we needed it for the first recording session. Any duplicate tape requiring preparation by the BBC would arrive too late and there wasn't much time to spare before we had to board. At the gate I made a couple of hurried telephone calls. The first was to the BBC Natural History Unit in Bristol to explain what had happened. Luckily I remembered the name of the cab company and asked the BBC whether they could phone them, trace the driver, and get the tape to Heathrow before we set off. It was a good idea but wasn't going to happen in the time we had left before boarding. A few minutes later the BBC called back to say they'd traced the company and the driver was still doing his rounds of hotels in the Heathrow area. I had to think quickly. I was determined to get the tape. I asked the BBC to ensure they were able to speak to the cab driver and to arrange for the tape to be dropped off at one of the reception areas of a Heathrow hotel. Once the tape was there, I asked the BBC to arrange for a motorbike courier to be sent from the BBC in London to pick up the tape. I was now hoping the third part of my plan would work and I made a hurried call only minutes before the flight. I remembered that Paul Talkington, who was based in Colchester, was flying out on a slightly later flight from Stansted Airport. In order for my plan to work, I had to count on Paul still being at home and for my phone call to connect with him. If he was at home, I could then arrange for the courier to drive the tape from Heathrow to Stansted where Paul could pick it up. What happened next made all the bells of synchronicity ring true.

Paul was standing outside his house waiting for his cab. As the cab pulled into his street, he heard his house phone ringing. These are moments when we usually ignore such a call. Who wants to unlock the door and go in again to answer a call when your cab is arriving? But something prompted him to do just that. He picked up the receiver and heard a frantic Martin Kiszko on the other end explaining the lost tape story at breakneck speed. If the tape was dropped off at the British Airways desk at Stansted, could he pick it up? Luckily that important call happened in the nick of time and Paul was then able to liaise with the BBC. But there were some peculiar twists and turns in the evolving drama. The courier arrived at Stansted and found the desk at which he was to drop the package marked for the attention of Paul. The person at the desk examined the package and listened to the courier's story, but since Paul wasn't there at that exact moment, the desk person wouldn't allow an unattended package to be left for pick up. The courier had to keep it. Sometime later, Paul arrived at the same desk now manned by a different person. He asked whether a package had been left for him but the desk person had no knowledge of such a delivery. Paul walked away. At this point, the courier decided to use one of the call phones on the wall to contact the BBC and explain how he was unable to drop the package. At the same time, Paul also decided to go to a call phone and contact the BBC to say the package hadn't turned up. Both men ended up standing next to each other at adjacent phones! As they both made their calls, the courier heard Paul say 'the package for Martin Kiszko hasn't arrived.' On hearing my name mentioned, the courier turned to Paul and asked, 'are you Martin Kiszko?' The extraordinary synchronicity of the moment became obvious to them and that is how the tape got to Munich!

Everything went perfectly for the recording sessions and Munich kept us well stocked up on weisswurst and lager. Sound engineer Keith Grant collected all the tapes to be mixed down to masters at his studio in the UK. A week later the master DAT tapes were sent to me but I was in shock as I listened. A number of the music cues sounded completely different to how I'd heard them on the monitor mix in Munich. The expansive sound of the music was no longer audible. I called Keith and mentioned that some of the cues sounded texturally weak and lack-lustre. He mentioned he would try and improve the mix but the results of the new mix were still unsatisfactory. It was then that he broke the bad news. One of the ADAT machines in Munich had a technical problem. It had recorded horn parts and the room sound on a misaligned recording head. This meant the tape would not play back correctly. We were both at a loss at what to do and after much discussion I decided to break the bad news to my producer. Steve was obviously very concerned but took the news calmly. We knew we had a serious problem. It would take tens of thousands of pounds to re-record the affected music cues again in Munich. The production didn't have the money for that or the time in the post production schedule to accommodate more sessions. The only other option was the re-composition and recording of all the affected cues as electronic cues, but as good as samples were in those days they would never match the expression of live orchestral players. We decided to think on it for a day or so before discussing the matter again with Keith.

Keith, however, was hatching another plan. He had approached the technical workshops of a major company involved with making tape machines. He explained to the tech team at the company's lab that his composer would kill him if he didn't get the sound sorted on the tape. Could they help in any way? One of the tech guys came up with a solution. They rang the recording engineers at the studio in Munich and asked them to measure by how much the recording head on their machine was misaligned. The measurement was sent back to London and the techies got hold of an Alesis ADAT multi-track and adjusted its head to the measurement of the angle of the head on the misaligned Munich machine. The techies' new misaligned machine now perfectly played back the faulty tape as both machines now had a recording head positioned at exactly the same angle. The expansiveness of the orchestral sound was immediately restored and recorded by another ADAT recorder with a correctly aligned head.

Keith rang me that afternoon. 'I've got it all back!'

'You've what?'

'I've got it all back.'

It was more than music to my ears and I had to hear it for myself. The newly mixed master tapes arrived the next day and sure enough everything was there exactly as I'd heard it on the session days. I could hardly believe I'd be giving this news to my producer and was over the moon to see the expression of relief on his face. Hopefully it was the end of the adventures I was to have on *Alien Empire* – until I ran into the newspapers.

The series had been a critical and public success. In the magazine *Music from the Movies* the score was described as 'one of the finest written for a British television production.' But there is always someone who will take a stab at something to project their own ego. A television critic from a major British newspaper chose to lambast the music. To my mind, the columnist was unnecessarily bullish and the piece had the air of a personal insult. Bombastic in tone, it pronounced the music was unsuitable because it was too 'feature film based' for a TV series. The reviewer panned the 'lush and dramatic expansive orchestration' and 'grand emotion producing musical gestures often found in feature film scores.' Unfortunately the reviewer failed to take note of the director's nod to feature film drama scores. Steve Nicholls had asked for an epic large scale score to represent miniature creatures that were actually 'beasts with armour' or 'sophisticated pieces of hardware'. There were also extraordinary natural phenomena such as the flight of millions and millions of monarch butterflies which in our minds required robust and expressive musical forces rather than a flute and a clarinet! In one sequence we included expressive romantic strings for the mating of two moths. In a nutshell, we were accused of anthropomorphism. The reviewer was also unaware of the pioneering work Steve and I had produced on previous projects in which we endeavoured to experiment with the role of music in wildlife films. The best endorsement one could wish for, however, is from viewers — this one from a viewer in Belgium:

'For the first time the music wasn't just background filling. The music played an emotional part in the events and though I'm not a weak person I couldn't prevent the tears from welling up when I heard your music, especially the first part of *Angels and Warriors*, *Slipstreams* and *Earthrise* which still grab me by the throat.'

In terms of music for natural history, I was ahead of my time and the film scoring world. It wasn't long before many major natural history documentaries and series were also using large orchestral forces for their scores. What we achieved in 1995 became a benchmark for the approach many composers would take in successive years. We all know art leads the way and often on a contrary trajectory to critical response. Nowadays, we don't bat an eyelid when we experience this style of dramatic and emotional music in the BBC's *Blue Planet* productions.

The BBC/EMI/Soundtrack Music Records release of my first album *The Ocellus Suite — Music from the BBC's Alien Empire* was released soon after the series was broadcast and eventually became a collectors' item for movie soundtrack buffs. But there were soundtrack aficionados who were collecting the music of *Alien Empire* and not just listening to it! Years after the broadcast and release of the album, I was amazed to see a You Tube video posted by someone I didn't know. The video had been posted by a fan of the *Alien Empire* music and posed the question of whether compositional and stylistic aspects of my score had been poached for a major Hollywood movie. This was extremely upsetting and too close for comfort. There were indeed similarities in terms of melodic motifs, harmonic language, and instrumental palette. Plagiarism is not unusual in the music business but I eventually put the episode down to coincidence. I thought no more of it until a few years later when I was asked whether I would assist a famous composer on a British feature film, a composer who had been indirectly involved with the earlier incident. In a telephone conversation, he asked what type of equipment I would require to work with his small team of composers in London. I outlined my needs and, at his request, sent a few of my albums for him to listen to — including *Alien Empire*. A few weeks later, I heard I would no longer be offered the job and a team of composers from the USA would be sent to London instead.

A couple of years later I was at the cinema watching a movie. I didn't know who had composed the soundtrack but I began to feel uncomfortable. If I had to name the composer of the movie's music it would be me! When I saw the credit on the end of the film, there was no great surprise. It was the composer who had intended to work with me. While I felt I should have the grace to put it down to coincidence again, overreaction or the possibility my album may have been used as a 'temp track' for the film, part of me felt a major opportunity to share my music with the feature film fraternity and audience had been usurped and lost — perhaps irrevocably affecting my short term sustainability and my long term career. A few days after, I was teaching my students when one of them asked me whether I had seen the movie I had concerns about. I said I had and my student replied,

'Don't you think the score sounded exactly like your score for *Alien Empire*?'

Was it more than coincidence again? I now wondered if I could do anything about it. I made a few exploratory calls to the US and it was suggested I might consider legal action to sue a major Hollywood studio. It was tempting but 'little me' against a major studio and a great film composer meant putting all I had on the line. I decided I was great at my craft, always ahead of my time and that if other composers didn't have enough imagination of their own then I felt sorry for them. I didn't want to be known in the US as someone who made a reputation via a legal case. I told myself I was resilient, never to be beaten, and that there was a wealth of original and newly imaginative music left in me no matter who poached my reserves. I wanted to be known for creating top rate film scores and if that meant me pulling another groundbreaking score out of the bag — so be it.

News of what had happened percolated into the film community. I was invited to give an interview for a US magazine and was asked whether I'd discuss the issue of plagiarism. I declined. In my reply to the interviewer's question about the *Alien Empire* score, I simply replied,

'Hey! If any of you Hollywood composers still have my *Alien Empire* album, send it straight back now!' Especially painful was watching many of my colleagues celebrating the work of said composer and not raising an eyebrow regarding his misdemeanours with intellectual copyright. Moreover, they employed him on projects on which I might normally be approached as a contender. The pain of the injustice never left me. It was a contributory factor in a breakdown later in my career.

The success of *Alien Empire*, however, produced a hefty new workload and the snowballing career that *Land of the Eagle* had started was now an unstoppable train. Furthermore, there were more aliens about to abduct me in *The Uninvited*, a four-part sci-fi drama directed by Norman Stone. I'd met Norman in the early eighties through the Arts Centre Group in London. He began his career as the youngest ever producer and director at the BBC and went on to direct many highly acclaimed film dramas including *Shadowlands* (1985), *Man Dancin'* (2003), *Florence Nightingale* (2008), films in the *Agatha Christie's Miss Marple* series, documentaries in the *Everyman* and *Omnibus* series, and the feature documentary *The Final Fix* (2020). For many years I badgered him for an opportunity to compose music and I was thrilled when he invited me to be interviewed by his production team. After the interview with producers Ruth Boswell and Archie Tait, Norman reiterated the challenge as described in the booklet notes he wrote for my soundtrack album *The Uninvited* (1997):

'The task was not an easy one. Here we were with an extremely contemporary 'Sci-Fi' script, full of computers, political intrigue and an alien invasion, and yet we also had sunken villages off the Norfolk coast, long forgotten skeletons and elements of the storyline which stretched back before the dawn of civilisation. Clearly we needed to dig beneath the techno-surface and pull out the older, deeper, and more genuinely human references in the music. The whole feel had to be more *Edge of Darkness* than *E.T.* Most of the action takes place in East Anglia not Los Angeles and we were definitely aiming to be more European than American.'

Norman also gave me a full synopsis of the four episodes and asked me to be inspired by the storyline and come up with a suite of music that would include themes for characters, locations, the world of the alien body-snatchers, and the world of the journalist who is embroiled in the alien invasion. I composed a twenty minute suite which Norman liked and which won me the commission to compose a seventy-two minute score for alto flute, oboe d'amore, piano, two violins, two cellos, two double basses, a group of singers and samples. The score used two of my favourite instruments: the alto flute and the oboe d'amore. The alto flute, which has a rich mellow tone, was used to carry the protagonist's 'investigative searching' theme whilst the oboe d'amore, with its serene and less assertive tone than the oboe, was used to highlight the idea of the mystery of missing villagers in the drama.

I conducted all four music sessions for the series. It was a tall order getting an average of eighteen minutes of music recorded in each three-hour session. In fact, less than three hours once one accounted for tuning up, setting levels, technical hitches and tea breaks. In the planning of how music cues are recorded in a recording session, there are different approaches one can take. The cues can be recorded in chronological order as they appear in the film's narrative; cues can be recorded with the main theme first followed by cues based on it so that the orchestra develops a familiarity with the material; cues can also be ordered with the easiest first progressing to more difficult ones mid-session thus getting the orchestra warmed up before tackling the more complex cues; cues may also be recorded with attention to which musicians have the least to play. Cues in which those players perform are then recorded first so that they can leave the session early. I try to organise my sessions taking all these things into account, but I usually place the more challenging pieces later in the session.

I also like to work out roughly how much time I'm going to spend on recording each cue. So, if I have ten cues in a three hour session, I can spend about fifteen minutes on each one. Fifteen minutes per cue may seem a long time to rehearse and record, but once you've had a go at a couple of takes, recorded a good one and checked it back for quality and how it fits with the picture, your time has gone. I know if a cue is challenging in terms of its tempo, time signature, duration or complexity then it is going to require more time allotted to it in the session. In such a scenario, one has got to be very careful not to spend too many minutes on a cue that will steal rehearsal time from subsequent cues. This can prove to be a dangerous situation in which one is racing to record the remainder of the cues, thus compromising quality. On the other hand, an attempt to give the remaining cues their original allotted time can easily push the session into overtime. An orchestra on overtime is a totally prohibitive scenario in terms of the extra expenditure for a production. One of the cues I composed for *The Uninvited* was for a chase. The piece had a very tricky time signature and a lively tempo. I'd estimated spending about twelve minutes on each cue in the session but this particular one wouldn't lie down. The string players and I found it difficult to get the absolute articulation required and we rehearsed it over and over. I spent thirty-five minutes trying to get the best we could pull out of it. I ended up with a less than perfect take but had to bail out at that point or put the rest of the session into jeopardy. This is the delicate balancing act of running a successful recording session.

The mid to late nineties was a demanding period for me and luckily my creative juices were still flowing. I composed a seventy-nine minute chamber score for David Bell's six-part BBC drama *Black Hearts in Battersea* based on Joan Aiken's (1924–2004) novel. Running alongside this I managed a feat of film score juggling and composed music for five natural history projects: *The Natural World's Bowerbird — Playboy of the Australian Forest*, *Himalaya*, and *Mandrills — Painted Faces of the Forest* as well as *The Natural World* series signature tune music. In the *Wildlife on One* series I scored director Bernard Walton's film *The Eagle Empire* which featured the voice of singer Cindy Stratton whose album *Only You* (1994) I'd fallen in love with. Luckily, my muse, inner child and energy kept me going and I also got to compose the signature tune music for HTV's *Freize Frame* series and Lesley Morgan's feature TV drama *The Levels*.

I was elated when, out of the blue, a cinematic feature film offer came in. I hoped it would be my break into the world of big movies. I went to a cutting room in Soho to view the film, a thriller. I knew it was a film for which I could compose an evocative score but I had reservations. There was a rape scene requiring music and I didn't feel comfortable about composing for the scene. I declined the offer. It was timely, however, as another fabulous film came my way. Steven Spielberg had developed an interest in how the drama of the animal world was portrayed on screen and requested a promo from the Natural History Unit. From their library stock of millions of images, the unit produced an eight-minute film entitled *Dreamworks*, with commentary by Sir David Attenborough. Again, it was wonderful to work with David and discuss the approach to the score with director Hilary Jeffkins. There were two versions of the film: one with David's voice and the music and one with music and sound effects only. The score was orchestral and I decided to record it with the City of Prague Philharmonic Orchestra conducted by Allan Wilson. The recording of the score brought out every nuance I'd written into the orchestration and remains one of my favourites. Hilary was impressed too. It was her first time working with a symphony orchestra and hearing back the music she had commissioned. She was also fascinated by the 'behind the scenes' world of the recording session: the harpist tied her dog up outside and then sat knitting during the session until it was time for her to play, the percussionists read their newspapers when they had endless bars of rests before an entry, and our UK recording engineer John Timperley (1941– 2006) brought a bag of knobs which he attached to the mixing desk. He was all too aware from previous visits that bits of the faders were missing. After the session, I offered to take Hilary to the opera to see Verdi's *Aida*. I hoped she'd be impressed with the lavish opera house, cast of over a hundred, and the champagne and caviar at the interval. At the end I asked her what she thought of this introduction to Verdi. Her response was,

'The diva looks like the TV presenter Valerie Singleton!'

The balance of work life and home life became more of a challenge as film projects continued to land on my composition pile. The children were well occupied with school and nursery as well as time with our childminder. I'd usually break work to pick them up and often played with them as I was composing. God knows how! Once, during the composing of a score and with one child on my knee and the other dancing around to the musical *Calamity Jane* (1953), I had to take a break to cook a meal for us. Whilst my daughter was still dancing and my son was hammering the piano keys, the phone rang. I was in the middle of frying eggs. It was a BBC producer for whom I was working.

'How's the score going?'

'Yes I'm on it now,' I replied, whilst flipping an egg and slowly going out of my mind with the mayhem in the background.

'I've been thinking about the closing credits music.'

I hoped this wasn't going to be a long conversation as I was juggling three pans and a grill. I also hoped he couldn't hear the kids.

'Yes. The closing credits.'

'Can we give the music a bit of a flourish when my credit appears?' asked the director.

'Sure. I'll add horns and a suspended cymbal. I'll send you a new version.'

That scenario wasn't unusual during what were my pre-burnout years, but a bundle of good news arrived in 1996 — our third child Zita was born. Named after my cousin Zyta, the daughter of my Aunt Serafina, Zita was born in our bathroom. It was quite a squeeze with mum and two midwives. The only place I could stand was on the corner of the bath from where I had to crouch down and cut the cord. She also complemented her brother and sister. We now had a redhead, a brown-haired boy, and a blonde!

Apart from the demands of a young family, it was a most wonderful time watching the children develop their interests and passions. Serafina was extremely creative with drawing, music, crafts, sewing, and dance. She loved the programme *Sesame Street* and the clothes her mum made for her. Like her father, she adored musicals and film dramas. Once when watching Fred Zinnemann's epic movie *The Nun's Story* (1959), it came to the point where Sister Luke was about to become a fully fledged nun. As one of the other sisters began the ritual of shaving off Sister Luke's hair, Serafina cried, 'Oh no! And she's not even a real hairdresser!'

One year she had a go at writing a song, *Star Shining Brightly,* for the Eurovision Song Contest. I arranged the song and Cindy Stratton sang the vocals. One of my students, Andrea Pejrolo, who went on to become a professor at Berklee College of Music, mixed the track. But with such a stellar line up, we still didn't get selected. It obviously just wasn't bad enough! Serafina also enjoyed a film on Mandrills which I scored. When it got to the mating sequence she turned to me,

'Yuk, Daddy, it's a good job humans don't do that!'

Meanwhile, my son Luka was busy developing his belief system,

'Daddy, how big is God?'

I stared at him.

'Well for those of us that have a faith and believe in God, he made the stars, the universe and created all those wonderful planets like those on your wall chart.'

He considered the answer.

'Yeah, but how did he make screws?'

He also had his plans settled for a future career,

'I want to do all the things in the world that people do — only on different days.'

Like most children, he developed particular passions that would go on for a year or so before a new one materialised: traffic cones, diggers, the film *Jason and the Argonauts* (1963), mazes, horror masks, skulls, guitars, skateboards, lighting design, the building of a two thousand seven hundred piece rollercoaster and street magic — we made monthly visits to the Magic Circle in London where he was a junior member and filmed his first magic video in Venice. Luka never touched any of the money saved in his piggy banks. When asked why, he would be adamant about saving up to buy his own theatre and lighting rig.

Zita was a wild and free-spirited toddler whose early years were a whirlwind of *Teletubbies, Barbies, Little Ponies, The Simpsons* and changing her clothes every ten minutes or dancing around in fairy dresses. Once on holiday, she decided to take part naked in the hotel's line dancing evening. She would often come home from primary school complaining of a hard day of tracing. Times were hard in those days! Somewhere in the mayhem of work and family life, we were lucky to have a child only go missing twice; every parent's nightmare. On a beach in Wales, Serafina followed a girl who had invited her to play. In a split second, she'd vanished into thin air. I frantically searched the beach. With my heart racing and before a call to the coastguard, I was relived to spot her in the distance. She was only recognisable due to her fluorescent green wetsuit. On a family trip to London, Luka got separated during a confusing sorting of bags and children. It was amidst crowds on Paddington Station. We quickly got staff looking but I found him casually standing on Platform One, watching the arrival of the eleven o' clock from Bristol as if he was a seasoned train-spotter.

As for the composer in the house, I was struggling under piles of manuscript with a problem with my eyes that involved ophthalmologists, scans and X-Rays. It turned out to be a precursor to a chronic eye condition that resulted in wearing a pirate patch whilst writing this book. Another ongoing challenge was the care of my parents. As an only child, and as much as I loved them, this always weighed heavy on me. My father was constantly in poor health so we decided to move my parents from the council estate on which I grew up to a home of their own in Morley near Leeds. My dad was in and out of hospital. It often meant quick trips up the motorway to see him and talk to a consultant when he was in for an operation. It became exhausting so we decided to sell up the Morley property and buy them a house in Bristol. They were able to move in by Spring 1996 and it was wonderful for them to be close to the children. My father was ecstatic about the move. He'd always wanted to live closer to me. My mother was reticent. She was leaving behind good friends, her tea-dance community, and the old haunts of the North of England she so loved. On arrival in Bristol, my father's health gradually deteriorated and by December he'd died.

Prior to his death, I visited him in hospital to explain that Prince Charles was going to make a visit to the University of Bristol's music department to see the work I was doing with my MA students. Although my father was not a royalist, he gave a satisfying nod and smile as if to say he was proud. I left the hospital and asked the staff to call me if there was any significant deterioration of his condition. Early the following morning, I awoke in bed with a repeating image of tumbling purple shapes playing over and over in my mind. It was probably one of those moments when one experiences random sounds or images prior to falling asleep or waking. Or was it? Somehow, I felt it had significance. I got up and drove straight to the hospital. I found my father taking his last breaths. The hospital had failed to inform me. It was Sunday morning and I struggled to find a priest to come and give a blessing — they were all at Mass but I finally found one. The aftermath of my father's death consumed me. I struggled to complete *The Eagle Empire* score I was working on as I was immersed in planning a funeral service at the Polish Catholic Church in Bristol and a burial. I followed Polish traditions my father expected. I dressed the interior of the coffin with flowers and photographed him for my relatives in Poland. Two days later I was supposed to be meeting Prince Charles. I was in two minds. I contacted the university to say I wasn't sure I was up to it, but remembering how my dad smiled when I mentioned the visit, I changed my mind. Prior to the meet, I was instructed to wear a jacket and a tie and only speak to Charles once he'd spoken to me. I didn't have time for that. I swept my hair back into a pony tail, put on my magpie bolo tie ('one for sorrow' as a tribute to dad), didn't bother with a jacket, and spoke to Prince Charles as soon as he came into the room. It was an immense pleasure to show him the work of my students and introduce him to the techniques of applying music to picture. He was now fully equipped for a new career as a film composer.

10

Sex, Moonshine, Rock 'n' Roll

I always mentioned to my friends that in any book I wrote, the sex, drugs and rock n' roll chapter would have to be renamed 'sex, my own happy hormones, and rock 'n roll.' Drugs or smoking have never interested me. I always told people 'I am my own drug!' As for sex, sometimes I have to explain myself. For a long time I kept a rather unusual item in my bedroom. It was a long broom handle on the end of which was an orange swimming cap. I often wondered what would happen if I popped my clogs during the night and the item was found. What conclusion would anyone come to? One day when my children were round I decided I had to tell them in case they ever discovered it. I took them into the bedroom and showed them the device. They smiled and looked perplexed.

'What is it?'

'I just want you to know it's not a sex toy.'

They laughed.

'Can you guess?'

They shook their heads. I explained my bedroom had a flat roof and crows landed on it early in the morning. Their marching up and down always woke me. To deter them I'd open the window, take my broom handle, and raise it to roof level so they'd be confronted with the sight of my swimming cap. I hope my kids believed me!

As for being my own drug, I guess I've always been lucky to get high on my art and my imagination as well as draw energy from within, from nature or from the transcendental realm. That energy kept me running the music marathon I was on and it wasn't even close to last lap. During one year I'd scored twenty films: the six-part HTV series *Hotel*, six-part series *The Human Sexes* with zoologist Desmond Morris, the episode *An Arctic Secret* in the series *Franz Josef Land — A*

Frozen Wilderness, the film *The Natural History of an Alien*, the signature tune for the BBC series *The Natural World Classics*, and *The Uninvited*, a four- part sci-fi drama for ITV. *The Human Sexes* was a journey through sex and gender throughout history and a plethora of different cultures. I had to research the music of different eras, countries and styles. One minute I was composing for a film sequence about ancient Greece or the sexual postures of sculptures at an Indian temple, and the next I was composing for gay clubbers, lap dancers or Japanese female wrestlers. One of the New York nightclub scenes which required music posed a problem. The production didn't want to pay for clearing the original music on the nightclub sequence so my job was to compose new music to fit with what the dancers were doing. This was the second time I'd been presented with such a challenge. The first time was on the BBC series *The Nineties* when I composed a dance arrangement to match black and white archive footage of WWII soldiers and their partners dancing at the Tower Ballroom in Blackpool.

The titles music for *The Human Sexes* required careful negotiation between me, the director Clive Bromhall, and the commissioners and production team in the USA. The picture sequence showed the beautifully sculpted forms of a man and a woman in perizoma – ancient Greek loincloths. I proposed to produce a classically based score for chamber orchestra. The score would be minimalist in style and have a Baroque feel to it. The team in America wasn't so keen. Their viewing audience was 'rock music aware' and the team felt anything else would bore the viewer. Furthermore, someone on the team didn't like trumpets, someone else didn't like mandolin and another person wasn't a fan of flute or piano – all instruments I was intending to use. Someone else, thrown in for good measure, didn't like my suggestion of a minimalist approach, 'baroque overtones' or the music falling into the same camp as composer Michael Nyman's very popular score for *The Draughtsman's Contract* (1982). Yet I was convinced I could produce a piece that would be accessible to an American audience and would be a memorable aural signature for the series. And I did! I threw caution to the wind and used all the instrumentation I'd originally proposed apart from mandolin. What's more they liked it.

It appeared I'd done such a good job on my score for *The Human Sexes* series that I was fast becoming the go to composer for music for sex and I don't mean the pornographic kind. Executive producer John Sparks at the BBC's Natural History Unit asked whether I'd compose an eighty-two minute score for their six-part series *Battle of the Sexes in the Animal World*. Along with John, I worked with producers Julian Hector, John Ruthven, and Hilary Jeffkins with whom I'd collaborated on the *Dreamworks* promo. The series covered the turbulent relationship between males and females in the animal world. John wanted the music to elucidate the stories, which unfolded in each episode, by the use of leitmotifs for 'competitive males' and 'caring females.'

The search for a theme that is able to develop into a score of over eighty minutes is a tremendous challenge for a composer. Some themes appear quickly, fully formed. Others creep upon you stealthily at a snail's pace and require constant honing. Fortunately the theme for *Battle of the Sexes* fell into the former category and was composed within the hour. Written in a time signature of three-four with a driving crotchet beat, the titles theme became the basis for the incidental music. It required careful thought to select timbres which would be capable of expressing both male and female characteristics. Played by a fifty-piece orchestra, the lilt of the melody line had a feminine feel whilst the many layers of orchestral colouring suggested aggressive males. Throughout the score, a variety of rhythmic patterns, harmonies and textures were used to illustrate the attributes of animal sexuality. The music also helped to communicate the size of the animals, which in purely visual terms is so difficult to portray on the small screen. I chose a large brass section backed by low string chords, bass drums and timpani to represent the majestic scale of a bull bison. For a delicate bird such as the weaver, I selected a xylophone accompanied by soft tremolando strings. The clarinet was often used to herald the medium-sized males on land, sea or air whilst the flute and alto flute usually signified the females. Montage sequences, where males and females appeared in quick succession, called for both a theme and palette to serve both sexes across a huge variety of species and habitats. This became known as the 'diversity theme' and appears throughout the series. In this day and age, amongst humans, male and female stereotyping is anathema. The soundtrack, however, made no excuses for its allegiance to the polarities of gender difference. It aimed to underline those distinctive traits that identify and distinguish the sexes in the animal world. Of course, there was always a dilemma that presented itself in the narrative: the pregnant male seahorse or the single-sexed organism! In these cases the orchestral palette represented the creatures' identities by a 'cross dressing' of musical leitmotifs or by using the 'diversity theme.'

It was Hilary who joined me at the music sessions with the City of Prague Philharmonic Orchestra. Hilary had provided wonderful briefs for the music in a language only she and I understood. When she asked for one sequence to have 'a bit of driving bosom but not too slushy,' I'm glad I was able to interpret and deliver the appropriate music! For one music sequence, I wondered whether my producers were winding me up. They had a long montage sequence of animal penises. Amongst the gallimaufry of penile wonders were microscopic shots of invertebrates whose penises had scoops and spikes. The producers couldn't decide what to put over the pictures – commentary, sound effects or music? It ended up on my composition pile with a day spent playing the picture back and forth hundreds of times until I came up with 'music for penises'. Even when I delivered the music, I wasn't sure whether they'd commissioned the cue for a laugh.

Hilary and I headed for the sessions in Prague. We took a stressful flight out of Bristol in eighty-miles-per-hour winds and rain. Nearly all departing flights were cancelled and travellers were packed into the departure lounge like sardines in a tin. Only one flight came in to land and it was from Brussels. We saw the pilot walk through the lounge. He was wearing a long trench coat and casually brushed off the rain from it as if to say, 'look at me, I'm the only one who made a landing'. Sometime later he was on his way out again. It seemed nothing was going to stop him and luckily it was our flight to Brussels (connecting for Prague) he was taking out. At Brussels we had a couple of hours to wait for our connecting flight. We thought we'd have a coffee, do a bit of reading, and browse the shops. What we didn't do was advance our watches an hour for the new time zone. We'd also failed to take note of any flight announcements. It was only whilst nonchalantly wandering around in duty free we heard the announcement, 'last call for Martin Kiszko.' We couldn't believe it and then, in horror, checked our watches. The gate was a long way from where we were and we broke into a frenzied run. Out of breath and perspiring, we were rushed across the tarmac to our flight. As we arrived, a plane full of disgruntled passengers gave us the evil eye.

We arrived in Prague with a long wait at baggage. As I watched everyone retrieve their bags and stare at the empty carousel, the *Alien Empire* lost tape incident came back to haunt. The DigiBeta time-coded videotape we needed to lock the music to picture was in my suitcase and my suitcase didn't arrive. It suddenly became imperative to buy new underpants, toothpaste and a razor. Luckily I had a back up VHS tape in my hand baggage. The tape had burnt-in vision timecode but no audio timecode for synchronisation purposes. We managed with the tape by lining it up with a rough pre roll start for the orchestra. Providing the engineer pressed it at exactly the right moment and the conductor started the one bar countdown at exactly the right moment in the pre-roll, we'd be as close as we could get.

Thankfully the suitcase arrived the next day and we set off with the DigiBeta tape to record three three-hour sessions at Smecky Music Studios. Getting all the music recorded was quite a tall order since we lost twenty minutes in the first session due to two trumpeters not turning up. Once they arrived we had to make up time. Harry more than rose to the challenge and drew expression and emotion out of the orchestra even when a few players began to flag in the final session.

In one cue Harry unexpectedly stopped the orchestra. At the age of eighty-one, Harry's next words made everyone sit up. He pointed his baton at a viola player in his mid-fifties who had been yawning during the take.

'You, my boy, are too young to be tired!'

Apart from one very weary viola player and the missing trumpets scenario, the music and series were well received and I released the *Battle of the Sexes* (1999) album soon after. Not wishing to leave Prague without a musical souvenir, the journey home involved a mad dash to get a wrought iron music stand to the airport. It failed to arrive in time for my departure from the hotel and was subsequently picked up by Harry's partner who drove it to the airport and luckily found me in the car park. The stand occupied three spare seats on the flight to Brussels and three on the flight to Bristol. I was lucky that seats were available and they weren't charged for, but to carry such as dangerous implement as a five-foot-high iron music stand as cabin baggage would never happen today.

Hardly taking a well earned breather, I released my album *The Age Demanded* (1999) a compilation of my work since the mid-eighties. I also burnt my already burnt out candle at both ends by taking on *Unification*, a film about King Abdul Aziz Al Saud that was presented alongside a laser show at the National Museum of Saudi Arabia. The film had a punishing schedule. I began scoring a thirteen and a half minute electronic mock-up of what would be an orchestral score on a Saturday morning. I played and recorded all the orchestral parts on my Emulator sampler and the mock-up had to be completed by Sunday afternoon when the director and producer visited to hear the score. The Sunday evening was spent making amendments and on Monday morning I began to orchestrate on manuscript paper. There were nine music cues. I worked on the basis of completing almost two cues per day over the next five days. At the end of each day I'd pass on my score to my copyist who would work through each night to produce all the instrumental parts. At the end of the week we flew to Prague on Saturday morning and recorded the score with the orchestra in the afternoon.

Hot on the back of that, the BBC asked me to compose music for images to be featured in the 'spiritual zone' of London's Millennium Dome. The commission prompted me to produce another album *The Millennium March* (1999). The album was a spoof. The premise for my project was that millennium revellers could use the march to dance through their houses, patios and workplaces in synchronism with people all over the world. I suggested the ensuing mass march would easily be seen if one was standing on the lunar surface. As we approached the millennium there was a great fear that all computers would stop working and planes would fall out of the sky. As a joke, I marked the CD as being 'not year 2000 compliant' and included a pair of cardboard goggles shaped as the numbers 2000. The goggles enabled the wearer to view the future as they were dancing! The third wonderful millennial project I developed was a millennium CD and CD-Rom which recorded the life of two hundred and sixty children at St. John's Primary School, Clifton, Bristol, throughout a whole year. The CD featured playground songs, poetry and jokes, sports events, lessons, register calls, fire drills, school trips, music lessons, school dinners, sick bay, fancy dress competitions, school fairs, and naughty children sitting outside the head-teacher's office. The album was buried in a time capsule on the school grounds as a record for future generations to see what life was like in a British school at the turn of the millennium. Another time capsule I was opening was my PhD. I'd spent eight years on the monster, an eighty-thousand word thesis replete with charts, graphs, photographs and manuscript examples. It was time to hand it in. The viva took place at the University of Bristol's music department. There were three examiners and each examiner required a copy of the PhD. The dissertation and appendices was comprised of four volumes, each volume was four centimetres thick. It required a porter with a massive trolley to wheel in all sixteen volumes, including my own set, for the viva. I was thrilled to pass.

As if this period of flat out music wasn't enough, my screenplay *The Bell* was resurfacing. I'd been developing the story I'd heard from a Polish priest when my father and I first visited Belarus. Initially I worked it into a documentary format, but later discarded this and began to think on a grander scale. I wrote a treatment for what I believed could be a feature film. I drew a blank with finding interest for the project until a chance encounter with the film director Vadim Jean who I'd first met in 1980 and with whom I'd lost contact. Vadim was visiting the Watershed cinema in Bristol and we caught up on old times and the directions our media careers had taken. It was an opportunity to pitch my film. Vadim not only loved the story but wanted to co-write the screenplay and direct it. Sometime after, we met in Bristol for our first screenwriting session. We approached the task in a time tested traditional way, writing the story outline on scene cards pinned on a wall. Each scene could then be moved around to a new position if necessary. Although screenwriting software in later years superseded this antiquated method, the method still holds good as it gives one the opportunity to take a global overview of the screenplay's structure. I often employ the same technique when I'm writing a substantial score. It's easy to write endless pages of manuscript on a music software programme, but to display fifty pages of a score to see how themes, instrumental solos and sectional distribution work throughout the piece just isn't possible.

Vadim and I made two trips to Belarus to collect images of the locations for our film, and interview villagers. A lot of my adventures have been as a result of mishaps with aeroplanes and our second trip was no different. Vadim and I planned on two full days in Belarus and we arrived at Heathrow to fly out to Minsk. Heathrow was fogbound for most of the day and our flight was cancelled. The available options offered for the afternoon were a crazy trip to Beijing and on to Minsk, which would have wiped out the whole weekend, or a flight to Vienna going on to Warsaw the next day and then changing for a flight to Minsk. We chose the Vienna flight and landed in the city early evening. At the hotel we met two people from the BBC and had a few drinks. I looked at my watch.

'Hey', I said. 'We're in Vienna. It's nearly seven. Why don't we go to the opera? We could just make it.'

Everyone agreed. We grabbed a cab and ended up at the box office a couple of minutes before curtain up. We hurriedly got tickets but had no idea which opera we were going to see. Breathless, we made it to the upper circle just in time. My three colleagues sat together on one row and my seat was in the row behind. The curtain went up to reveal four baths on stage and in each was a naked couple. As the brass of the orchestra played a flourish, a naked baritone protagonist appeared from the wings to deliver the first aria. I leaned over to my friends in front of me,

'I bring you to all the best shows in Europe.'

Whatever the opera was, it was stunning in terms of production and design. The next day we caught the flight to Warsaw and transferred to an old Tupolev airliner bound for Minsk. The aircraft's aisle carpet was threadbare and raggedy. Mid-flight, a hostess not dissimilar to Mrs. Doyle in sit-com *Father Ted*, wheeled a wobbly gold trolley down the aisles and served up caviar and vodka.

We arrived at my cousin's house in Volkolata in the evening. With only one day left for our important research we began with a meeting with some of the young of the village. We were plied with vodka. When the young people weren't looking, most of mine went into the plant pot next to me, but Vadim was still downing his out of politeness. We soon realised the conversation was veering to one where we were being asked if we wanted sex for dollars. We excused ourselves and moved on to our next meeting at the village hall. The hall had a table, chairs, and a piano at the side of which was a redundant bust of Lenin. Our contact at the village hall immediately offered us 'moonshine' a lethal home-brewed high-proof distilled spirit made from potatoes or sugar beet. It was fit to be weed-killer. I felt I could manage one or two as I'd avoided drinking at the previous meeting. Vadim, however, was again polite and respectful and accepted the toast. We downed it in one and within seconds, as if suddenly struck from behind, Vadim toppled forward with a thud onto the table. His Russian hat rolled off his head, bounced across the table and managed to almost land on the head of Lenin's bust.

I called my cousin over. Step by step on slippery ice and snow, we dragged Vadim back to the house where a grand table of food had been set out for the family and our special guest movie director. Vadim was legless, semi-conscious and already beginning to puke. We sat him in a corner with a washing up bowl for company and a bucket between his legs. As the evening's dining continued, the retches and gurgles emanated from the corner. Fortunately he was sober enough to make the flight back to the UK the next day, a flight that ended with an aborted landing for the aircraft and a sudden swoop back into the air since another plane was on our runway. So, we arrived home with no research or significant interviews achieved from our recce. We still managed, however, to produce a few more drafts of the script and introduced material based on the moonshine experience.

Around the turn of the century my music career began to dismantle as a result of internal and external pressures. After receiving accolade for my large scale scores, I found it increasingly difficult to secure similar projects. The film and television industry is renowned for being cut-throat and nepotistic, and the egos of those at the top often turn a reasonable human being into a control freak. One of the contributory factors to my fall was related to an eminent producer who decided to bring in a composer friend to score films. This ousted other composers as well as me and did considerable damage to my income stream. I heard from film editors and programme directors that the producer was spreading the word my music was too lavishly orchestrated. This was odd since the producer's composer friend was also a dab hand with a large scale orchestral palette and the producer later chose to employ another composer who was world-renowned for his dense layers of orchestration. The influential hand of the producer quickly wiped out any future commissions for me. The experience made me consider the power of words. One phrase or line can create mayhem in another person's life. I was devastated. The second factor was the increasing democratisation of music technology. As samplers and software became accessible at low cost, everyone fancied themselves as a composer. The same had happened with photographers with the advent of Photoshop software. The floodgates were now open to 'whistling composers', now known as 'topliners', who had a tune but couldn't create a harmonic structure or orchestrate. It was also open to musicians with a computer but no knowledge of the intricacies of applying music to picture. Alongside that, TV film music budgets were slashed and often the only composers that could be afforded by productions were drawn from this new group of hopefuls. It led to poorly conceived scores and reduced the production value of films. The third factor was my own burnout both mentally and physically.

For many years, as I laboured over scribing millions of music notes, I'd faced a farrago of ailments. Some were annoying and went on for months; others involved being sent in for ultrasounds, MRI scans, or being rushed to a CT scan. A few didn't clear up for a year or so, such as the sting from a weever. The weeverfish is the most venomous fish found in British waters and injects a neuro-toxic venom from its spines. In my case it caused excruciating pain, a year with a numb big toe and nerve damage in my leg and hip. There were also times with my health issues when I'd avoid a recommended surgery. A scan would show a problem but I would endeavour to wish, pray or self heal it away. One scan showed a cyst in an organ. On a successive scan the cyst had disappeared. On another occasion a year spent with a hard ganglion at the side of my plantar fascia meant I couldn't comfortably wear shoes. I was determined to avoid surgery and spent half an hour every day pressing hard against the ganglion and massaging it. At the point my ultrasound scan finally came through as a precursor to having the ganglion surgically removed, the scan showed what a great job I'd done as the affected foot now looked identical to the good foot. Like my mother, whose response to illness and accident was 'it'll pass,' I believe the mind plays a crucial role in self healing and wellbeing and I've been convinced of this during times I've tried to assist others with their healing. I don't regard myself as a healer but as an empath who is easily moved by the predicaments and life problems of others. Unfortunately, I'm also able to develop phantom symptoms of the illnesses of others. This always placed me on the horns of a dilemma. Help or ignore? Many of my own ailments have been phantom. I'd present with all the symptoms of a disease, have all the tests and scans and discover I had nothing. Parts of my burnout were related to depression and I was still affected by the death of my father. There was also an ongoing internal battle about my faith and I began to revisit the big questions about life. A therapist friend told me that men always arrive on the couch with three problems: the need to be a hero, the need to be loved, and a fear of death. It was the question of mortality that haunted me. If my faith was dwindling, with what would I replace it that held any meaning?

Other pressures mounted as life at home with three young children became demanding yet still full of the joy of creativity, imagination and play. I also had to ensure my mother was coping and I took on the gardening and shopping she could no longer manage. There was also a move afoot and I needed new premises for my studio. I'd made sufficient income from my music to buy the Coach House Recording Studios in Clifton, Bristol. The building, originally a nineteenth-century coach house was remodelled as a studio by recording engineer Andy Allan. The studio had quite a reputation. It was regarded as the home of the 'Bristol sound'. Most of the tracks on Massive Attack's debut album *Blue Lines* (1991) had been recorded there in addition to the first album released by band Portishead, *Dummy*

(1994). I used the studio's main room to house my studio equipment and rented the other rooms to composers, songwriters, filmmakers, graphic designers and bands. During the time I owned the studios, the Coach House still enjoyed national and international acclaim. One day there was a knock on the door. Outside stood four young Japanese guys, two of them holding guitar cases. They were all almost identically dressed and looked like a throwback to *The Beatles*.

'We've heard about the Coach House,' they said. 'We want you to produce us.' I hoped they hadn't come all the way from Tokyo, and I turned them away explaining the studio was no longer producing bands.

The beginning of the Coach House years marked the start of what I hoped would be an era in which my skills as a writer and director would come to the fore. I was spurred on by the hope of *The Bell* one day becoming a feature film and I wondered whether I could spawn a parallel career in screenwriting and directing. Others had done it. Film directors Clint Eastwood and John Carpenter also composed their own film music so why shouldn't I? I'd only just emerged from the success of the world premiere of my cantata *Sea Star*, when I decided to apply for a scheme HTV were running for filmmakers. They were looking to commission four thirty-minute dramas. My story submission, *Steps*, was based on a sign I saw at the coastal resort of Brean. The sign read 'Caravan Steps Made Here.' It's the simple chance sighting something this random that has often been the catalyst for a project. Brean has a very large number of static caravans and I wondered what would happen if someone had their caravan steps stolen. Not by anyone, but by a soldier who was not aware WWII had ended and had been hiding out in secret in the old fort at Brean Down. The script was chosen for production with my colleague Tim Francis as co-writer and Lee Cox as producer. I was thrilled to be able to try my hand at directing again but this time it was the real thing.

The auditioning of actors took place at my studio. Well over a thousand actors sent CVs and photos. Amongst those that were invited for interview were actress and singer Bonnie Langford and actress Kacey Ainsworth who went on to play Maureen 'Little Mo' Slater in the BBC's soap *Eastenders*. We finally chose Canadian actress Joanne McQuinn to play our protagonist. The production also collected a stellar line up for the other roles. We managed to secure one of my favourite screen stars, the Oscar nominated actor Ron Moody (1924–2015) who played Fagin in the musical *Oliver* (1968) as well as Stephen Lewis (1926–2015) who played Inspector Blakey in the TV series *On the Buses* and 'Smiler' in the long running sitcom *Last of the Summer Wine*.

The film's locations were the old fort at Brean Down, the caravan site, the leisure park, and the village hall. The demands of the filming were great since the shoot took place in the worst week of weather in any April since anyone could remember. Furthermore, I required two children, an owl and weapons. My son and eldest daughter acted in the film. My son was a huge fan of Ron Moody and had spent months watching him every day in *Oliver*. The big moment came when I introduced Luka to Ron. I knew he'd be blown away. It was at a lunch and my son was sitting opposite him.

'Luka, do you recognise this gentleman?'

My seven-year-old gave Ron a hard stare and announced,

'I've never seen this man in my life!'

The gusting wind and torrential rain at the location meant we had to protect our stars from being blown off a cliff. The cliff edge was near an entrance to a secret cellar which was the location for the soldier's hideout in the film. A few weeks prior to shooting the film I'd been in Woolworth's store and happened to bump into an old friend from college, Christine Wright, who had been in my folk group The Ossett Quartet. She introduced me to her husband Duncan. We got chatting and I discovered he was a bit of a handyman. I asked whether he'd like to do some carpentry on the production. I needed a barrier to stop Ron Moody or Joanne McQuinn falling off a cliff and I also required three sets of decorated caravan steps. Duncan became indispensable on the crew and came up with a do-it-yourself fix for many of the props or location carpentry issues that cropped up.

The demands of filming began to take their toll. Ron became, well to put it bluntly, 'moody.' Perhaps it was my directing or perhaps it was all the hours he had to spend in wind and rain. I'd heard he could be a challenging actor to work with and he decided he was going to abandon the shoot. In the hope of sorting out Ron's issues, my producer set up a meal at a hotel for Ron, me and cameraman Mike Fox. It was only during dinner conversation that Ron and I shared we both had Russian ancestry and from that point the Russian connection sealed our friendship and trust. Later, in a letter, Ron mentioned how he had 'loved every rain-soaked, thermally-insulated minute,' and even gave the director an accolade:

'You gathered around you some first class talents and gave them their lead, and I feel, brought out the best in everyone. I love working like that, and I've always been given that degree of freedom by the best directors! So there!'

He was also over the moon about the hotel he stayed in and especially since it was on *Steps* that he began to formulate the direction of his new book and began to write it. But what Ron wasn't aware of was the behind-the-scenes mutiny from an overworked crew. The incident deeply upset me and demolished the confidence I'd spent a long time building in terms of training myself up as a director. Having initially pointed out we would be doing incredibly long hours above the call of duty, I had my knuckles severely rapped for the long days. It was at that point I made the decision that directing wasn't going to become my future career. In hindsight perhaps I made the wrong decision. I remember the actor Michael Caine was also told by friends and colleagues not to bother with an acting career after his early attempts. Michael ignored the comments and, believing in his talents, went on to become one of the greatest British actors. To succeed, one has to ignore the criticism. Yet, as a hyper-sensitive person, I couldn't take it. Years later at the Toronto Film Festival, I got into a lift and the only person in it was Michael Caine. I should have mentioned to him I wished I'd followed his bullish determination to ignore criticism, but I didn't. I couldn't say anything to him except 'hello'.

I may have left directing behind but I didn't leave screenwriting. Spurred on by the modest success of *Steps*, I set about writing my second feature-length movie script *Junkworld*. *Junkworld* drew on my childhood adventures on the council estate where I grew up. The story follows four children who become the recipients of special powers and discover a world of junk in which their parents will be eternally dumped. I made a decision to go to the Cannes Film Festival to make contacts for the screenplay and was lucky enough to win a place in a session where writers pitched their scripts to producers, directors, and an audience. I nervously stood up to pitch and received positive feedback from the panel. As I was packing up my things, a woman from the audience approached me. Shirani Le Mercier was the assistant producer to John Calley (1930–2011) who was chairman and chief executive at Sony Pictures. Shirani asked to read the screenplay, loved it and presented it to John. Unfortunately, it didn't go any further.

Back in London I managed to win a literary agent on the strength of the screenplay. The script was presented to several companies including Ridley Scott's company Scott Free Productions. I was asked to meet with a young director in the company who was interested in my work and the script made it to Ridley's slate of films to be presented to Fox in the US. Again it failed to make it through to the funding stage. Years later, the script made a journey around Hollywood to Paramount Pictures and Walden Media but again failed to be taken up for production. My next stop was at David Heyman's company Heyday Films. David had all the *Harry Potter* film rights and was beginning to produce all eight films. David and his development executive liked the script and the executive commented, 'Martin, you may not realise it, but you've written a children's classic!'

Great encouragement but there was no way the company could take on more material with production on the *Harry Potter* films looming. Instead, it was suggested I should write *Junkworld* the novel and present it to book publisher Puffin. That summer, I placed a chair and desk outside my studio and began to scribble down the novel. It was a wonderful time, taking in the sunshine and feeling a magical flow of words writing themselves onto the page. I got a draft of the novel to Puffin and they liked it but asked me to reduce the number of pages. Once I'd laboured on the edit, I heard the news that the board of Puffin had changed and the new team were not going to proceed with any writers they'd taken on during the previous year – including me.

It's often difficult for friends and colleagues to understand the excessive hours of hard work that go into trying to launch a film or literary project, only to be met by rejections and bitter disappointments. As these setbacks continued, along with dwindling music work, I hit rock bottom. For the first time, I felt I was treading water. Again and again I attempted to reignite my career and struggled with fanning the flames of a new one. I was exhausted from all I'd achieved and anxious about what the future might hold. I felt I'd reached breaking point and needed to get away. I wanted wilderness, escape and time to reset my compass. I knew exactly where I wanted to go. I thought I'd be going alone but it didn't turn out that way. One day I'd popped out of the studio to buy a pint of milk. I bumped into film editor David McCormick with whom I worked on *Zastrozzi*. He was in a hurry so our conversation was brief. After the hellos, I said I was going to Antarctica. 'Want to come along?' David immediately said yes. A few days later I was having a drink with Aardman's *Wallace and Gromit* animator Nick Park and, before I knew it, he was on board too. Aardman animator and owner David Sproxton joined up next followed by an enthusiastic Duncan Wright who had worked with me on my film *Steps*. The expedition now wasn't a solo journey of self- discovery, but was more like material for a bestseller or travelogue: *Five go Mad in Antarctica!*

11

Ship, Shamans, Champagne, Trains

We boarded the *Akademik Ioffe,* a 364-foot-long Russian research vessel at Ushuaia, Argentina, on January 14th, 2001. The round trip to the Antarctic Peninsula would be 1991.6 nautical miles. The ship, carrying eighty-five passengers, was under charter as a polar cruise vessel from the Shirshov Institute of Oceanology, part of the Russian Academy of Sciences. The ship was usually used for experiments on the long-range transmission of sound in the ocean – a fitting vessel for a composer to travel on. The evening sail out of port was accompanied by the sighting of magellanic penguins, kelp geese, South American terns and imperial shags. In the early hours of the morning, the ship made a turn to starboard and headed south towards Antarctica.

The next morning, as rain came in and the ship began to rock, I awoke to see a royal albatross glide on a thirty knot breeze past my cabin window. The fly past was the herald for what came next: a Black browed albatross, Southern giant petrel, and a flock of Wilson's storm petrel – a small seabird that will follow ships as it flies close to the ocean's surface and often in the troughs of waves. The almost musical pattern of the flock in motion was beautiful to behold. I couldn't get enough of watching them whenever the cry of petrels on port or starboard came up. Later that morning the wind got up to twenty-five knots and the sea became choppy, but I was still able to stand upright on deck and watch a whale breaching. The following day was a force-eight gale. Fighting the sea-sickness and rocking ship, the only place I felt comfortable was as near to the bow as possible. Given I was responsible for bringing my group to Antarctica, I thought it best to introduce them to other passengers at mealtimes or other events on board ship. So, before leaving the UK, I had business cards made which they could hand out:

Nick Park
Snow Shoveller.
Drives or whole continents.
Glaciers sensitively removed.
Pengy poop by contract.

David Sproxton
Albatross Photobooths Inc.
Photo-U with albatross.
Discreet cabin darkroom.
Lighting choice – on or off.

Duncan Wright
Whalewrighter.
Right whales a speciality.
Whales while-u-wait.
Call me on my Moby.

David McCormick
Ice Cutter.
Big begs or G&Ts.
Discounts on pack ice.
Ask for 'Yo Daddy Ice'.

I'm not sure whether they received any commissions but at least everyone got to know us.

We finally arrived at 66 degrees 33 minutes south, the Antarctic Circle, at 11.30am the next day. Our arrival was greeted by snow petrels, Antarctic fulmars, and two whales. The bergs were magnificent. Some were jagged and looked like a witch's hat and fingers; others stood tall and ornate like the façade of a cathedral. There were white bergs, blue bergs and floating bergy bits drifting past the ship. My first impression of this land and seascape was one of entering a lost continent and I marvelled at what Captain James Cook's (1728–1779) impression must have been when he approached the first ghostly icebergs as they appeared through shifting fog. Our crossing of the Antarctic Circle was exactly two hundred and twenty-eight years to the day that Cook crossed it for the first time in 1773 and eighty-nine years to the day that Scott reached the South Pole.

Before turning northwards along the coast of the Antarctic Peninsula, we sailed farther south to 66 minutes 52 minutes to Detaille Island, home to a colony of Adélie penguins and a group of derelict huts and outbuildings which were part of British research stations in the 1950s. Our first trip out in the zodiacs was thrilling as we navigated the bergs as well as meeting imperial cormorants and Weddell seals on ice floes. We also spotted a pod of killer whales and a humpback whale in the distance. The next day's visit to Vernadsky station, a Ukrainian research post, had a somewhat different flavour. We were greeted by a welcoming group of Ukrainian scientists who plied us with pepper vodka and encouraged the women in our party to donate underwear to the line of bras and panties draped above the bar. There was only one taker and it wasn't me.

After a pit-stop back at the ship, we took the zodiacs to Pleneau Island where there were plentiful gentoo and chinstrap penguins as well as skuas, large aggressive birds that swoop down and kill penguin chicks. They also like to have a go at dive-bombing the heads of tourists. With two in pursuit of me, I broke into a frenetic run with my hands covering my head. Back on board ship we were lucky to avoid the obstacle of thick ice and gain clear passage through the Lemaire Channel. Here, huge black mountains rise three thousand feet on either side of what is a narrow waterway. The majestic range was perfectly mirrored in the still water and we all stood on deck in awe as the setting sun changed the colours of the landscape from orange and red to pink and purple. We also spent one evening at a barbecue on deck. The weather was warm enough for us to wear T-shirts and shorts and it highlighted and starkly brought home to us the effects of climate change.

The next morning was a brilliant blue sky day. We sailed through the Gerlache Strait and into Paradise Bay with mountains, glaciers, snowfields and icebergs reflected in the water. We climbed a big hill for panoramic views across the bay and slid back down the slopes on our bums. One of the things to watch out for as we returned to the zodiacs was the calving of icebergs. It was spectacular to watch, but the ensuing wave created by the collapse meant we had to get the zodiacs away quickly to avoid being deluged. As we moved on to Neko Harbour on the Antarctic continent, a huge glacier calved and a wall of ice crashed into the sea. The wave it produced was powerful enough to reach our landing site half a kilometre away from the glacier. Later that day was the long awaited (for some!) trip to Dorian Bay to dig snow-holes, erect tents, and show off our mettle as we prepared to brave an Antarctic night beneath the stars. It sounded like hard graft to me and David McCormick, but we still went ahead with all the other Antarctic heroes and left the ship at ten o' clock in the evening to avoid taking any food ashore.

The setting up camp in Antarctica scene was fitting for a silent comedy. The wind picked up and made the erection of tents a challenge. Tents blew upside down, inside out, and in our faces as we tried in vain to look as if we knew what we were doing. David and I didn't have a clue.

'Did you ever camp as a cub scout?'

'No, did you?'

'No. Do you know how to put this thing up?'

'No. Hey Nick, Duncan, can you give us a hand?'

No reply.

We poured ourselves a whisky instead and watched the drama as the wind blew tents, poles, sleeping bags, gloves and hats towards the ocean as if they were kites or tumbleweed. Better still was watching those who chased them. It was like a movie chase playing at breakneck speed. Even though David Sproxton had already dug his snow-hole, erected his tent and was already snug as a bug in his sleeping bag before anyone else, McCormick and I took it easy with our whisky, wondering when someone would arrive to help us with our tents. By midnight, everyone was settling down. I'd just got my tent to stand up when we were saved by the ship's horn which sounded the signal to abandon camp as the gusts had now reached forty knots. McCormick and I celebrated with another whisky — we'd be returning to the ship. We arrived back on board at half past midnight with those who had managed to erect their tent and get into a sleeping bag claiming they'd actually camped on the Antarctic continent, albeit for only ten minutes.

With twenty-two hours of near daylight outside the porthole, there was plenty of time for contemplation and reflection. I'd come to this wilderness to ask myself questions, recharge my batteries, commune with nature, and search for inner resolve to move on despite the setbacks I'd encountered. I found that spending time in wilderness helped to centre one's energy in a positive way. The experience of Antarctica is perhaps the closest one can feel to being in a totally different world and the environment announces that we belong to nature and not it to us. Unless one has the experience of being in the depths of the ocean or in space, being on this 'lost continent' was the closest one could get to feeling vulnerable as well as at one with the elements, the land, sea and wildlife. On the other hand, I hadn't laughed so much for a very long time. There was a great sense of camaraderie in our group and a letting go of any pretensions, status or trappings of the world back home. I couldn't stop myself from creating some playtime on board and composed the *Antarctic Rap* which I performed to my fellow sojourners after lunch one day. I think it may have been the first rap performed live in Antarctica. Alongside that, I had another plan for a composition. It occurred to me no-one had ever written the International Anthem of Antarctica! There was another first waiting for me. I put the request out for a motley crew-cum-choir to write the lyrics and perform. Our rehearsals took place in the ship's library. It wasn't long before the first meeting erupted into surreal humour and hilarity which inspired the lyrics for what became a spoof anthem.

International Anthem of Antarctica

Home of the Gentoo,
Seat of the Shag,
Land of the Chinstrap,
Realm of the Whale.

Chorus:

Antarctica.
I said Antarctica!
You are so cold,
Rock and ice befriend you,
Your bottom they enthrone.
All hail Antarctica!
I said Antarctica,
Protector of the Pole.

Mountains are big here,
Slippery is the ice,
Bergs are the bestest,
Glaciers are nice.

Chorus.

Zodiacs are racing,
Over the waves,
A soaking we are facing,
No worries, we're so brave.

Chorus.

Drake cleared his passage,
So said Scott's log,
James cooked the circle,
Shacky ate the dogs.

Chorus.

I set about composing the melody for the lyrics, rehearsed the choir a few times and decided we could go for the big time. Why not make a music video of the song? There happened to be a filmmaker from New York on board, Roger Leigh, who was strangely enough more than happy to shoot and direct the anthem. Even better, we discovered there was a video editing suite on board and we had a film editor with us — David McCormick. The video featured the choir singing on land, in the zodiacs, ship's decks, the bow, the stern, the bridge, the cabins and the library. I even choreographed a few cool moves into the anthem. As if we didn't have anything better to do! The passengers were subjected to the live performance and the music video. Returning to the UK, in true polar fashion, I claimed the International Anthem of Antarctica as a first by registering it with the Performing Right Society in London. I've never heard the anthem performed at global events. Shame.

The *Akademik Ioffe* anchored at many places for us to explore wildlife and icebergs. From Cuverville Island, with Antarctica's largest colony of forty thousand pairs of gentoo penguins, we set sail for what was to become one of my favourite visits: Deception Island — the caldera of what is a live volcano. It was a bleak, grey day, with a blizzard setting in as the ship approached Neptune's Bellows, a channel on the southeast side. From a mile offshore, the narrow 1300-foot entrance to the caldera of the island was barely visible through the snow and cloud. The captain wasn't sure the ship could enter but he succeeded. The zodiacs were lowered and our first encounter with the island was the pungent sulphuric smell of hot steaming pools at Whalers Bay. Once a whaling station, the bay had derelict rusty huts and the sad legacy of whalebones scattered on a beach of black volcanic ash. The blizzard of snow and wind was blinding, chilling our faces as we headed down the beach past lines of marching chinstrap penguins, then up the valley towards a viewpoint. But the wind suddenly grew stronger, gusting at forty-six knots. Messages from the ship informed us it was having difficulty holding anchor. By now, the snow was sheeting across us and we could barely see the shoreline never mind the ship. Soaked through to the skin, we had to make a run for the zodiacs before the weather worsened. Back on board and homeward bound to Argentina, the dreaded Drake Passage was thankfully benign until the winds rapidly increased as we approached Cape Horn. As we turned into what was a gale, the bow plunged deep into the oncoming waves and a few of the larger ones drenched us to the skin.

Back in Ushuaia, we gathered our things and set off for four days in Buenos Aires. In the mood for having a good time, we took a trip to a tango club. Unfortunately I hadn't learned to tango at this stage in life, but on the way there McCormick and

I met two women who were also on their way to the club. They asked if they could sit with us for dinner. As the evening progressed, we watched the stage dancers and exchanged very little conversation with the two women. That is, until they heard a few lines David and I exchanged.

'Remember that heart transplant we did in Jo'burg?'

'That was a challenging one. Heart flown from Paris.'

'Still flying your jet?'

'Caribbean in January.'

The women cocked their ears. David and I were in full swing with one of our wind ups.

'Remember how you suddenly announced you had to leave for a ski trip?'

'Mid surgery.'

'Yes. It certainly put the pressure on me and the surgical team to finish off.'

We left it there and continued with our meals, confident in the fact the ladies were chatting away in whispers about the 'internationally acclaimed transplant surgeons' with whom they were dining.

On another evening, the five of us were walking through a park. McCormick and I had long hair and were suddenly singled out by a group of young people.

'Hey, aren't you the famous band...'

They named whatever band it was, I don't remember who. Or maybe it was The Who. We looked them in the eye, paused for a moment, and then David and I said, 'yes we are', and walked away.

I arrived back in London with the usual air travel drama with lost things — my suitcase hadn't arrived and I hoped it wasn't in Argentina. I had special mementoes inside for the children. No penguins, seals or whales! Luckily the luggage showed up a couple of days later. Of course, any trip to a pristine wilderness poses the question of tourism in such environments. We had been on a small ship with a small number of people as opposed to the growing number of super vessels beginning to show up in Antarctic waters. Are there any easy answers except not to travel or discover non-polluting means of travel? Those would be questions I'd be asking myself for quite a while. The big question was had the journey changed anything for me? Apart from recognition of how climate change was affecting Antarctica, I came back revived and ready to grow a parallel career in screenwriting against the backdrop of sporadic music commissions.

Musically, the years of famine were approaching and after rising to the top of my TV film composing career, I was now grasping at straws. Over the next couple of years only a few projects trickled in. I scored director Vadim Jean's amusing animated pilot *The Nutter Tales* and his three-part insightful documentary series

Skin Deep in which Anita Roddick, founder of The Body Shop, goes undercover as a vagrant on the streets of London to show how the other half lives. I also scored one of TV's first explorations of life drawing, the seven-part HTV series *Life Class*. I began looking for new ways to market my work, and as someone who has always pioneered new approaches to projects, I collaborated with producer Robert Copeland and wrote, directed and performed in what became the UK's first video tutorial for young film composers *The Art of the Film Score*. The video became a teaching aid for my students on the MA in the Composition of Music for Film and Television at the University of Bristol as well as being available for sale to other teaching institutions and the general public.

The video covered many aspects of film music composition from orchestration to the placement of music cues in film narratives. Of special interest for me has always been the subliminal use of music — the use of music to trigger ideas, thoughts and emotions below the threshold of consciousness and thus elicit a viewer's response without them being aware of why they might be making it. Such devices were used in film and often escaped the beady eye of the censor. For example, to make a car chase film sequence more dramatic, a film-maker might insert a single frame here and there of serious injuries. Due to censorship, the graphic horror of those injuries couldn't normally be shown, but in the placement of single frames scenario, the viewer would find themselves disturbed by the chase sequence because their brain had registered a subliminal image their eye was not quick enough to spot. The technique was often applied in porn films such as *Deep Throat* (1972) where images of fellatio embedded as single frames excite the brain but are invisible to the eye unless the picture is stopped and a frame by frame search is made. Product advertising campaigns also used the placement of subliminal imagery as part of their film commercials.

The technique, however, is not new and Russian filmmaker Sergei Eisenstein (1898–1948) and his composer colleague Sergei Prokofiev (1891–1953) developed a method of subliminally placing intervallic, melodic, rhythmic or textural patterns in music to persuade the audience they were experiencing a near perfect marriage of music and picture. Eisenstein and Prokofiev used the technique on their film *Alexander Nevsky* (1938). In planning the score, graphic diagrams, which used simple lines such as horizontals, verticals, diagonals and curves, were used to portray the composition of a shot or the movement within a shot. Prokofiev used these diagrams to find similar graphic representations in the contour of melody, the duration of music notes or in the spatial distribution of notes in a chord. The curve of a melodic line might represent the curve of a winding river in the picture, a constant line of repeated notes a marching army, or ascending harmonies may represent floating clouds. As a result, there was a hidden audiovisual correspondence between the images and the music score.

I've used this technique of Eisenteinian correspondence many times in my scores. Most notably I used it in *Living on the Edge*, episode six of the *Land of the Eagle* series. For one shot I decided a moving sidewinder snake had a curving shape and looked for an equivalent curving timbre on the synthesiser. For another, I created a melodic phrase on electric guitar that copied the pattern a lasso made as it was thrown into the air. I also shaped an electronic sound to match a camera move over shadows cast by rocks. All these devices were not recognisable by the viewer who only sensed a good match of image and sound. I also used the technique in episode two *Taming the Iron Monster* in the BBC series *Locomotion*. A continuous sustained chord in the score represented the landscape behind the on screen presenter and a series of arched-shaped melodic motifs in the string parts of the score represented the arches of a viaduct in the background of the shot. My teaching video also uses this approach in a short sequence of film I shot in Antarctica. Although the video has been extremely useful in the teaching environment, it failed to bring in any sufficient income to plug the years of what looked like the demise of my music career. At times like that, when one is not on a roll, it's often difficult to muster the energy and confidence to participate in anything let alone a TV interview, but I agreed to appear on the long running *Songs of Praise* series. As I finished my piece with the programme's presenter, I felt like a hypocrite. I knew deep inside my faith had fractured and the fault lines were clearly visible.

Based on the positive responses to the scripts *The Bell* and *Junkworld*, I turned my attention to writing. Graphic designer Richard Higgs and I collaborated on my opera project *Tectonic Plates*. Richard produced set designs and I produced a treatment for the opera but couldn't garner any funding interest. We did, however, receive funding to develop and shoot a promo for my short film *Shadowed*, but we were unable to secure backing to get it into production. Time flies by when you're writing screenplays and over the next few years I wrote several feature film scripts: a black comedy *The Fleabert Inheritence*, an animated feature *Spyders*, and a children's adventure *Tranimal* optioned by a natural history production company. Again, my screenplay didn't attract sufficient funding to go into production. My screenplay with Vadim Jean *The Bell* was now doing the rounds of actors with a view to someone coming on board as our protagonist but we had passes from Ralph Fiennes, Ewan McGregor, Daniel Craig and Gerard Butler even though the script had been nominated by the British Film Council as Best British Screenplay to represent the UK in the Hartley-Merrill Screenwriting Competition at the

Cannes Film Festival. It was a kind of Eurovision song contest for screenplays and great to be nominated, but *The Bell* didn't end up as the 'greatest story ever tolled!' In the midst of gloom about income and not being able to launch a screenplay into production, the universe shook its dice and out rolled a lucky music one.

My mentor Edward Williams had been pressing on with the development of his ultrasonic instrument Soundbeam and his organisation Elektrodome. Elektrodome commissioned me to compose a work for year-eight pupils at Bishop Perowne School in Worcester. The completed work would be performed at Worcester Cathedral. It was the first time such a challenging and technically complex performance had been realised with children. The piece gave me the opportunity to build on my background in natural history and revisit my interests in environmentalism, Native American spirituality, and shamanism. I chose to call the piece *Inua*, the word used by the Inuit peoples of the Arctic regions for the soul or spirit. The inua is sought by shamans, professional healers who plead with higher forces to obtain powers to heal an individual, a community or the environment. In seeking out these higher forces, the shaman requires three attributes to complete the journey: spirit allies, power songs, and a drum on which to ride. I chose to use the shaman's quest as a structural story arc for the work. I also wanted to create a piece about healing the wounds incurred by the destructive forces threatening our planet.

The opening processional introit of the piece introduced a single candle flame and musical motif — the notion of the universe emerging from dark into light. The theme and flickering projections of the candle were controlled by the performer's hand moving through invisible ultrasonic beams which, when interrupted, converted those interruptions into MIDI instructions for playing an electronic musical instrument and projecting an image. The introit was followed by the arrival of four elements: fire, wind, sea, and earth which were quickly subdued by the negative impact of humankind's intervention with wars, poverty, deforestation, and ecological disaster. The loss was marked by a musical and visual lament for nature created by movement in Soundbeam. The performers then used Soundbeam's floor switches to trigger sounds of rattles and drums which became the musical material for a circle dance announcing the arrival of a shaman. The shaman ended the dance by striking a drum in the beam to create thunder and lightning — a phenomenon which the shaman believes will give his drum the power to make the journey to the 'world tree'. The tree allows spirits to pass from one world to the other and acts as a bridge that connects heaven, earth, and the underworld. A power song and drum ride accompanied the journey to the world tree where the shaman received healing artefacts in the form of musical instruments and themes from three spirits: peace, love, and wisdom. The final section of the work described the journey back to earth and the successful healing of the natural world.

Inua not only helped children understand the environmental issues facing our planet but also introduced them to the belief system of indigenous peoples who felt an intrinsic connection to the natural world. Furthermore, it enabled young people to explore and combine live performance with the electronic arts of sound and light. The piece was nominated for the 2004 British Academy of Songwriters, Composers and Authors (now known as The Ivors Academy) Composer of the Year Award in the community and education category. The event took place at the Ironmongers' Hall, London and the awards were presented by the cellist Julian Lloyd Webber. The evening was a star-studded affair with musicians, composers and broadcasters. I straightened my tie and checked my suit prior to entering the hall where guests were being greeted for a champagne reception. As I moved through the crowd, a wine waitress opened a bottle of champagne. The cork popped, skimmed my head, and champagne splurted out and drenched my suit. I brushed off the bubbly and for a split second I paused. I told myself I could feel embarrassed and annoyed by the incident, regard it as a simple accident or imbue the incident with meaning. I chose to laugh it off and read it as a sign: drenched in champagne means I am going to win an award! Twenty minutes later I heard my name announced as the winner of the 2004 British Academy of Composers and Songwriters Composer of the Year Award. Better still, it was the only award in all the categories that carried a cash prize of £5000.

Composing a piece about a shaman, the healing of the natural world and the journey to the world tree enabled me, as did my Antarctic voyage, to ground myself in nature rather than a world suffocated by materialism. From the world tree to the four towering pines I look out on from my dining room window, trees are important to me and I regard them as my friends. The pines are eighty feet tall, majestic, lofty, and distinguished. I like to celebrate their uplifting and positive energy drawn from Mother Earth. I often ask to soak up some of it for myself, especially when I'm extremely low. The beauty, shape and dance of a tree canopy in the wind can also imbue a feeling of wellbeing. As I walk or run around the nature reserve close to my home, I thank trees for their contribution to pharmaceuticals, which provide healing for us, as well as their role in fighting climate change by removing carbon dioxide from the atmosphere. I'm reminded by the oaks, cedars, cypresses and redwoods that I should do more to contribute to carbon reduction. I also enjoy walking by a nearby river. It's often just me and the river. I'm there seeking reflection and focus without the intrusion of transient thoughts. The slow moving waters assuage my turbulent river of consciousness which is often near to breaking its banks.

Many great thinkers received revelation and wisdom as a result of being in nature. Buddah received enlightenment by sitting under a tree, the ancient Greek philosophers wandered olive groves where they held discourse on their ideas, Isaac Newton (1643–1727) watched an apple fall from a tree, and Charles Darwin (1809–1882) walked the Sandwalk, his 'thinking path', a perimeter track around a small wood at his home in Kent. I believe our disconnection with the natural world has a negative effect on our emotional and psychological health. Certainly during the spread of Covid 19 and the subsequent lockdown during 2020, people had the opportunity to rediscover nature, commune with the environment, and benefit from ecopsychology. Yet after the lockdown, as I wandered open green spaces, woods and beaches, I saw litter and plastics left behind. Some people didn't learn lessons from the pandemic about how we might adopt new values, begin to reframe our attitudes, and rebuild our relationship with nature. Nature was kind to us during our moment of need but was often treated with little respect in return. Reciprocation is essential. Planet Earth which has so faithfully sustained us should be rightfully sustained by us.

As much as I was feeling fulfilled and rejuvenated by the success of *Inua*, I was still floundering and grasping for a solid single career trajectory. Ping ponging the worlds of music, writing, academic work and in later life my work as a poet caused confusion for potential commissioners who were at a loss to identify whether I had a primary career. For them, it was safer to employ someone who practised one discipline rather than a polymath with fingers in lots of pies. I'd always been ahead of my time in my approach to music scores, but others — except for a few visionary directors with whom I'd worked — failed to embrace the benefits of my ability to communicate themes and issues by combining media — something that became common place in the arts years later.

Like the captain on the *RMS* Titanic, I went full steam ahead with my writing in the hope I could turn around a ship that was heading for icebergs. I immersed myself in writing a book of short stories for children, *Stories for Ghosts*, but it didn't find a publisher. I also developed a children's TV series, *Godz*, which got to the final round of being commissioned by ITV. In the end, I was pipped to the post by an already established writer of children's drama. Soon after, I was invited to a concert by artist friends Dr. P J Crook and Richard Parker-Crook. The concert was given by legendary guitarist Robert Fripp who founded the progressive rock band King Crimson. It was an enormous pleasure to meet and discuss music with him and then, coincidentally, sometime later at a lunch event in Bristol, I was introduced to his partner English singer, songwriter, actress, author and producer

Toyah Willcox. Toyah has, to date, released twenty albums and has appeared in forty stage plays as well as numerous television shows. Her best known hit singles were *It's a Mystery* (1981) and *I Want to be Free* (1981). Our meeting was like two fireworks going off. There was an immediate connection in our conversation about art, writing, films and music. Toyah also had the type of playful and fertile imagination with which I resonated. When she asked me whether I would consider being a writing partner, I jumped at the opportunity. Supported by coffee and chocolate biscuits we spent numerous sessions developing TV dramas. Our most promising was a psychic thriller, *The China Detective*, but again in the fickle unpredictable world of the film industry, it didn't secure finance. The best opportunity that came out of the collaboration was the introduction of Toyah to my film director friend Yvonne Deutschman with a view to her starring in Yvonne's feature film *The Power of Three* (2011). Toyah secured the role. Because of co-producers, I never got a look in for the music and it was yet another disappointment for me.

Sometimes it feels you can only take so much and desperation sets in. I became like a gambler courting addiction. I resorted to investing more time and savings into writing more material which included a children's drama *Clan*, the story of a boy and a hare. *Clan* was submitted to a UK Film Council scheme which was looking for new animal dramas. It reached joint first in the selection process, but following an interview and a requested second draft, the organisation decided not to award the commission and scrapped their plans of looking for animal drama. If one believes in bad luck or not, this was another very painful rejection. As a creative you're expected to get used to the rejections and knocks and I've a found I'm usually resilient in coming back after losing an opportunity. What is much more difficult than coming back from a few punches in the ring is trying to find your feet after you've hit the canvas and are being counted out.

After getting up and coming round to creative consciousness again, I took a different tack and pitched an idea for a sci-fi radio drama. *Scramble* (2006) was a tale of love, treachery, and the self-realisation of an individual pitted against enormous odds. In the drama, music is considered subversive and is utterly forbidden and outlawed by the government of a futuristic 'big brother' Britain. The protagonist, a composer, faces a race against time in which music lies at the heart of a battle between the forces of good and evil. BBC producer Mark Smalley loved the concept and we decided the format would be three thirty-minute episodes. The series has been broadcast many times. Thankfully my muse was working overtime and another pitch application resulted in a commission from the City of Bristol's Brunel 200 celebrations. The commission enabled me to compose a cantata for soloist, choir, orchestra and film to mark the 200th anniversary of the birth of Isambard Kingdom Brunel (1806–1859), one of the most inspirational engineers of the nineteenth century.

I based my piece on Brunel's construction of the Great Western Railway, the railway track from London's Paddington station to Bristol's Temple Meads station. Brunel was the Sir Richard Branson of his day with a plan to build a railway to connect London to Bristol where passengers would then board his steamship the *SS Great Britain* for the transatlantic voyage to New York. I was able to research material for the libretto in the Brunel Collection at the University of Bristol. My work *A Radius of Curves* (2006) became a cantata in eight sections divided into two stories. The first told of Brunel's personal battle to build the railway, his hopes, setbacks, turmoil and anxieties during the construction of the track and ultimately his success. The second parallel story followed the journey from a geological perspective and described every type of rock and sand over which the track travelled as well as the inclines and declines. Many of the words written for soloist Martin Le Poivedin and the Exultate Singers were Brunel's actual words from his books of calculations and drawings, budgets, reports, correspondence and diaries.

The idea for the title came from the 'radius of curves', an essential measurement deemed important by engineers and especially by Brunel. The advantage of determining curves of a larger radius for the GWR resulted in smoother curves which enabled locomotives to travel at speed. The term, for me, also stood as a metaphor for the twists and turns that occurred both personally and professionally in Brunel's life. A few of the most wonderful sections to write were the *The Estimate*, *Coffee*, and *Maidenhead Bridge* sections of the cantata. At the cantata's opening, the choir sings the words from Brunel's original estimate for the construction of the railway: 'two million eight hundred and five thousand three hundred and thirty pounds.' In *Coffee*, Brunel celebrates the possibility of drinking coffee without spillage on a train travelling at forty-five miles per hour. In *Maidenhead Bridge*, the choir sing the measurements from the equation Brunel calculated for the bridge's construction. I also wanted the work to have a visual element. Filmmakers David Parker, Scott Tibbles and Robin Toyne contributed images filmed in Brunel's archive. The icing on the cake was a film we shot from the driver's cab of a train travelling from London Paddington to Bristol Temple Meads. The film was speeded up to match the duration of the cantata and projected behind the orchestra – the Bristol Ensemble conducted by David Ogden. A tremendous bonus for the world premiere was the attendance of artist John Austin, one of the world's greatest artists specialising in the depiction of the steam railway. John exhibited his large painting *King John at Dawlish* alongside the choir and orchestra

12

Blue Notes

Things don't often land at an apposite time and the offer to compose the score for the movie *The Killing of John Lennon* landed at a point in my life when I was in a bad place due to the break-up of my marriage. After twenty-seven years in a relationship, I couldn't bear the upheaval and the sense of having failed. I'd fallen out of love and the ensuing tumble from that fall would be emotionally and psychologically costly for all of us. I was also very aware of how two very demanding careers can cause abrasion in a family unit. Most of all, it was painful to think about how the children would get through it.

At the point I felt I could never lift a pen again or write another music note, the phone rang. It was the film producer Rakha Singh. I'd met Rakha a couple of years earlier at the Cannes Film Festival. A friend had said to me, 'You see the guy sitting over there at the bar, go and have a chat to him.' So I did. Rakha was immediately friendly, a great communicator, and well read. We got on well and didn't initially talk about film. We discussed astronomy, cosmology and life. Towards the end of the conversation Rakha mentioned he was producing a movie in New York and Hawaii about the killing of John Lennon (1940–1980). I must have been worn out by rejections at that point and didn't even bother to chase the project but Rakha insisted we kept in touch.

A few months later we exchanged an email, and a year after that Rakha and the film's director Andrew Piddington got in touch. They mentioned they were close to completing their film and invited me to a viewing theatre in Soho to see the final cut of the movie.

'Can you come to London and see the movie. It's got temp tracks on it and we'd like to know if you could replace them.'

The film's score was made up of 'temp tracks'. These are pieces of music which a director places as temporary guidetracks in a film and are usually, but not always, replaced by original music commissioned from a composer. There was about an hour's worth of temp tracks that needed replacing. A few tracks in the film were going to stay. These were the ones in the Hawaii scenes and featured Hawaiian guitar. All the other tracks were disparate pieces with no thematic connective tissue. They would also have been prohibitively expensive for the film's budget to clear so had to be left behind at the checkout. Rakha and Andrew asked whether I could compose the new score in three weeks. Psychologically, I was on the precipice of a particularly dark point in my life. I wondered whether I could cope with the project on top of the emotional angst I was going through. I could easily have given up, but the film required a very dark brooding score and this resonated with my blue if not black period. I accepted the job and wondered whether it might also reignite my film music career.

Although my early music background was in electronic music, I'm best known as a composer of orchestral scores. So, the return to a largely electronic palette created an opportunity to experiment with synthesisers again. The fact the film was based in 1980 didn't affect my approach to the score. My only nod to the period was to include a sampled guitar or piano here and there as a tribute to Lennon, but it was incredibly subtle and the main thrust of the underscore was to highlight the psychological state of an assassin and create emotional impact as the tragic events leading to Lennon's death unfolded. I decided to put together a music team and compose and record the score in Bristol. The electronic portion was composed in my studio and then transferred to the studios at the Victoria Rooms, Bristol. I employed Jonathan Scott, with whom I'd worked with in the university's music department, to mix the score. Composer Jean Hasse was hired as music copyist and Claire Louise Sibley joined on her first outing as a feature film runner.

The score required the usual speedy delivery. I planned to compose sixty minutes of music sketches in one week so the director would have a further few days to make and approve any adjustments. That left around ten days to complete the MIDI programming, the composition of the live instrumental parts, and the recording sessions with the Bristol Ensemble. I'd been used to employing MIDI programmers on my projects to adjust any music notes which may have been imprecise due to the nuances of expressive performance or as a result of sketching the material too quickly. The process of correcting any note misalignments or timing issues is known as quantisation. One of my former film composing students answered my call to work as my assistant and concentrate on the MIDI quantisation and programming. At the informal interview at my studio

I mentioned the task ahead.

'I'm going to pay you for the three weeks but I require you with me lock, stock and barrel. You'll follow me everywhere.'

He nodded.

'I want to do it.'

'It's going to be full on,' I said. 'It will take you out of all social activities.'

He was still enthusiastic. I looked him in the eye.

'Have you got a girlfriend?'

He looked back quizzically.

'Yes.'

I smiled.

'You haven't now.'

My score evolved into an ominous ambient arrangement overdubbed with chamber ensemble: alto flute, oboe, piano, strings, soprano, and counter-tenor. The main melodic theme on strings was made up of a repeating and cycling pattern of descending tones to represent the assassin's internal descent into obsession and madness. I composed a few of the tracks at a moment's notice. One morning, the director rang to say he required a new cue and would come in within a couple of hours to hear it. I frantically jotted down a piece for violin, guitar, oboe d'amore and soprano in less than a few minutes and called in the musicians I had on standby. I followed that with the same lightning delivery service on the counter-tenor cue, which wasn't used in the film but made the album. Another challenge was the director's thoughts on the relationship between sound effects and music. He'd included sound effects at specific pitches and wanted incoming or outgoing music cues to match the pitches in the sound design. Although the film was nominated for a BAFTA award, there were those who felt it wrong to make a movie that gave media exposure to Lennon's killer. I knew my involvement with the film might draw criticism, but I believed the content of the film was robustly and sensitively handled by the director and I was an aficionado of John Lennon. I can prove it! I still have my dinner plate bought when I was five years old with an image of The Beatles on it!

The divorce proceedings pre and post the John Lennon project broke me into tiny pieces. Furthermore, music work I expected to pour in on the back of the movie didn't materialise. The whole world was suddenly looking very different as I endeavoured to find my feet after such an emotional, psychological and financial upheaval. Every day I was haunted by the toll it would take on the children. My wife and I decided they should have the least amount of upheaval so, on selling the house, we used a major portion of the sale for her and the children to move to a property close to their school. Before I could buy a new place, I had to wait for the sale of my studio premises to go through. I moved with what was only essential: my piano, musical instruments, recording equipment, a bed, a sofa from the studio, bookshelves, a couple of chairs, a few paintings and my bicycle. A number of friends were happy to store items for me, including my grand piano! The day the removal van arrived was a very tough day. It was raining. I stood with my bicycle opposite the house and watched as the furniture was loaded up. I couldn't bear to say goodbye to the happy days and playful times with the children in the garden and on the street. I could hardly contain the tears as I left the place where two of our children were born. I thought about all the music I'd composed in the basement studio in the house – some of my finest scores. I thought about how the walls and atmosphere of the house had soaked up that music and the laughter of the children and I would have given anything to have got it back.

The rain soaked me. I cycled to my studio to be greeted with tenants who were refusing to move their possessions. It was hugely stressful. They left me with damaged rooms and I had to dispose of over thirty bin liners full of their rubbish. I had only my bicycle for transporting it. I felt as if I was being punished and the world was against me. To add to the stress, Stan, a friend and dance partner of my mum's was dying. My mum couldn't face the hospital visits, nor could Stan's family be bothered to visit so it fell to me to be with him in his last week and hours. It brought back all the memories of my father's death and was an extra burden at a time I was extremely low. It took a few months before the studio was sold. Friends helped out. My music mentor Edward and his wife Judy gave me accommodation for a month whilst they were on vacation. I was put in charge of keeping an orchid alive. I'm not the world's best guardian of houseplants so I talked to it every day and begged it to stay alive until my friends returned. My estate agents also offered me accommodation in their house whilst they were away and I then moved on to look after a guinea pig for a few weeks. I must have got a good recommendation from the orchid owner! Unable to find a suitable house to take a recording studio, I moved in with my mother. I'd always thought that when a guy has to go back to his mum then he's hit a really tough patch.

Trying to revive a music career and grow a writing one from a dormer bungalow bedroom was a tremendous challenge amidst my emotional turmoil. I had no studio set up so couldn't do a music project even if one came in. Something else gnawed away at me too: my failure to get to Hollywood and work on studio movies. I wanted to work amongst my peers and be challenged by scoring a major movie. I knew my music was good enough for Hollywood since it had received favourable responses and had been plagiarised by a couple of big name composers out there, but somehow I never got the contacts or breaks even when I was in LA. *The Killing of John Lennon* film could have been my passport to Hollywood as it was nominated for a BAFTA award. If the film had won, it might have opened possibilities in LA – but it didn't. Personally and professionally I felt I'd hit rock bottom, but when you're down in the dumps you can either stay there or start to move the crap around and tunnel your way out. A year later a suitable house turned up and I moved to a quiet leafy green location close to the centre of Bristol. It became a safe haven where I could recover from the instability of previous years.

It was some time after my move that one of the cues, *Psychoanalysis*, a slow waltz from *The Killing of John Lennon* was picked up by a Los Angeles director. He grew attached to it and asked whether I'd compose music for his new movie. I was hopeful and excited. The screenplay arrived. It was a slasher-horror and extremely graphic in terms of violence. I was in two minds about it. I needed a calling card to get me into Hollywood and the film might have delivered that. A few colleagues advised it didn't matter about the genre or content of the film as my score would shine through and get me other films in LA. I read the script again, but on a meet with the director and producer at their office in LA, I came clean and said that in my heart of hearts I couldn't work with the material. *The Killing of John Lennon* (2007) album, on which that track is featured, was a timely cathartic project. I felt the album reinvented me as a composer and could possibly assist my renaissance. In my view, the album worked not only musically but conceptually and graphically. By having no photograph of me on the cover or in the booklet, the listener may have assumed the composer and conductor was a young one! Interestingly, it is mostly young people who have found the score stimulating and the oldies comment that they sit in the bath surrounded with tea lights with the score massaging their innermost psyche. In a good way! Suitable accolade came from a seventeen-year-old who approached me in a cinema,

'Excuse me, I've seen you give a talk on film music. Aren't you the composer of *The Killing of John Lennon* score?'

'Yes.'

'Oh man that is such a fucking awesome score.'

I returned home immediately to tell my fifteen-year-old son what this young man had said. My son, who had paid little attention to my orchestral achievements over the years, thought it was 'so cool.' Finally I'd received accolade from my own boy! In the eyes of the young I was now a cool composer. I felt as if I was on the next step of my journey as a composer albeit briefly – the film and album failed to secure any new work.

I turned to writing screenplays again. Two screenplays raised a smidgen of interest: a musical fantasy *Planet Pants* and a thriller *Obscura* written with director Vadim Jean. At this time, I became obsessed with the life of Darwin and bought every book I could find about him. I was interested in writing an opera including aspects of Darwin's life which many Darwin movies and TV series had omitted. I had a different take on the story and developed a treatment and synopsis as well as a condensed screenplay for a Los Angeles company — which came to nothing. There were funds available, however, via a scheme in London that funded art and science based projects. I decided to apply with my opera *Darwin — the Odyssey* and another Darwin based project set in the future, *2222*. The scheme required a scientific consultant to be attached to any proposal and I didn't know anyone. I searched the net and came across one of the world's greatest scientists, the Nobel laureate Frances Arnold. I pinged off an email thinking nothing ventured, nothing gained. A week later I had a reply. Frances said her two favourite things were 'opera and Darwin'! What a strike. She was on board.

The next step was to find a director for my opera. One night I happened to be at the Watershed arts venue in Bristol to see a new film by veteran and maverick director Ken Russell (1927–2011). I'd remembered the incredible output of his work including *Women in Love* (1969), *The Devils* (1971) and *Tommy* (1975). At the end of giving a talk about his current film, Ken's entourage and other media 'luvvies' were going on to an after party. Ken's chaperone, a PR person I knew, had other things to do so she asked if I'd take Ken along with me. It was a perfect opportunity to ask him whether he'd like to direct my film opera. He said he'd love to direct it. I wasn't even bothered whether it might have ended up in Russelleque style with Darwin and twenty-five naked nuns on a hallucinogenic sailing ship. In fact, that was what I was hoping for! Only three works were going to be made by the organisation putting up the funding. Both my Darwin projects made it to the final six but neither made it to the final three. That's showbiz! Sadly, sometime later, Ken died.

As I worked on my Darwin project I began to identify with Darwin's own questions about faith and his musings helped to smother the final fading ember of my Christianity. As the husband of a devout Christian, Darwin moved from a theist point of view to one of atheism. I found I was on the same trajectory. I was also deeply affected by a traumatic incident that challenged my faith and I rejected my evangelicalism — the belief that God could personally intervene in one's life or the lives of others. I exchanged evangelicalism for Theism, which accepts an intelligent designer who is active but doesn't personally intervene in our lives. From there I took the highway to non-belief. The struggle to declare myself as staunchly atheistic was difficult. I was still hanging on to a stray thread of Christianity. Furthermore, I loved challenging the apologetics of my Christian friends:

'Look. I know you regard God as sinless and he/she can't sin but here's a take on it. Humankind was supposedly made in God's image and humans are sinners – so does that mean there is a constituent of God that is sin? It would be great if that were so, that God is vulnerable and open to making mistakes. If it were so, I could accept a vulnerable God who makes errors and thus I could accept human suffering.'

Questions about meaning and purpose bugged me. I began to reframe my worldview and looked at life as a mirror of what happens in the life of stars. The seeds of star birth happen in the gas and dust clouds in our galaxy. The clouds remain dormant until an encounter with an exploding supernova or a passing star sets them in motion – a motion that is a trajectory to 'stardom'. This process in our universe reminded me of our chance encounters with experiences or people that often set us on our trajectories to whatever our personal stardoms might be. Stars, like all of us, have different stages of life. In a star's adolescence hydrogen fusion and energy from the star's core causes it to balloon. We also experience this ballooning of energy in our own adolescence. Some of the stars in our galaxy are pulsating stars. They maintain a balance of outward pressure from radiation alongside an inward pull of gravity that can throw the star into a period of instability. Sometimes the star can be ruled by pressure, sometimes by gravity. Metaphorically, it's not dissimilar to our own mental health issues as we tussle between the pressure of the world around us and the internal battles raging within us. When a star reaches its middle age, however, it becomes a red giant. The red giant shines with a constant brightness for perhaps billions of years until it eventually collapses –not unlike my glorious years in mid-life when I was creating one music score after another before my burnout. The star, however, has a second chance. It expands and contracts and re-expands, but this second expansion leads to disintegration as the star throws off layers which become some of the most beautiful sights in the universe: planetary nebulae. Out of disintegration, beauty and new purpose can be born. Perhaps I too could find a new purpose.

There are also stars that are superstars just like the 'stars' on Earth. These stars balloon into red supergiants but have a sudden ending. Perhaps the supergiants on Earth have over worked and over indulged or perhaps they've been unlucky and have ballooned at too great a rate? Such a star ends up as a supernova explosion. The gas, dust and other materials from supernovae and planetary nebulae can eventually combine with other materials to form new stars. Is this a model of what happens in life? Do we form new 'stars' by passing on what we once were? A legacy of our genes, knowledge and experience? Perhaps my director friend David Hopkins, with whom I worked on *Zastrozzi*, was right when he told me to be happy with the fact that 'you're simply stardust!' I can certainly see the pattern of star life in the universe as an imprint in my own life and the lives of others.

There is also a metaphorical pattern that resonates with me at a cellular level too. Cellular life has displayed a long running battle between pathogens and hosts. We still don't know whether viruses evolved before cells but the evolutionary process has been driven by viruses. A population affected by the virus in a pandemic either dies or adapts. Scientists who have identified all the proteins that interact with viruses have discovered adaptations occurred three times as frequently in virus-interacting proteins compared with other proteins. In a sense, viruses have shaped us. We wouldn't be where we are today without this ongoing battle with our ancient foe. I view this pattern of cell versus virus relationship as a metaphor for society. Although we do not wish to confront antagonistic or evil forces in society, those forces, like viruses, enable us to re-evaluate and develop greater resilience as well as new strategies. Such improvements may be in the psychological, interpersonal or communal realm and perhaps allow us to create a more robust society. Do bad things exist purely for good to overcome and prosper? I like to explore these questions but I believe good will always prosper even though our world and lives appear to have a pattern built on polarities which have been with us since the Big Bang. There are of course bad things to which we have given a helping hand: we've exploited animals and destroyed habitats, which has in turn contributed to climate breakdown.

As I worked hard to formulate a new belief system, I had to eradicate an echo of Christianity still reverberating in the back room of my psyche. This 'leftover' did its best to kindle guilt as I strove to find my way in the big wide world again. Franciscan friar and author Richard Rohr mentions in one of his talks that guilt is one of the worst aspects of Christianity. It spawns a certain negativism rather than creating a positive and happy faith. One is never good enough and always working to earn more points to be allowed 'into the kingdom.' In my new world of singleness, I would, for the first time in many years, be doing the opposite of what Christian doctrine taught. I would have to try out new partners, not simply in terms of psychological compatibility but sexually too. It was three years since I'd been intimate with anyone and I would now have to move on and dump any burden of guilt that held me back. I was certainly going to learn how to be naughty in the noughties and beyond.

Recording *Realms of the Russian Bear* in Moscow

Working on *Land of the Eagle*

Photoshoot for *Millennium March* album

Alien Empire session in Munich

With Prince Charles at the University of Bristol recording studio

A Radius of Curves world premiere

Dreamworks promo recording in Prague

Sketch of Martin by Nick Park

Performance in Dubai

Performing as Poet in Residence for Bristol 2015, European Green Capital

Green Poems for a Blue Planet performance in India

Performing in London for Triodos Bank

Portrait of Martin Kiszko by Martin Rose

I tentatively entered the world of online dating: a world where everybody loves walking their dogs, bungy jumping, sunsets, red wine, and an Indian takeaway on the sofa whilst watching box sets of American and Scandinavian TV dramas. Oh, and don't forget the 'fine dining'. The fine dining always troubled me as it's a crazy thing to put on a dating profile. *Everyone* enjoys fine dining! Yet I would suggest not everyone enjoys paying for it. On my dates I was usually the one who ended up paying for fine dining. It appeared that 'going dutch' had been thrown out of social etiquette a long time back. I was lucky, however, to date women from a variety of ethnic and cultural backgrounds. Some were kind and sensitive, some strong and demanding; some were quiet and introverted and some were bundles of energy. What each person requires from a relationship is obviously different and there were certainly surprises. One woman wanted, after two weeks of dating, to get married and have a child, another got me started on the *Karma Sutra*, another wanted me to swim naked in the sea at midnight beneath a full moon. It was magical. There were endless companions who craved coffee time conversations and one partner who appeared to enjoy only my friends, vacations and the events to which I took her — my emotional availability wasn't required. Some relationships were wonderfully spontaneous, igniting in a flash, only to die out in days — others had a spark which couldn't be kindled.

Once, when starting off on a coach journey from London to Bristol, I noticed a bohemian-looking woman boarding the bus. There were only two seats left on the coach and one was next to me. She walked the length of the coach and then turned back and sat down next to me. As the coach set off, she dived into conversation.

'You look like a musician.'

'I am.'

And so we continued chatting. She was on her way to an ayahuasca ceremony and asked me whether I would like to join her. I declined and replied with my usual mantra,

'I am my own drug.'

She was somewhat disappointed and tried to persuade me. Before the coach pulled into Bristol she took off her necklace which contained two blue agate stones. She removed one stone from its setting, gave it to me and kissed me goodbye.

My relationships fuelled a learning curve in how to navigate the worldviews of others or the annoying quirky things that cropped up in relationships. I found it difficult, however, to go into a relationship where physical looks weren't a priority. Friends told me personality was more important, but it never quite worked like that for me. The physical attraction had to come first. This was a throwback to my personal battle in dealing with aesthetics whether in my craft or in women. A close friend chastised me, 'Your problem,' she said, 'is dating beautiful women. Choose someone not for their looks.'

It was indeed a problem especially at social events when men took a fancy to my partner and would approach me and ask, 'Is she with you?'

Were they surprised I was lucky enough to date an attractive woman or was it a cruel jibe of 'you're not good enough for her'. The latter is how I often felt.

Equally problematic was why I couldn't continue relationships with the kind, sensitive, yet sexually timid women, but favoured the adventurous and unpredictable ones. Failure wasn't always because I was making the wrong choices. I had relationships where I met compatible lovers, but later learnt I was dating closet alcoholics or drug users. As a result of abuse due to their addictions, I ended those relationships. In one relationship that meant the world to me, I never received a spontaneous hug or embrace. My partner told me I was useless and asked me why I didn't have a six-pack like her ex-husband! Even though I gave all I had to her, I told myself that to give love and not have it reciprocated should be a signal to move on, but those are cruel words when you love a person with all your heart and hope they might one day fall in love with you.

Six-pack aside (though I did a reasonable job with my tum at the gym) I took encouragement for my physical attributes when a television production company approached me to be a hand model for a TV feature drama. I didn't realise my hands were in such good shape or I that could make money out of them! My hands were filmed in a couple of scenes where a celebrity actor had to leave the shoot for work in the US and wasn't available for a few close-ups of his hands. Amazingly, his costume ring fitted my ring finger perfectly and my hands were similar in shape and skin tone. As I was waiting for my scene, I watched a scene being filmed where the missing actor was supposed to be a bed with a beautiful woman. I thought it was going to be my lucky day when the director asked whether I'd also like to replace the star and shoot a scene naked in the bed with the actress. I agreed, but an hour later I was most disappointed to hear the scene was no longer necessary. Perhaps the crew decided they didn't want to be subjected to my physique!

There were occasional flickers of hope for new romance. I was once standing on the platform at Belsize Park Underground. A woman approached and stood next to me. It was her gloves that first caught my eye. They were chic, black, and with exquisitely tied bows. For some reason I felt a magnetic pull to this lady. The train arrived jam-packed. The carriage doors opened and we both spotted the only two vacant seats. They were together and we rushed for them. She made it to one but I didn't get the other. I ended up stepping on her toe as I stood in front of her. There was, I thought, an awkward glance that hid a smile and perhaps a coy connection. After a while a seat became free opposite her. I sat and watched her through the gap between standing commuters. She removed her gloves to fiddle with her mobile, and as the train suddenly pulled into Charing Cross, she got up and left. Another woman boarded the train and sat in the exact same seat. At her feet I noticed a pair of gloves. I hesitated before I made my move. Was it the same pair of chic black gloves or a different pair dropped by the new passenger? She bent down, picked them up and threw them in the tray behind her. I immediately knew they were the gloves that belonged to *my* lady. I got up, grabbed them, and headed for the exit in the hope I could meet the Belsize Park lady on the platform. But the doors closed and the train sped on to Goodge Street.

I sat down again and considered a plan. I assumed the lady on whom I bestowed my secret love had reached the stairs at Charing Cross, realised her gloves were gone, and turned back to see if she'd dropped them on the platform. In the time it would take her to assess her loss and begin a search, I would arrive at Goodge Street, cross to the opposite platform and take a train back to Charing Cross and alight to find her looking for her gloves. At Charing Cross I looked everywhere along the platform and the stairs. She wasn't there. At the station's exit I found a member of staff. Before handing the gloves over as lost property, I had another idea. I took one of my business cards, rolled it up, and inserted it into the middle finger of one of the gloves. What a start of a love story that would be: if she collected them from lost property and found my card. I checked my answerphone messages every day but nothing from her came my way. Many others would not have pursued this idle whim. Yet why live with the fantasy as if it is an imaginary scene from a film when there's a possibility of living it out? I was pleased to have acted on that 'glove story' romance but I was sad the events had not brought love back into my life. I had to put all my relationship experiences down to bad luck whatever that is.

Amidst the relationship flux, I looked for escape and any new opportunities at the Cannes Film Festival. It was the year there was a guy wandering around the festival with a small box covering one ear. On the box were two words: 'bullshit protector.' Extremely on point I thought. It's often the case that there are people who have created nothing and who pose as directors and producers. The business cards they hand out don't mean a thing when you've checked out on the net what they've actually made. However, we all have to sell ourselves somehow. It was also the year my film producer friend Luke Walton hit Cannes. Unfortunately I introduced him to too many parties, got myself sozzled on G&Ts and ended up pushing him into a viewing theatre to watch a movie. I could barely stand up, but I saw a spare seat on the front row, stumbled in front of everyone's view, slumped in the seat, fell asleep, and awoke to applause on the final credit of the film. That year was also the year of an almighty thunderstorm. It rained for a week and my boots were so wet they were stuffed with newspaper every night. I knew all those magazines I was given in the Cannes festival bag would be useful! It was during one of those flash storms that I ran for shelter to a pavilion in the festival village. It was the Thai pavilion, one of the smallest but the closest for cover. The pavilion was packed and I found myself pressed up against a glamorous looking lady in large sunglasses and a leopard-skin jacket. It was somewhat embarrassing being so close to her as her partner was right next to me, but we got talking. She introduced herself as Shere. The conversation went everywhere: the arts, film, writing, relationships, hopes, dreams, you name it. We got on like a house on fire. As the storm subsided and the crowd began to disperse, the lady's partner Paul turned to me and said,

'Do you know who you've been talking to?'

I shook my head.

'This is Shere Hite.'

The penny started to drop. It was the famous sex educator and feminist Shere Hite (1942–2020). As we left the pavilion, Shere asked whether I'd be interested in meeting her in London and I agreed. Who wouldn't want to meet up with one of the world's greatest sexologists and advocates for readdressing the consensus on women's sexuality? I knew it was going to be a great meet and it didn't disappoint.

We met for lunch in the restaurant at BAFTA. After the hello and the ordering of a drink, Shere began the conversation with this question,

'So tell me Martin, what do you think about clitoral stimulation?'

I'm used to taking any kind of question from anyone and I knew what she was probing for but my answer was,

'I like it.'

Shere's career trajectory was an extraordinary one: top fashion model to a women's movement activist. She had posed as a model for *Playboy* and for a well known Olivetti typewriter advertisement which later appeared in the magazine and carried the strapline, 'The typewriter so smart, she doesn't have to be.' Feminists in the USA rose up in protest against the ad and Shere joined in. Shere's legacy as a sex educator lies in the pioneering work she did in organising a survey of American women which concluded seventy percent of women do not have orgasms purely as a result of penetration. The results of the research showed women achieved orgasms much easier through clitoral stimulation. Earlier work by sexologists suggested orgasm was mainly reached as a result of penetration. If not, it was deemed to be a sign of a sexually dysfunctional female. The results of Shere's research became her first book. *The Hite Report* (1976) was the first in depth piece of scientific analysis written by a woman to concentrate on women's sexuality and re-defined our understanding of the female sexual experience. The book has sold over forty-eight million copies and was followed by *The Hite Report on Male Sexuality* (1981) and *The Hite Report on the Family* (1994). Seen as a threat to the male dominated media and men's perception of female sexuality, Shere found her character assassinated by the media and was closely watched by the FBI and the CIA. In fear of losing her life, she fled America, gave up her US citizenship, lived in Paris and finally settled in London.

At our lunchtime conversation, Shere discussed many aspects of sexuality and we got talking about our backgrounds both in terms of sexuality and family life. She asked me whether I'd be interested in writing a screenplay about her life. For many years, along with her partner Paul, it was something we hoped to realise but never got to start. One weekend, when Shere and Paul came to stay with me in Bristol, Shere gave me copies of *The Hite Report*. Over Sunday breakfast I asked her to sign the first page of *The Hite Report on Male Sexuality* and she wrote, 'For Martin, love, Shere Hite. THANKS FOR LAST NIGHT. She meant, of course, our wonderful evening of conversation and music, but the words read like an innuendo and I was very pleased to receive that 'double entendre' from a famous sexologist! It was unfortunate when a few years later such a wonderful woman was struck down with a degenerative brain disease that left her incapable of communicating. At one point, I went to visit her in hospital in London and played my clarinet for her. Although she had been given around six months to live, Paul decided to take her out of hospital and care for her with help from his friend Bill. The few more years she lived were a testament to their love and commitment.

There are always fascinating people at Cannes. One year, I bumped into film festival producers Rosana Golden and Dean Bentley. They asked me to be a judge at the Angel Film Awards at the Monaco Film Festival. Not only did I judge but I wrote linking script for the presenter of the awards. I knew one of my favourite singer-songwriters from the sixties and seventies would be there too. Donovan had reached fame with hits such as *Mellow Yellow* (1966), *Hurdy Gurdy Man* (1968), and *Jennifer Juniper* (1968). I made sure I took my EP of *Jennifer Juniper*, bought in 1968, along with me and got Donavan to sign it. Another year, whilst chatting in the Carlton hotel bar with one of my best friends *One Love* (2003) producer Shelaagh Ferrell and a couple of friends, I could feel someone pushing me. I hate pushy and obnoxious people elbowing me around bar areas and tried to ignore it, but gradually the pressure increased and my guests were feeling it too. I was getting annoyed. At the point we were being shunted forwards I turned around to find a guy with his face almost in mine. I recognised him from somewhere but just couldn't place him. Behind him were a line of security guards pushing, and behind them was the general public giving everyone a good shove. It appeared I was the person they needed to push past. I looked at the guy again and then opened my arms towards him in annoyance exclaiming,

'So what's all your pushing about?'

At that point the facial recognition part of my memory kicked into play and I realised I was talking to film director Quentin Tarantino. The security guards pushed him through my group of guests. If only I'd been quicker off the mark at recognising Quentin. I would have introduced him to my music and asked for a meet!

13

Poetry in Motion

Welcome greenies, non-greenies and inbetweenies,
Welcome all those who have recycled your Lamborghinis,
Welcome those of you toasting your new biofuels with a martini,
Welcome all of you hippies with holes in your jeanies,
Welcome all of you fans of organic beanies,
Welcome you chilled classic fans of Boccherini, Puccini, Rossini, Paganini,
Welcome those of you selling off your Giovanni Bellinis,
To sustainably invest for your future bambini,
Welcome all of you who've given up your lattes and paninis
To fit into your boxers and your bikinis,
Welcome all of you who've shed pounds of fettucine and linguini,
To keep your butts and your tums teeny and weeny,
Welcome all you green warriors with the heart of an eco-Athene,
Welcome those who'd like to see the green genie
Grant a wish to set the world free like a Houdini,
From the exploitation of those naughty non-greenies.
You know what I meanie?
That's the best I can do rhyming with greenie!

It's this poem I use to open all my eco-poetry shows or events and it gives me great joy to receive positive feedback and laughter from greenies, non-greenies and inbetweenies alike. But the modulation from music to becoming a professional eco-poet was accidental. That doesn't mean I tripped over the kerb, fell, and suddenly I was a professional poet. It was an accident always about to happen and it happened one day in 2009 when there was a different kind of call to the ones

I'd been used to when directors and producers phoned to commission a score. This other call was either from within or from out of the air. I was working on a writing project when out of nowhere the words *Green Poems for a Blue Planet* popped into my head. All of us have those times when thoughts meander through our minds: what we might do or what ideas or dreams we have. Often a thought is fleeting and in a split second is discarded. We fail, I believe, to recognise when we are perhaps being prompted to take note and receive what is offered. My call was a pivotal moment. I had an immediate intuition those words were of relevance and should be grasped and used. This was the seed of my career as a professional poet and it chose me. I wrote the words down. I knew they had meaning.

I returned to the words a couple of weeks later. I decided to read up on environmental topics and write poetry about the challenges our planet was facing. Over a period of a year, I spent my evenings away from the temptations of TV or the net and ended up writing a poem every week about an issue I knew little about. I guess I was green behind the ears at being green! It was a self-education. I'd grown up with a father who had inspired me to connect with nature and I had a background in working in natural history films, but at the start of my green poems journey in no way did I regard myself as an eco-warrior. I saw myself as an eco-pilgrim who was 'greening up.' I hoped that once I'd committed these subjects to poetry, my own children would also find it useful to read about serious topics in an accessible and light-hearted manner. Although the state of the planet is not a laughing matter, there's ample room for the eco-chuckle and it's a very welcome injection to lift us from the doom-laden eco agenda where our lives are heavy with the burdens of the world. Even though the content of what was to become my first book, *Green Poems for a Blue Planet*, has a serious message, the garments it wears are a smirk, a smile, entertainment and laughter. So, a year later I had fifty-six green poems and named the collection *Green Poems for a Blue Planet*!

Many of the poems were written whilst I was out and about. I'd be struck by something and would write on any piece of paper that came to hand. My poem *Fruit Miles* started its life on the back of a supermarket receipt after shopping for fruit and veg. Out of the thirty or so fruits on display, only one came from the UK: Cox's apples. My poem *Takeaway Carbon* was dreamt up as I watched skateboarders skating to school. It prompted me to write about how we can all travel around in different ways without using a car. I enjoy writing my poems on junk that will either be recycled or land-filled and wrote *Takeaway Carbon* on the back of my son's old skateboard. Once I'd read about how energy could be created from animal or human poo, I couldn't resist writing my poem *Poo Power* which has become a hit worldwide with children in schools and at festivals. Every time I give a live reading of the poem, the thought of generating power from poo seldom leaves the mind's eye of the audience, and what's more they remember it! The poem has a 'poo power salute' which children shout out at the end of its performance, but teachers are somewhat jaded by hearing the salute shouted in school corridors months after I've left. But this is the power of poetry: its ability to create a 'snapshot' of an idea or scenario; the encapsulation of an all-encompassing thought or vision into a succinct piece. Poems are like postcard or text messages that a reader or hearer often remembers. Poems are also portable, easily carried around in the brain and can be verbalised in full at a moment's notice.

The process of writing a poem is very satisfying as a literary, mathematical and aesthetic challenge. First I have to be moved by something: an event, a person, an emotion, a notion. It might simply be a thought triggered by a walk during which I haven't seen many butterflies. I'll ask myself, 'Why are so many butterflies losing their habitats? That's not right! I know, I'll write a poem about it. They can't do it themselves can they? And I'm sure they'd like to complain somehow.' Once I have my subject, I experiment with the world in which the poem will be set. For example, with my poem *The Board of Butterflies at the Annual Moth Meeting* I'd asked myself whether the poem should describe the loss of habitats or should the butterflies be anthropomorphised and tell their story as we might? Sometimes I think laterally and might choose an approach which is the opposite of what might seem the way forward. I'm fascinated by the approach of using material which I've initially rejected whether it is an initial idea or a draft. In terms of the butterfly poem I imagined the butterflies as if they were trade unionists demanding their rights at a meeting! Next, I usually think about structure. Will the poem be a ballad, a villanelle, a kyrielle, a sestina? Rhythm and pace are important considerations too. On the whole that's easy as I've spent my life with all that stuff going on inside me as a musician. It's intuitive. Then it's a case of deciding on any rhyming scheme. A poetic structure often dictates a metre and rhyme so one must follow that form. Once the skeletal structure of the poem is on the page, often with words still missing from stanzas, I concentrate on the words I want to use. I often choose words because of their aesthetic. I like the way they look alongside others in a line, the way they balance the length or sound of other words or perhaps deliberately unbalance them — like washing on a clothes line. I'm always tinkering and honing even when I think I've nailed the poem.

So, I'd written the collection, but I had no idea how it might find its way in the world. I was now busy getting my new home together and the days seemed full with builders, plumbers, and furniture deliveries. As an attempt to kick life back into my music career, I'd booked to go to Los Angeles to meet music executives at film studios and music synchronisation agencies. I'd put together a list of directors and producers I wanted to meet. This meant a lot of cold call emails and telephone calls but I managed to set up a fantastic list of people who would meet me or let me down at the last minute. That's typical of the industry. I once took a train journey from Bristol to London for a meet with a BBC director who cancelled the meet as my train was pulling into Paddington Station. I had to turn round and go home because they had someone more important to see. My plan for the LA trip also involved adding a week in New York. Scientist Frances Arnold, who had come on board my *Darwin – the Odyssey* project, was working there and was happy to meet me for the first time. I was full of great expectations for the trip. We met on W.55th Street at restaurant *Serafina*, which coincidentally shared the same name as my eldest daughter. We sat down at a table outside for brunch and talked music, science, Darwin, children, and poetry. I told Frances about *Green Poems for a Blue Planet* and about how I believed in the power of poetry to help save the planet. There and then, I asked whether I could perform a few poems for her on the sidewalk. I stood up and performed some of my favourites. Three poems later, Frances laughed, applauded, and invited me to her home in Los Angeles to perform for an invited audience. I gratefully accepted and wondered what new opportunities might emerge.

The flight from New York to Los Angeles was full except for one vacant seat next to me. For the first time in my flying history I felt the great god of empty airline seats had finally heard my prayers. No longer would I have to face someone falling asleep on me, nudging me or endlessly squeezing past to go to the loo. Everyone was seated and I took a sigh of relief as I saw the cabin door was about to close. I relished the thought of that empty seat until a late passenger suddenly boarded. I looked down the aisle to see who it was. She was beautiful. I looked behind me and down the plane to double-check the seat alongside me was the only free one. Could my luck be in? It was indeed. I knew the late passenger was going to be sitting next to me. Maybe there was a god after all. The plane took off. My travelling companion soon booted up her laptop and was busily typing away. I was re-reading Flaubert's novel *A Sentimental Education*. I wondered whether there would be an opportunity to speak to my neighbour, but she seemed totally focussed and engrossed. I knew I had to act or the opportunity would be lost. As I reached one of my favourite romantic paragraphs in the novel, I turned to her and said, 'Excuse me. I'm reading a French novel, Flaubert's *A Sentimental Education*, and have come to one of my favourite paragraphs. May I read it to you?'

I don't know how I managed to pluck up the courage but have always believed there is no point in imagining what could have been. Best live out the fantasy as long as it's legal! She broke off from her typing.

'Yes, please do.'

After I read the passage we chatted all the way from New York to LA. She was a film director, and on arriving at LAX we exchanged cards and agreed to meet up in town. A couple of emails later we still hadn't managed to arrange a date. I thought that was the end of it until I was returning from North of the city on Halloween to attend a party with friends.

My mobile rang. It was her. She had two tickets for the theatre that evening and asked whether I'd join her. Idiot I then was, I said no. Why? For some reason which goes back to my needy 'only child mindset' of wishing to be loyal to friends and for them to reciprocate the same, I felt I couldn't let down the friends who had invited me to their party. In terms of forging any companionship with my lady friend, the opportunity was lost. Worse still, the Halloween party was dull and I went home early. I truly learned a lesson and realised my friends would have been pleased for me to have gone out on a date rather than be with them. I never made the same mistake again.

My performance in LA created momentum and back in the UK I was fired up to push on with the project. If it was to become a book it would be the world's first collection of ecopoems for children. It needed great illustrations and I knew exactly whose arm I was going to twist. *Wallace and Gromit* animator and director Nick Park had been a friend for many years though I knew it was still going to be difficult to get such a busy person on board. I hoped to broach the subject at one of our evening meets during which we usually watched a movie and gave its narrative a 'story analysis beating'. Nick and I often talked for hours about narrative structure. The architecture of a screenplay, the character arc, and the emotional beats of the drama are cornerstones in creating a solid story. Screenwriters use various models of structure on which they base their stories. There is the eight-part sequence structure based on the ten-minute-long film reels that made up a feature film in the early days of cinema. There is also 'displaced narrative' where the story is not told in chronological order. By far the most popular approach evident in most feature films and TV drama is three act structure based on the Aristotelian principles of story structure described in Aristotle's *Poetics*, the earliest surviving work of dramatic and literary theory. Three act structure involves using the first act to set up what is often referred to as the protagonist's 'ordinary world'. This is the world in which he or she has grown up, lives in or works in. Here, we learn something of the 'backstory' of our protagonist. Usually, not far into the first act is what is known as an 'inciting incident'. This is an incident that will irrevocably change the character's life and provoke an audience to question how the protagonist will cope. It could be a loss of job, a divorce, a disease, an injury or a death threat, indeed anything whether internal or external. At the end of act one the protagonist must make a decision often known as the 'call to adventure' and the call is usually placed at the point of the character standing on the threshold of what is his or her ordinary world and the 'special world' of act two.

Act two worlds are places where protagonists meet allies and enemies, obstacles, re-evaluate their aims or ambitions (known as the 'midpoint' of the film) and experience loss and come close to death. The protagonist's move into the special world is as a hero who makes his own decision to take on the new world or as a 'reluctant hero' in which case he is guided into the special world by a mentor. At the end of act two the protagonist has usually exhausted his physical and mental resources. To move into act three, the character must search inner reserves and draw strength to endure a descent to where a climactic battle will be fought with the antagonist. The result of this climactic scene answers the audience's question asked at the inciting incident at the film's opening: can the protagonist survive and destroy the antagonist whether that antagonist is an internal or external force? Act three is the journey home to the protagonist's ordinary world. But the rules of narrative structure dictate the character must have experienced an epiphany, a realisation of what it is he or she really required to change their life. The character must also experience an apotheosis. This isn't the literal biblical definition of the word meaning 'a transformation into becoming godlike', but it is a recognition witnessed by the protagonist's ordinary world community that the character has been truly transformed by his journey and has returned with a reward: treasure, a relationship, a battle won or a mind restored. Most movies follow this template. Not only would Nick and I rattle on about what makes good story and where these story beats fall in a film, but it was often put into good practice in helping young filmmakers develop their projects. For a few years Nick and I worked at Pinewood Studios with actors David Suchet and David Oyelowo *OBE* and producers Mark Blaney and Jackie Sheppard. We were all 'story judges' looking for the best short film idea on producer Luke Walton's *The Pitch*, an annual film competition which gave one winning filmmaker the opportunity to make a short film and present their finished work to Hollywood producers.

So, it was after one of those movie narrative structure conversations with Nick that I finally raised the question of the illustrations for *Green Poems for a Blue Planet*. I used my best opener and told him the world would end or there would be a significant environmental catastrophe if he didn't illustrate the book! But then I told him all about the poems and read a few. Nick was excited about the ethos of the work and especially that it conveyed its message with humour. Once he agreed, I initially asked for a cover illustration plus a few for the inside. Nick got captivated by the characters in the poems and enthusiastically drew many more illustrations than I could have wished for including one of my favourites: Leo. P. Ardseal, a Leopard seal who writes a letter of complaint about a 500 billion ton ice shelf falling on his head. On the strength of the poems, illustrations and the performance in LA everything was lined up to secure book layout artist Simon Bishop and publisher John Sansom of *Redcliffe Press*.

The first proper outing of the book came swiftly. Nick and I were invited to be interviewed on one of the UK's flagship children's programmes *Blue Peter*. The producer asked whether I'd perform a poem to complement their on line green poems poetry competition. I had no intention whatsoever of becoming a performer! I looked around for a young actor to perform my work but there were only a few days before filming the item at BBC TV Centre in London. Before I knew it, I was in make-up, shaking with nerves, and about to perform on a programme me and all child-dom had watched for many years. I came away thinking 'well, I'm never going to do that again,' only to be offered, soon after, a performance to a live audience on BBC Radio Four and a live full-length performance at the Ilkley Literature Festival. Again, I wondered who I could find to take my place, but there was no time to scout around for talent. As I waited in the wings to go on stage, I was super nervous. Yet I grew to love performing poetry with physical vigour — not like a daisy drooped over a book. My show at Ilkley was high energy and I somehow made it through the forty-five minutes stand-up and escaped backstage. Afterwards, someone came up to me from the audience, complimented me on all my on stage gesticulations and movement, and asked where I'd trained.

'Nowhere,' I said. 'It's just me. How I perform is just me.'

'It's great,' they continued, 'so you must be the UK's Green Poet?'

Again, as when the title of my book first came to me from the ether, those words appeared imbued with what I believed to be meaning and significance. I accepted the appellation with a wink and a dose of tongue in cheek humour and have continued to use the title.

I began to gain confidence in growing what was becoming an environmental campaign. Despite my nerves, I knew I'd have to embrace the performance element and run with it. Another early performance for organisation *Climateworks* was at the Arnolfini in Bristol. An eminent panel of scientists and eco-commentators was set up to be grilled by the audience. My job was to open and close the proceedings with green mirth. It went well, but after my opening performance I was surprised when I was asked to join the panel. I was no expert but sat alongside the others. The first question from the audience was about population growth. There didn't appear to be a population expert on the panel so the chairperson asked me to respond. I felt that 'ouch' moment followed by perspiration and a galloping heart. I didn't know what to say but I started by saying I was the least qualified to reply as I had three children! I then fumbled through my memory banks for something I'd heard Sir David Attenborough say about population growth. I think I just about got away with putting a short answer together and wished the ground had swallowed me up. At least that would be one less member of the population. About twenty minutes later someone else in the audience asked a question about population numbers. It was as if the chairperson was saying, 'now let's go to our resident population expert', as unfortunately the question was again directed to me. This time I was well out of my depth.

One of the biggest challenges was memorising around twenty-five poems for a show. That doesn't seem too arduous a task, but when nearly all of your content is rhyme there are many opportunities to come unstuck. There's no prompt, no back up, and if a word is forgotten at the end of a line, any word can't be used as a replacement. The chance of finding a new rhyming word that makes sense of the preceding line is impossible. Yet somehow I managed to develop my memory and always ended my show with my thirty-five stanza audience participatory poem *Around the World in Eighty Ways*. Writing poetry that keeps the audience awake and waiting for the next one was always a challenge in terms of the poem's content, structure, and its delivery whether solo or participatory. Eco topics are often overly repeated, well worn, and become 'old hat', an old hat that badly needs recycling into something that throws a few unexpected punches. We require a wake-up call from eco-fatigue. At one festival I gave the same performance slot at 2pm over two days. On the second day a young boy turned up again and was seated well before the start of my performance. He'd returned to hear one of the poems he'd heard the day before. It's essential to keep the content accessible, entertaining and engaging in the hope they come back for more.

Invitations to perform came in thick and fast especially after the publication of my second book *Verse for the Earth*. I performed at schools, on radio, business events, award ceremonies, arts festivals, charity events, private dinners, and on the street. The campaign began to touch hearts and minds. It was emotions that so urgently required a prompt since the endless streams of dense and arid factual information on ecological issues can often make us bury our heads in the sand. We're often so busy keeping our own brick-and-mortar homes in order that we forget about our most important home. Our relationship with nature must be rebuilt through a genuine desire and commitment to love our planet. Whenever I toured my show, people young or old would always ask the same question,

'What else can we do to save our planet?'

My answer was simple.

'Do you know what it feels like to love a parent, a sibling, a child, a devoted pet?'

The answer was, 'yes'.

'Then you must feel that love for planet Earth. It's only through an emotional connection that we will want to care for our planet. Instead of an obsession with control, we must grow an authentic relationship with nature.'

It was William Wordsworth who said, 'Nature never did betray the heart that loved her.'

It was the work of the British romantic poets in the late eighteenth and early nineteenth century that inspired me to keep writing and continue performing my show. Poets William Wordsworth (1770–1850), Percy Bysshe Shelley (1792–1822), and John Keats (1795–1821) explored the countryside and reflected on nature. When city dwellers read their poetry, they too were able to connect with and begin to explore nature. Similarly, I hoped my poetry might encourage readers to reflect on how we can protect our environment. This will encourage a generation to engage with nature and help others reframe their attitudes about how we treat the planet and its creatures. *Green Poems for a Blue Planet* is about planting seeds in readers and listeners. It allows them to be entertained and to go away and consider what contributions they might make in helping to achieve a sustainable world. I am simply a prompter sowing seed for successive generations and providing a much needed prompt for our current one.

It wasn't only the romantic poets who were pioneers in prompting social change. Poets throughout the ages have been protestors and revolutionaries. They've often represented the voice of the oppressed, campaigned for change and have spoken the truth before anyone else dare speak out. They have imagined new worlds and possibilities. Messages, morals or lessons relating to human flaws were, of course, prominent in ancient Greek poetry relating to mythical adventures of the gods and the heroic deeds of humans. The Greek slave Aesop also sought to communicate lessons about life through his fables. Further down the centuries we have the debating poems of the medieval period. In the last few hundred years there have been remarkable poems of vision and social protest. The poem *Protest* by Emma Wheeler Wilcox (1850–1919) reminds us that we sin when we stay silent rather than protest. *The Man with the Hoe* by poet Edward Markham (1852–1940) discusses the exploitation of labourers in the USA at a time they had few rights and little protection. Carl Sandburg's (1878–1967) 1922 poem *The Mayor of Gary* contrasted workers in Gary, Indiana, who worked twelve hour days seven days a week to the Mayor of Gary who always had time for a shampoo and a shave.

The Beat Generation, a literary movement of the 1960s, which grew alongside the American civil rights movement, also fanned the flame of revolution as it heralded the demand for greater human rights. Amongst the most powerful Beat poems penned was Nikki Giovanni's *My Poem*. The poem is resolute and defiant in proclaiming that whatever is metered out to her by the police, the army or the government, it will not stop the revolution. There is not only power in the poet's vision but a change of circumstance. The passage of time or new worldviews can often give poetry another power — the power of irony. The poem *The New Colossus*, a Petrarchan sonnet, was written by Emma Lazurus (1849–1887) for an auction of art and literary works to fund the building of the pedestal for the Statue of Liberty. A plaque bearing the text was mounted on the pedestal in 1903 in memory of Lazurus. The poem mentions the statue as the 'mother of exiles' who welcomes the 'huddled masses' to her shores. The current political climate in the USA with regard to immigration policy now breathes a different ironic meaning into the poem and reminds us of the faults and prejudices of policy makers. This is the power of poetry! It was the poet Percy Bysshe Shelley who said, 'poets are the unacknowledged legislators of the world.' This is a maxim I embrace.

In a similar vein to those trailblazing protestors and campaigners, I hoped my *Green Poems for a Blue Planet* show would become a positive force in encouraging, along with other environmentalists, an eco revolution. It wasn't too long before new opportunities emerged for other performances for larger audiences at prestigious venues: the Eden Project in Cornwall, the Natural History Museum in London, and Latitude Festival. Producer Adam Glen also came on board to create *Green Poems for a Blue Planet* 'poemprints' which were sold at events. He also arranged for me to give performances and workshops on the Isle of Man and to work with school children in Devon on a poetry project on which I encouraged children to write their poetry on junk. I like to write on plastic bags, plastic bottles, old skateboards, used greetings cards and even old fish and chips paper — almost anything. The children did the same with items connected to issues with which they were concerned. They wrote on plastics, litter, junk, and even banana skins and nappies. We exhibited their work as a gallery exhibition at the Plough Arts Centre, Great Torrington.

There were also wonderful opportunities to work with the ethical bank Triodos and with Richard Collins of Ecobrand on the Green Apple Awards Ceremony and the International CSR Excellence Awards Ceremony at The Crystal and at RADA, London. My work with charity WaterAid was especially rewarding. I performed for young people at different UK Water Authority venues and ran an international poetry competition with the charity which reached more than a million people, inspired young writers, and spread awareness about the water crisis and WaterAid's work. I was especially pleased to perform at the book launch of one of my friends, Polly Higgins (1968-2019), who was known as Earth's lawyer. Polly lobbied the United Nations Law Commission to recognise ecocide as an international crime. She wished to create an international law that would hold business executives and governments accountable and criminally liable for the environmental harm they cause. Sadly her work was cut short by her death but her organisation Stop Ecocide, co-founded with environmental activist Jojo Mehta, continues this important mission.

One of the most significant fillips for the *Green Poems for a Blue Planet* campaign was my year as Resident Green Poet for Bristol 2015 European Green Capital. Bristol became the UK's first ever European Green Capital in recognition of what its citizens achieved in working towards a healthier, happier, and more sustainable city. My role was to write poetry about environmental issues and perform eco-poems at city events, usually alongside Mayor George Ferguson. At the opening ceremony for the year I gave a rallying call for green endeavour with my poem *Big Gap* which looked at how we might bridge the gap between our green intentions and our green actions. It compared that gap to the one across Bristol's Avon Gorge between Clifton and Leigh Woods — a gap engineer Isambard Kingdom Brunel closed with the construction of the Clifton Suspension Bridge, completed in 1864. I also took to the streets with poetry. In a performance in Bristol's Millennium Square, I dressed as a medieval poet and had a large red and white warning road sign at my side: DANGER — POET AT WORK. It was also wonderful to ride my green bicycle around the streets, stop pedestrians and engage them with on the spot poetry.

The year was also the one in which Aardman Animation produced their *Shaun the Sheep* trail in Bristol and London. The trail's producers decided to include a *Green Poems for a Blue Planet* Shaun the Sheep decorated with my poetry and Nick Park's illustrations. The sculpture was placed on Bristol's waterfront and encouraged visitors to bring out their inner eco warriors! I was also starting work at this time on *King Frank and the Knights of the Ecoquest*, a ten-thousand-word poem in rhyming couplets which would become the world's first eco epic poem. I began writing the work whilst Poet in Residence for *Frank Water*, a Bristol based charity which has worked on water issues for ten years across six states in India. Their work has enabled nearly 360,000 people across three hundred and eighty-six communities to have access to safe water and sanitation. The opening act of the poem is based on the experience of the charity's founder Katie Alcott MBE who founded *Frank Water* after contracting dysentery from drinking dirty water in India.

Green Poems for a Blue Planet was now attracting international attention and invitations came in to perform at overseas festivals or events: three times in India, in Malta, China, and in Dubai. My first trip was to Mumbai to perform at a literature festival at the National Centre for Performing Arts. I arrived at my accommodation at the Royal Bombay Yacht Club overlooking the waterfront. The first morning I went straight out to explore the magnificent *Gateway of India* arch directly opposite. On my way back, a 'holy man' stopped me and wished to give me a blessing. I stopped. He promptly tied a string bracelet around my wrist and painted a red bindi dot on my forehead. He then asked for a fistful of rupees. I had several meetings that day with people connected to the festival and also a business lunch at a restaurant. I'd forgotten I was wearing sunscreen and wasn't aware the red paint had smudged with sweat and lotion to create what I only noticed at the end of the day: a movie make-up artist's dream face-paint job — a Pulp Fictionesque splattered gunshot entry wound on my forehead! Not one person throughout the whole day mentioned it. They were probably having a good laugh behind my back. My first performance in Mumbai went down well. Festival goers even asked whether it could be repeated the next day.

My second trip to India was again to Mumbai and onwards to the Bookaroo Literature Festival in Pune where I performed for thousands of children who were enthusiastic about how to save our planet. My third visit was to the Neev Literature Festival in Bangalore to give performances, interviews, and take part in panel discussions. The festival is the brainchild of Neev Academy's founder Kavita Gupta Sabharwal, a pioneering educationalist who, frustrated with the state of pre-schools in India and unable to find education for her own children, started her own preschool in 2005. Kavita's remarkable vision expanded into five preschools and one academy campus employing over two hundred teaching professionals. Following the success of the poetry in India, an invitation from the Bookworm Literature Festival in China arrived. I was booked to give festival performances as well as performances and workshops in schools. One of the most magical moments was climbing the steps up to the Great Wall of China and giving an interview to camera at the top. It was a beautiful spring day with the bloom of early blossoms. Within moments, a wind whipped up and blew petals through the air. Exactly on cue with that shower of pink, snowflakes began to fall. Ten minutes later it was as if someone had suddenly turned a page back to a beautiful spring day.

The next invitation took me to the Emirates Literature Festival in Dubai. My programme included performances, interviews, panel participation, and the judging of poetry writing and performance competitions. A highlight was meeting one of my natural history icons, primatologist and anthropologist Dame Jane

Goodall. Jane is best known for her sixty-year study of social and family interactions of wild chimpanzees in Tanzania. I saw her reading over her lecture notes for a talk in New York and plucked up the courage to interrupt and introduce myself. It was fantastic to hear about her Roots and Shoots organisation which brings together youth from preschool to university age to work on environmental, conservation, and humanitarian issues. There was also time for sightseeing. One day I joined a festival excursion to the *Burg Khalifa*, which at 829.8 metres is the tallest building in the world. On the way up I was privileged to share conversation with one of the world's greatest mountaineers, Sir Chris Bonington, whose remarkable career included nineteen expeditions to the Himalayas and four to Mount Everest. I mentioned to him I could now brag to friends that I'd made a north-face ascent of the *Burg Khalifa* with Sir Chris Bonington! As for ascents, I hope *Green Poems for a Blue Planet* will continue to make its ascent as a campaign which will help a new generation to understand and grasp the environmental challenges ahead and will encourage a search for solutions that can create a sustainable future for all.

I arrived back in the UK to find a wonderful invitation to perform at the Royal Albert Hall and at a festival in Yorkshire. There was also the opportunity to write a poem for Voices of Future Generations (Arabia), a unique writing initiative under the patronage of UNESCO and which was created to promote sustainability and the UN convention on the rights of the child. My eco-poem *The Arabian Horse (The Thousand and Second Tale from the Arabian Nights)* explored the attributes of the Arabian horse and the relationship between a king and his stallion. Another exciting project was my 'pipe poems' project. I'd been developing it with James Sterling, Communications, Engagement and Partnership Manager for Bristol City Council's Energy Service. Our project fell under the banner of Bristol's City Leap scheme which planned to make Bristol the UK's first carbon neutral city. Part of the scheme involved the laying of a new network of underground pipes to deliver low-carbon heat and energy across the city. I suggested etching my specially commissioned eco-poem *Made in Bristol* onto one of the underground pipes that would be made visible to the public. It would also celebrate the opening of the heat network.

14

Breast-Hoard

In my poetry workshops I often work with a short verse form known as the kenning. The kenning is usually a one-line metaphor. I also like to write extended kennings of perhaps two or more lines. The kenning was often used in Anglo-Saxon and Norse poetry. The idea behind the kenning is to write a two-word phrase that describes an object without naming it. It's like a riddle. Examples found in Anglo-Saxon and Norse poetry include 'whale-road', which means the sea or 'sky-candle' which means the sun. One of my favourite kennings is 'breast-hoard' which means breast-treasure. So what is this breast treasure? Breast-hoard can be a kenning for the body or breast – the outer shell which contains the soul and spirit. It can also be a kenning for the 'treasure of the breast' – the soul and spirit, and even a person's inner feelings and thoughts. Research has shown that there are connections between the heart and the brain neurologically through nerve impulses, biochemically via hormones and neurotransmitters, biophysically through pressure waves, and energetically as a result of electromagnetic field interactions. Whilst much of what had happened to me personally and professionally ruminated in my mind – it was somewhere deeper where all these experiences played out. It was in the heart, the soul or whatever one might wish to call it. I prefer to use the word breast-hoard and I truly felt my hoard was filled to the brim with successes, blessings, challenges, love, disappointments, rejections, heartache and loss.

During the period of my *Green Poems for a Blue Planet* environmental campaign, my breast-hoard carried an undertow of depression which I'd managed to hide in my professional life. I wore the daily mask of continuing success by publishing all my achievements on social media whilst deep down I could barely start the day, get myself on stage or give a lecture without being gripped by the deep distress I was experiencing. I didn't even know how things would pan out for my poetry. I'd sunk savings into it and had accepted work for little or no fee. I told myself everyone happily talks the talk about environmental issues but no-one supports a campaigner at the heart of it. I was also working in total isolation, a place I hated as a child and as a composer. I felt as if I was floating on driftwood on an endless ocean. I could see no land ahead, had no vision of where I was heading, and no-one was going to rescue me. I lost all desire to go on. I was still affected by the loss of a relationship and I required mental health help for a long time. Sometimes I lay on the floor like the psalmist of Biblical times and begged the universe to bring back my partner. I cried out to anyone who might hear. I was haunted by the memories of our laughter, our discussions, and the touching of hands. I couldn't bear the empty house I'd come back to after an evening out. I hated the meals alone. Even as I cooked, the preparation of food reminded me of the way she prepared food or drink. Every memory pervaded my innermost being. I once heard psychotherapist Julia Samuel speak at an event. She explained that when one loses a person, the level of loss is equivalent to the amount of love one had for the person. My level seemed immeasurable. Friends worried about my welfare, supported me and paid for therapy to get me through, but the feeling of loss was so great I couldn't bear it. I found it impossible to move on and was unable to function on a daily basis. The prevailing sadness and loneliness put me in a place it is too painful to write about.

It became difficult to find solace and structure for my life. A book concept was stolen which someone else turned into a bestseller; friends passed away; my mentor Edward died and my mother's health deteriorated. The onset of my mum's dementia was followed by many falls and two broken hips. It meant much of my time was dedicated to hospital visits, cleaning, shopping, cooking, and turning up in the middle of the night when she had falls. In one three- month period she made two hundred and fifty-six emergency calls. Some were genuine; others made because she wasn't aware of what she was doing. My clothes were always at the ready for the quick dash during the night to her place where I'd often find her injured. Some days I'd take her out in her wheelchair. We'd go for a meal or coffee and cake, but she couldn't use cutlery and her communication was down to only a few words. Sadly, she would chime them out to anyone who knew her and stopped to say hello. The words were, 'I've got dementia'. I couldn't help her with toilets when we were out and found the whole situation deeply upsetting. I became exhausted by it all.

One night she had a bad fall and the ambulance crew turned up. Fortunately she had only light injuries but had soiled herself and the carpet and bed. I was used to cleaning up the bedroom but not her. As the ambulance crew packed up

I thought they would wash my mum but they told me it was my job. It broke the dignity and privacy there had always been in our relationship. As an only child, the pressures of being a carer (alongside carers who visited to dress mum in the morning and evening) became all consuming. I stayed with my mother through every accident or problem. She filled a great part of my 'breast treasure.' She was proud of my achievements but wise enough to keep me grounded by not celebrating them. She was a kind and generous woman and my confidante in times of trouble. Whenever I approached her worried, confused or tearful she would simply wave a hand and say, 'you'll get over it!' Her spirit, having suffered much in the war years, was indomitable.

During my mother's last week, I was at her bedside the whole time and cancelled performances to be there. I had, however, four days of performances set up at the Edinburgh Fringe Festival. My mum had understood this and as she deteriorated in hospital, the time got closer for my departure to Scotland. I took advice from the medical team and was advised to go ahead and I explained to my mum I would be going. I left to get my train a few hours before mum died. Although the medical team and I thought I was doing the right thing, I later deeply regretted it and believed I was selfish. It was whilst I was on the train at a station stop at Leeds that my phone rang. It was my ex-wife with the news my mum had just died. I looked out of the window. There was a certain synchronicity. The train had stopped not more than a half mile from where my mum was born. The rest of the journey was torturous: self-blame, grief, and uncontrollable tears that concerned the guard and passengers. I felt lost. As the train approached Scotland I was still in pieces. I then rang the only person in Scotland I had a number for, the film director Norman Stone who was based in Glasgow. I couldn't hold back the tears. He suggested I stay on the train to Glasgow where he'd pick me up. I arrived at the station as a totally broken man. Norman suggested I should stay overnight at the farm where he and his family lived. The house provided solace in the midst of despair. Norman carried my bags in and then ran me a bath, lit a few candles around it, and brought me a double whisky. I knew I'd have to pull myself together somehow to perform my shows at the Edinburgh Fringe, but all my mind could focus on were the three most important women in my life I had loved and lost: my wife, a post divorce long-term partner and my mother.

It was in Canada and the USA that synchronicity or intuition seemed to play a role in the loss of that partner. We'd spent a wonderful time in Vancouver with my relatives who'd taken us on a vacation in the Rockies. The meet with them was in itself extraordinary. When I'd met them back in the seventies and nineties, I was an evangelical Christian and I can remember sharing my faith with them. Who would have believed that on my visit in 2017 I'd find they had all become Christians whilst I'd turned atheist. If there is a God, it was a mighty fine joke! It was after the Rockies trip that my partner and I went on to Vancouver Island. At a meal in a restaurant a large glass jug was dropped by a waiter at an adjoining table. The explosion was dramatic and ripped between me and my partner, throwing glass fragments into our meals and drinks. This is the sort of event one would normally pass off as random and accidental, but I felt it had resonance and meaning. Call it coincidence or my overactive imagination, but I began to believe I was having premonitions about the end of our relationship.

The same happened on our flight to Los Angeles a couple of days later. As the plane reached cruising altitude, I felt something hit my toe. It was a mobile phone. I picked it up.

'Someone won't be happy losing their essential means of communication.' But then a very strange thought hit me and the words 'loss of communication' repeated in my head. At first, I regarded it as an idle thought, but then I wondered whether it could be some kind of sign? Did it mean my partner and I would be losing communication with each other? I'm not a superstitious person and reprimanded myself for being so at the time. I asked the passengers in front and behind whether they had lost a phone. No-one had so I passed it on to the cabin crew who ascertained no-one on the flight had lost it. Again, I was haunted by the thought of losing communication with my loved one. The plane landed. By the time we'd gone through immigration, another loss of communication kicked in: I'd totally lost my voice. A super-fast laryngitis rendered me unable to speak to my partner or anyone else for a week. Two weeks later, on returning back to the UK, my partner walked away with no explanation or closure. I believe something on that LA flight gave me foresight of what was going to happen.

There was someone else I loved and lost too: Barney. Barney had been our family cat and came to us from a rescue organisation. He was a timid gentle giant marmalade ginger tom. I adore cats and somehow got to be his close 'cat whisperer' by default. He wouldn't leave the room he arrived in and it was months before he'd venture through the other rooms in the house and explore the garden. During this time I spoke to him gently — encouraging him to do so. I would often lie with him and whisper 'roll over Barney', and he would. My mum made a harness and lead for him. Bit by bit we'd introduce him to each room and finally take him on walks around the garden. When Barney's health failed, my son and I took him to the vet. He was taken into a back room. I was expecting his death to take a few minutes rather than a sudden reaction to the needle. My son and I were devastated — we were not able to say goodbye as he was put to sleep. I cried for many days after.

My mother's funeral was somewhat tricky to set up but it was my ex-wife who managed to make the arrangements whilst I was away performing in Edinburgh. One thing I had to find was a church. The minister at the local church my mum attended was away so I asked my local church whether they could take the service. They weren't sure whether their vicar or curate would be available so I booked my friend Luke Walton to officiate. Just prior to the day, the church decided its vicar and curate were available so mum ended up with three vicars on the day! It's strange to look back on a life. Even in writing this book and looking back over the years, everything seems to have gone by in the blink of an eye. We often hear about how we shouldn't focus on the past – an attachment to historical nostalgia, the longing for a particular era. We are also told not to be preoccupied about the future – being in the 'now' is the preferred state. Yet personal nostalgia, as distinct from historical nostalgia, can be of benefit. Perhaps some of us don't wish to remember our past. I like to replay the days of my childhood as if I am playing old records of songs I love. It was the same for my mum. On October 22nd 1977, she was sitting in our car in a car park, and waiting for me and dad to return. As she waited, she realised the car was parked opposite a spot where the house in which she was born once stood. The moment triggered a recollection of her childhood which she wrote down as a six-page memoir. She remembered her gas-lit bedroom, the broken windows, scrubbing her father's back as he bathed after coming in from the pit, the odour of his pit clothes drying on the fireplace, receiving a bowl of soup when the family had nothing and being evacuated as a child to Hooton Pagnell village near Doncaster. At the end of my mum's memoir she said:

'It's a funny thing. We suffered nothing but hardship in those years yet I miss them, in fact, as I sat in the car waiting for my husband and son I realised that forty years had gone since I played on that spot and I must confess I cried for times gone by.'

Research into personal nostalgia has hailed its benefits. Personal nostalgia doesn't lock us into the past. Positive nostalgic recollections actually stabilise us during the transitional periods in life. According to scientists, such memories of our early connectedness to positive people and experiences remain more crystallised than negative or neutral ones. As a result, we use such memories to promote personal growth. During the writing of this book, in very challenging personal times, my own nostalgia has reminded me of what I've been able to achieve with the help of loved ones, friends and professional colleagues. It is these memories that must become the essential fuel for my future energy and self-belief.

Even so, one can often be put on the spot and any self-belief restored can suddenly be challenged again as it was a few years ago when I was closing a lecture on film music. I asked the group of students whether there were any further questions. One student raised a hand and asked why the group was being taught by someone who hadn't composed any film music for ten years. The comment cut deep into me and within a few seconds I felt as if I was redundant, a fake, a 'has been'. It was, however, a legitimate question and certainly an embarrassing one to answer in front of the whole class who eagerly awaited my reply. I took a deep breath.

'Do you really want to know?'

The student nodded. I considered whether I'd answer and then...

'Then I'll share this with you. For five years I took care of my mum. I was massively affected by the time commitment to her, her death, and also struggled with personal relationship problems. I lost a partner I deeply loved. These issues affected what work I could manage or pitch for. Against that backdrop, I was also trying to grow my performance poetry career. But I have composed over two hundred film and television scores, released ten albums, pioneered music composition and recording approaches in natural history filmmaking, won a Composer of the Year award, travelled the world with my one-man show, have a PhD and an honorary doctorate and co-founded the very course you are on. If that's not good enough for you then I don't know what else to say. Sometimes life doesn't quite work out how you plan it and you will find that there are times when it interrupts your golden trajectory of becoming a famous film composer. Thanks for asking the question.'

Despite the question, the student and I went on to become best friends.

In the midst of melancholia I sought refuge in movies — sitting alone in the cinema night after night. Art galleries were my other places for distraction or contemplation. I've always had an immense pleasure in looking at art and was lucky enough to be able to commission a portrait from artist and friend Martin Rose. Martin had two paintings in the National Portrait Gallery: one of Olympic gold medallist Sebastian Coe and the other of composer Sir Michael Tippett (1905–1998). He agreed to paint mine. The portrait shows me working in my studio, but Martin gave me three arms! One hand is holding my head as I contemplate composition, one is holding a stopwatch to measure film sections for music, and the third hand is holding what looks like a quill. At the side of me is a TV screen on which a tern is flying. This represents my work in natural history. Behind me is a swirling mass of colour which represents the imagination — from which I am plucking ideas. The style of the painting is loose in terms of how the paint is applied to the canvas. At the time of painting, Martin was going through a transitional phase. As a result of breaking a wrist, certain mark-making on the canvas became impossible. It was at this point he began to use his fingers and a palette knife to create the work. One day, many years after buying the painting, I had a party. One of my guests looked at the painting and said,

'I'm interested in the huge head of the baby alongside you. What's that about?'

It was the first time I'd ever seen it. The artist hadn't intended to paint a baby's head, but amongst the swirling mass of palette knife and finger strokes, my friend had spotted a face straight away. From that moment on, it was perfectly visible every time I looked at the painting. I regarded the 'hidden head' as a subliminal portrayal of my inner child and was pleased the painting reminded me of my inner sibling and best buddy! Given I always preferred to buy a painting than buy a car, I saw another painting I liked. *Journey of the Magi* was painted by Martin's wife Kate Rose. It was one of a hundred or so paintings Kate was going to exhibit in London. I couldn't decide whether I could afford it. The exhibition went to London, and whilst it was there, I changed my mind and decided to buy it. But *Journey of the Magi* was the only painting sold in the exhibition and to a well-known celebrity. There was, however, a companion painting, *Windows of Heaven*. I didn't think twice about it and snapped it up.

Although I hate travelling on my own, I also sought to alleviate my depression by going on vacation. One Christmas I booked a room in a spa hotel near Albufeira in Portugal. It was as I anticipated. I was lonely and my only conversations were with the waitress or the barman. The usually crowded coastline of the summer months was deserted. I attempted to make the best of each day. I strolled along the beach and made it my mission to find the best shell during my daily walks. The weather was chilly, but it was gloriously sunny and the silvery blue sea was always so inviting. I was the only person swimming every day. Afterwards, I'd go to a café at the top of the cliff to eat and read. One lunchtime, a local artist called at the restaurant and tried to sell a large oil painting to the owner. He stopped near my table on the terrace and delivered his sales pitch to the restaurant manager. The picture he wanted to sell was of a naval battle — most probably one of the Portuguese and Dutch battles in the seventeenth century. As the artist waxed lyrical about the painting, I felt the image had a synchronistic significance for me. In the scene were several Portuguese men-of-war galleons. A few had been blown to pieces with Dutch cannons and were either aflame or sinking. In the centre of the painting, one galleon stood intact — proud and imposing with its flag and majestic sails catching the wind. I looked at the beaten sinking ships around the galleon and said to myself that I didn't want to be like them. I wanted to be the resilient galleon in the centre. I endeavoured to hold the image in my mind.

I fed a lot of the aftermath of breakups, loss and therapy into poetry. As well as the two hundred green poems I'd written, I wrote a collection which I performed at the Royal West of England Academy against the backdrop of artist PJ Crook's exhibition *Metamorphoses* — an apposite title for changes in my own life. The exhibition included Greek mythological stories with themes as potent now as they were to the ancient Greeks. I titled my collection of poems *Heartchery*. I'd recently taken up archery and the symbol of arrows piercing targets was so obviously an outward manifestation of my subconscious mind replaying the heart-piercing experience of losing a precious relationship. The collection revealed the 'story of my heart'. All the poems were based on the theme of love — love for people, family, Earth, and the creatures on it. I believe love, along with peace, are attributes with the power to truly transform an individual, a community, and humankind. The poems also covered themes of love lost, unreciprocated, and the experiences of brokenness in life — a rite of passage that may or may not transform us for the better. The collection also gave a nod to my environmental work about developing a love for our planet and not a list of things to do or an investment in the hope politicians will sort it out. What needs to be done can be done by us the worker ants, putting aside our disagreements and self-interested political rants which spawn discrimination and fear. In their place we can redirect our energy into relationships, community and environment.

I made no excuses for the heart on my sleeve emotions expressed in the poems. I was emotionally raw at the time. That is what being human is all about — living a full life that explores the negatives, the positives, and the territory in between. The writing of one my poems in the collection, *Broken Things*, helped me with mental health issues around the loss of relationship, music career and self-esteem. The poem is about the Japanese art of *Kintsugi* in which broken pottery is mended with lacquer mixed with powdered gold. It celebrates breakage and repair as part of the history of an object and features this imperfection as valuable and beautiful.

Broken Things

A shattered pot –
fractured, fragmented,
splintered, chipped.
Is this the end of its service?

In the Japanese art of *Kintsugi*,
the piece is mended with a lacquer mixed with powdered gold –
golden joinery transforming what was broken
into something much more beautiful.

We are vulnerable to breakage:
mental, physical, deliberate, accidental.
Damage spawns awareness of fragility –
the gift of change is thrust upon us.
Flawlessness is irrelevant.

These gold seams that fill the cracks,
embrace and illuminate imperfection.
The repaired vessel draws attention to its scars –
shows off an unconventional beauty,
and boasts that in our brokenness
there is gold dust.

Another place in which I found refuge was dance. My mum had always been a great ballroom dancer and encouraged me to learn so I could go dancing with her. I didn't have the inclination or the time, but a few months before she died I promised her I was going to learn. I took ballroom and Latin lessons and really enjoyed the quickstep, rhythm foxtrot and waltz. Many of my evenings were spent taking Argentine tango lessons and dancing at milongas – the social gatherings where tango is danced. I loved the music as it reminded me of the times in my childhood when my father played tangos on his accordion. Yet, whilst the dancing was wonderful, it always heightened my feeling of being alone. I'd watch couples dancing, dance the night away myself, but then return home feeling so terribly alone in the world. I'm convinced that loneliness is one of the greatest burdens to bear and many are not aware of what it is like if you cannot live with your own company.

During those times the arts came to the rescue as a sibling or partner. Creativity's pool is always available to us as long as we look into it and are still playful enough to cast a stone and let a ripple stir. How I once played and imagined as a child is a reservoir for inspiration I still draw upon. As for successfully moving on with the artist's life, chance, luck, and contacts come into it, but so does moving step by step. I remember seeing a statuette of Milo of Croton in my local gym. It was a visual reminder to those pushing weights of what can be achieved. Milo of Croton was a sixth-century Greek wrestler who won many victories in the athletic festivals of ancient Greece. Milo's super-human strength was attributed to his daily childhood regime of lifting and carrying a new born calf on his shoulders until it developed into maturity. At that point, Milo found he could carry a bull! Start small, move step by step, never give up and you will achieve!

Tenacity and holding on to one's passion are cornerstones on which an artist builds a career. Someone once told me I was unable to let go and will keep searching for the pearl of great price whether in life or art. It's true. I will go on when others have given up. I can't help it. This is how I was coded. Let me give you an example. I once went to Weston-super-Mare pier with a girlfriend. She asked whether I would go on the 'robotic arm ride'. The ride was a two-seater spinning arm that turned you through a series of twists, swoops and revolutions. I hate rollercoaster type rides but finally plucked up the courage to get on. After we'd done the ride and all the others on the pier and got home, my partner realised she'd lost an earring that had sentimental value.

The next morning, before the pier opened, I managed to reach staff by phone. I was able to check whether any of the cleaners had swept or hoovered up the earring. No luck. I asked whether I could make a search once the pier opened to the public. They agreed and I drove over from Bristol and painstakingly explored every ride, carriage, walkway, dodgem, go-kart and machine we'd been on. I even walked the ghost train's track. Nothing. Yet I believed I would find the earring. Finally, I stood under the robotic arm. I remembered in which ear my partner had the earring and I watched and noted each move of the robotic arm. I watched again. This time I closely observed the movement angles of the ride and how it might throw the earring during any of the moves. One move in particular repeated at great force. I was convinced it was the move that threw the earring. I followed an imaginary line from the position of the robotic arm at that point. It led to a tall slot machine standing by the fairground entrance. I knew the earring was under that machine. I walked over and knelt down. The bottom of the machine had a tiny gap between its base and the floor, but I saw something under there — no more than a few millimetres in. I took out a credit card, slid it under the machine and flicked out the earring!

Whether it is in the finding of earrings, the composing of music and poetry or in trying to understand my place and purpose in the world, I would like to determine whether I'm a slave to the evolutionary process or a part of a greater mystery. In the first millionth of a second after the big bang, matter and anti-matter were created and transformed into pairs of particles and anti-particles. These particles annihilated each other and returned to energy. But small quantities of a particle called the X boson were produced and were biased towards matter rather than antimatter. Cosmologists tell us it was from this tiny amount of matter that the universe was formed. I would like to work out what happened prior to that first millionth of a second and who or what was responsible for causing such a great party atmosphere at the beginning of time. I want to know all about the tiny particles known as the up quark and the down quark. These are particles that combine in threes to form protons and neutrons which reside in the nucleus at the centre of atoms. Each proton has two up quarks which are positive and one down quark which is negative; each neutron has one up quark which is positive and two down quarks which are negative. In that quantum world I see someone or something at play and I would love to be invited to their next games night.

This book started out as a short memoir for my children yet it somehow grew a lot more pages. I suppose I've ended up writing about what's been important to me, what I've learned, what and who I have loved, what I still believe to be important, what I still need to learn and what I wish to pass on that may be helpful to others. In writing it, I've reprimanded myself in the same way I would take issue with any piece of storytelling for omitting contentious content, the 'juicy bits', and for not telling the full story — the 'story of my heart' — the cargo of my breast-hoard which would make me totally vulnerable. I haven't recovered from wounds I've received and to mention them is, to some extent, an embarrassing and worthless task. Like a Native American warrior injured in battle, I like to think I bear the scars of the wounds well. And though they might have faded, it's difficult to forget them when I catch a glimpse of a scar or revisit it as the fingers of memory rub over it.

I'm not fearful in the midst of unfolding events in the world. I simply plough my furrow and do the best I can to love my children, my friends, Earth and its creatures more than I did the day before. I believe we all have opportunities to change things for the better and I hope I can continue to contribute to a better world. Perhaps I should have learnt by now how to take a rest or to pace myself, but I have to be honest, the world is not enough for me and I'm sure my inner child will tell me which ride to jump onto next. There's so much more I want to achieve in the arts and in life. Most of all, I would like to see everyone working together for good. Big dream I know, but I will not wake from it. I'm a dreamer but one who puts dreams into action. If a lad from a council estate in Leeds can do it, anyone can. I'm still playing as the only child I was sixty years ago and I'm still learning to 'breathe deep with the joy of wellbeing'. What's the next chapter in Lah Lah Land? I'm about to dream it up.

Acknowledgments

I'd like to thank Simon Bishop for the design and typesetting of *Major and Minor Adventures in Lah Lah Land*. Thanks to Mark Simmons for the cover photograph, and Pat Aithie for the *Land of the Eagle* session image. Thank you to publisher Richard Jones of Tangent Books and John Garrad and Nick Garrad of Akcent Media Ltd for advice along the way. Special thanks to my first-draft readers Ken and Marcy Baron, Viv Eaden, and Sophie Howard.